Lecture Notes in Artificial Intelligence   1647

Subseries of Lecture Notes in Computer Science
Edited by J. G. Carbonell and J. Siekmann

Lecture Notes in Computer Science

Edited by G. Goos, J. Hartmanis and J. van Leeuwen

Springer

Berlin
Heidelberg
New York
Barcelona
Hong Kong
London
Milan
Paris
Singapore
Tokyo

Francisco J. Garijo   Magnus Boman (Eds.)

Multi-Agent System Engineering

9th European Workshop
on Modelling Autonomous Agents
in a Multi-Agent World, MAAMAW'99
Valencia, Spain, June 30 – July 2, 1999
Proceedings

Springer

Series Editors

Jaime G. Carbonell, Carnegie Mellon University, Pittsburgh, PA, USA
Jörg Siekmann, University of Saarland, Saarbrücken, Germany

Volume Editors

Francisco J. Garijo
Telefónica Investigación y Desarrollo
C/Emilio Vargas 6, E-28043 Madrid, Spain
E-mail: fgarijo@tid.es

Magnus Boman
DSV, SU/KTH
Electrum 230, SE-16440 Kista, Sweden
E-mail: mab@dsv.su.se

Cataloging-in-Publication data applied for

Die Deutsche Bibliothek - CIP-Einheitsaufnahme

Multi-agent systems engineering : proceedings / 9th European Workshop on
Modelling Autonomous Agents in a Multi-Agent World, MAAMAW '99, Valencia,
Spain, June 30 - July 2, 1999. Francisco J. Garijo ; Magnus Boman (ed.). -
Berlin ; Heidelberg ; New York ; Barcelona ; Hong Kong ; London ; Milan ; Paris
; Singapore ; Tokyo : Springer, 1999
  (Lecture notes in computer science ; Vol. 1647 : Lecture notes in artificial
  intelligence)
  ISBN 3-540-66281-2

CR Subject Classification (1998): I.2.11, C.2, D.2, D.1.3

ISBN 3-540-66281-2 Springer-Verlag Berlin Heidelberg New York

© Springer-Verlag Berlin Heidelberg 1999
Printed in Germany

Typesetting: Camera-ready by author
SPIN 10703846   06/3142 – 5 4 3 2 1 0   Printed on acid-free paper

Preface

In the ten years since the first MAAMAW was held in 1989, at King's College, Cambridge, the field of Multi-Agent Systems (MAS) has flourished. It has attracted an increasing amount of theoretical and applied research.

During this decade, important efforts have been made to establish the scientific and technical foundations of MAS. MAAMAW publications are testimony to the progress achieved in key areas such as agent modelling and reasoning, multi-agent interaction and communication, and multi-agent organisation and social structure. Research results have covered a wide range of inter-related topics in each area including agent architectures, reasoning models, logics, conflict resolution, negotiation, resource allocation, load balancing, learning, social behaviour and interaction, languages and protocols, interagent and agent-human communication, social models, agent roles, norms and social laws, and static and dynamic organisational structures.

The feasibility and the viability of the proposed models and techniques have been demonstrated through MAS applications in heterogeneous domains including electronic commerce, co-operative work, telecommunications, social and biological systems, robotics, office and business automation, public administration, social simulations and banking.

As the applicability of the technology became understood, the multi-agent paradigm has been progressively accepted by product managers and system developers, giving rise to a considerable amount of business expectation from industry. These expectations do not rest on the concept or metaphor of agent, but on the development of MAS useful in an industrial setting, with real-time systems presenting the biggest challenge.

The choice of MAS engineering as the central theme of the MAAMAW'99 underlines the need of workable solutions for incorporating the scientific and technological knowledge on MAS into useful systems, according to industrial and customers' demands.

The need for pragmatic approaches that allow for the rapid development of large MAS applications and services will continue to increase in the first decades of the next century, when most of the economical and social activity can be carried out over the global networks. It seems natural to imagine this emergent world of services and "virtual" goods populated by organisations of intelligent and mobile agents managing resources and services, carrying out tedious, repetitive and laborious tasks, negotiating with other agents for finding cost-effective solutions, helping service providers to get new clients, performing security tasks and achieving trading, commerce and information task on behalf of users.

Building this complex virtual world with its organised inhabitants will only be possible if there is a solid engineering discipline for agent development. This will require tight collaboration between researchers and engineers in order to know what the real problems are. Feedback from engineering will raise two related challenges to the MAS research community. First to extend existing models to large scale MAS applications, and second to elaborate and validate new techniques and theories considering a variety of new MAS aspects such as stability, robustness, reliability, scalability, reusability, security, performance, life-cycle, cost-effectiveness efficiency, and usability.

In software engineering, practical development of large complex systems have been much faster than in the research community. However, when scientific knowledge contributes to improve the production process or the quality of products, this knowledge is quickly assimilated by engineers into routine development.

The last MAAMAW of this millennium aims at providing the environment and the rich atmosphere needed for presenting innovative contributions and for debating new ideas for MAS engineering and other related topics. The city of Valencia will host this meeting, giving to the workshop participants the opportunity of enjoying the richness of its historical and cultural atmosphere. This book contains the seventeen papers selected by the program committee for presentation during the workshop. It also includes an invited text by Nick Jennings, who kindly accepted to participate as MAAMAW'99 keynote speaker. The volume is structured into five thematic groups according to the topics addressed by the papers.

The section on the engineering aspects of MAS starts out with the contribution by Jennings. The paper develops the concept of agent-oriented software engineering, addressing its advantages, as well as the limitations that must be overcome.

Three more papers then address engineering issues such as the specification of behavioural requirements, agent-oriented design, and analysis of experiences in the development of software agents in different domains. The MAS framework section comprises three papers. The first contribution presents an open environment based on FIPA recommendations. The second addresses the modelling of real-time agents, and the third discusses mobile agent co-operation and co-ordination issues on the Internet. Four papers in the Languages and protocols section address several related topics: MAS engineering, the design of agent communication languages, the definition of a temporal agent communication language, and the use of multi-paradigm languages for MAS development. The section on negotiation and co-operation contains four papers, two of which describe different models of agent negotiation. The first paper proposes a model based on argumentation, while the second is based on generic negotiation architecture to automate the agreement between parties. The two remaining articles focus on co-operation models. The first addresses plan selection in BDI-like agents, and the second presents an extension of existing reasoning mechanisms to cope with multiple partner coalition in MAS. The last group contains four papers addressing formal aspects of MAS. The first paper focuses on clarification and systematisation of mental attitudes in agents, proposing an integrated and coherent model. The second paper describes a doxastic logic based on subjective situations, to avoid logical omniscience. A formal framework for the analysis and specification of models for the dynamics of trust based on experiences is presented in the last paper.

June 1999

Francisco J. Garijo, Magnus Boman
Scientific Co-Chairs

Acknowledgments

We would like to thank all the people who helped bring about MAAMAW'99. First of all, thanks to the contributing authors for ensuring the richness of the workshop and for their co-operation in the preparation of this volume.

Special thanks are due to the members of the program committee, aided by the auxiliary reviewers, for their professionalism and their dedication in selecting the best papers for the workshop.

Thanks also to the MAAMAW Advisory Board for their guidance and their continuous support.

We owe particular gratitude to the invited speakers for sharing with us their experiences and most recent research results.

Nothing would have been possible without the initiative and dedication of the organising committee at the DSIC Department in the Universidad Politecnica de Valencia. The chair Vicente Botti and his team did a great job.

We would like to thank Telefonica I+D for providing the environment and the technical facilities to prepare the book. We are very grateful to Loreto Rodriguez, the AEPIA secretary, for her assistance in the review process. She ensured communication with reviewers and authors, and handled text formatting according to Springer-Verlag guidelines.

Finally, we would like to acknowledge the role of the Workshop sponsors Generalitat de Valencia, Spanish Council of Science and Technology (CICYT), Department of Sistemes Informatics i Computacio (DSIC) of the Universidad Politecnica de Valencia, Adjuntament de Valencia, the Spanish Association for Artificial Intelligence (AEPIA), AgentLink, the Springer-Verlag staff, Iberia, and Telefonica. All of them have provided continuous support for both workshop organisation and the publication of this book.

MAAMAW'99 Program Committee

Abe Mamdani, United Kingdom	John Perram, Denmark
Aldo Dragoni, Italy	Judith Masthoff, United Kingdom
Amal ElFallah, France	Juergen Mueller, Germany
Barbara Dunin-Keplicz, Poland	Krzysztof Cetnarowicz, Poland
Carles Sierra, Spain	Love Ekenberg, Sweden
Cristiano Castelfranchi, Italy	Marie-Pierre Gleizes, France
Divine Ndumu, United Kingdom	Nick Jennings, United Kingdom
Donald Steiner, Germany	Rune Gustavsson, Sweden
Eugenio Oliveira, Portugal	Thierry Bouron, France
Helder Coelho, Portugal	Vladimir Gorodetski, Russia
Jan Treur, The Netherlands	Yves Demazeau, France
Jeffrey Rosenschein, Israel	

Organisation Chair
Vicente Botti
DSIC. Polytechnic University
Valencia, Spain

Reviewers

Table of Contents

Negotiation and Cooperation

Formal Models

Agent-Oriented Software Engineering

Nicholas R. Jennings

Dept. Electronic Engineering, Queen Mary & Westfield College,
University of London, London E1 4NS, UK.
n.r.jennings@qmw.ac.uk

1 Introduction

Increasingly many computer systems are being viewed in terms of autonomous agents. Agents are being espoused as a new theoretical model of computation that more closely reflects current computing reality than Turing Machines. Agents are being advocated as the next generation model for engineering complex, distributed systems. Agents are also being used as an overarching framework for bringing together the component AI sub-disciplines that are necessary to design and build intelligent entities. Despite this intense interest, however, a number of fundamental questions about the nature and the use of agents remain unanswered.
In particular:

- what is the essence of agent-based computing?
- what makes agents an appealing and powerful conceptual model?
- what are the drawbacks of adopting an agent-oriented approach?
- what are the wider implications for AI of agent-based computing?

These questions can be tackled from many different perspectives; ranging from the philosophical to the pragmatic. This paper proceeds from the standpoint of using agent-based software to solve complex, real-world problems. Building high quality software for complex real-world applications is difficult. Indeed, it has been argued that such developments are one of the most complex construction tasks humans undertake (both in terms of the number and the flexibility of the constituent components and in the complex way in which they are interconnected). Moreover, this statement is true no matter what models and techniques are applied: it is a consequence of the "essential complexity of software" [2]. Such complexity manifests itself in the fact that software has a large number of parts that have many interactions [8]. Given this state of affairs, the role of software engineering is to provide models and techniques that make it easier to handle this complexity. To this end, a wide range of software engineering paradigms have been devised (e.g. object-orientation [1] [7], component-ware [9], design patterns [4] and software architectures [3]). Each successive development either claims to make the engineering process easier or to extend the complexity of applications that can feasibly be built. Although evidence is emerging to support these claims, researchers continue to strive for more efficient and powerful techniques, especially as solutions for ever more demanding applications are sought.

In this article, it is argued that although current methods are a step in the right direction, when it comes to developing complex, distributed systems they fall short in one of three main ways: (i) the basic building blocks are too fine grained; (ii) the interactions are too rigidly defined; or (iii) they posses insufficient mechanisms for dealing with organisational structure. Furthermore, it will be argued that: *agent-oriented approaches can significantly enhance our ability to model, design and build complex (distributed) software systems.*

2   The Essence of Agent-Based Computing

The first step in arguing for an agent-oriented approach to software engineering is to precisely identify and define the key concepts of agent-oriented computing. Here the key definitional problem relates to the term *"agent"*. At present, there is much debate, and little consensus, about exactly what constitutes agenthood. However, an increasing number of researchers find the following characterisation useful [10]:

> *an agent is an encapsulated computer system that is situated in some environment, and that is capable of flexible, autonomous action in that environment in order to meet its design objectives*

There are a number of points about this definition that require further explanation. Agents are: (i) clearly identifiable problem solving entities with well-defined boundaries and interfaces; (ii) situated (embedded) in a particular environment—they receive inputs related to the state of their environment through sensors and they act on the environment through effectors; (iii) designed to fulfil a specific purpose—they have particular objectives (goals) to achieve; (iv) autonomous—they have control both over their internal state and over their own behaviour; (v) capable of exhibiting flexible problem solving behaviour in pursuit of their design objectives—they need to be both reactive (able to respond in a timely fashion to changes that occur in their environment) and proactive (able to opportunistically adopt new goals) [11].

When adopting an agent-oriented view of the world, it soon becomes apparent that most problems require or involve multiple agents: to represent the decentralised nature of the problem, the multiple loci of control, the multiple perspectives, or the competing interests. Moreover, the agents will need to interact with one another: either to achieve their individual objectives or to manage the dependencies that ensue from being situated in a common environment. These interactions can vary from simple information interchanges, to requests for particular actions to be performed and on to cooperation, coordination and negotiation in order to arrange inter-dependent activities. Whatever the nature of the social process, however, there are two points that qualitatively differentiate agent interactions from those that occur in other software engineering paradigms. Firstly, agent-oriented interactions occur through a high-level (declarative) agent communication language. Consequently, interactions are conducted at the knowledge level [6]: in terms of which goals should be followed, at what time, and by whom (cf. method invocation or function calls that operate at a purely syntactic level). Secondly, as agents are flexible problem solvers, operating in an environment over which they have only partial control and observability, interactions need to be handled in a similarly flexible manner. Thus, agents need the computational apparatus to make context-dependent decisions about the nature and scope of their interactions and to initiate (and respond to) interactions that were not foreseen at design time.

In most cases, agents act to achieve objectives either on behalf of individuals/companies or as part of some wider problem solving initiative. Thus, when agents interact there is typically some underpinning organisational context. This context defines the nature of the relationship between the agents. For example, they may be peers working together in a team or one may be the boss of the others. In any case, this context influences an agent's behaviour. Thus it is important to explicitly represent the relationship. In many cases, relationships are subject to ongoing change: social interaction means existing relationships evolve and new relations are created. The temporal extent of relationships can also vary significantly: from just long enough to deliver a particular service once, to a permanent bond. To cope with this variety and dynamic, agent researchers have: devised protocols that enable organisational groupings to be formed and disbanded, specified mechanisms to ensure groupings act together in a coherent fashion, and developed structures to characterise the macro behaviour of collectives [5] [11].

3 Agent-Oriented Software Engineering

The most compelling argument that could be made for adopting an agent-oriented approach to software development would be to have a range of quantitative data that showed, on a standard set of software metrics, the superiority of the agent-based approach over a range of other techniques. However such data simply does not exist. Hence arguments must be qualitative in nature.

The structure of the argument that will be used here is as follows. On one hand, there are a number of well-known techniques for tackling complexity in software. Also the nature of complex software systems is (reasonably) well understood. On the other hand, the key characteristics of the agent-based paradigm have been elucidated. Thus an argument can be made by examining the degree of match between these two perspectives.

Before this argument can be made, however, the techniques for tackling complexity in software need to be introduced. Booch identifies three such tools [1]:

- *Decomposition:* The most basic technique for tackling any large problem is to divide it into smaller, more manageable chunks each of which can then be dealt with in relative isolation.
- *Abstraction:* The process of defining a simplified model of the system that emphasises some of the details or properties, while suppressing others.

- *Organisation*[1]: The process of identifying and managing interrelationships between various problem-solving components.

Next, the characteristics of complex systems need to be enumerated [8]:

- Complexity frequently takes the form of a hierarchy. That is, a system that is composed of inter-related sub-systems, each of which is in turn hierarchic in structure, until the lowest level of elementary sub-system is reached. The precise nature of these organisational relationships varies between sub-systems, however some generic forms (such as client-server, peer, team, etc.) can be identified. These relationships are not static: they often vary over time.
- The choice of which components in the system are primitive is relatively arbitrary and is defined by the observer's aims and objectives.
- Hierarchic systems evolve more quickly than non-hierarchic ones of comparable size. In other words, complex systems will evolve from simple systems more rapidly if there are *stable intermediate forms*, than if there are not.
- It is possible to distinguish between the interactions *among* sub-systems and the interactions *within* sub-systems. The latter are both more frequent (typically at least an order of magnitude more) and more predictable than the former. This gives rise to the view that complex systems are *nearly decomposable*: sub-systems can be treated almost as if they are independent of one another, but not quite since there are some interactions between them. Moreover, although many of these interactions can be predicted at design time, some cannot.

With these two characterisations in place, the form of the argument can be expressed: (i) show agent-oriented decompositions are an effective way of partitioning the problem space of a complex system; (ii) show that the key abstractions of the agent-oriented mindset are a natural means of modelling complex systems; and (iii) show the agent-oriented philosophy for dealing with organisational relationships is appropriate for complex systems.

3.1 Merits of Agent-Oriented Decomposition

Complex systems consist of a number of related sub-systems organised in a hierarchical fashion. At any given level, sub-systems work together to achieve the functionality of their parent system. Moreover, within a sub-system, the constituent components work together to deliver the overall functionality. Thus, the same basic model of interacting components, working together to achieve particular objectives occurs throughout the system.

Given this fact, it is entirely natural to modularise the components in terms of the objectives they achieve[2]. In other words, each component can be thought of as

---

1 Booch actually uses the term "hierarchy" for this final point [1]. However, the more neutral term "organisation" is used here.

achieving one or more objectives. A second important observation is that complex systems have multiple loci of control: "real systems have no top" [7] pg. 47. Applying this philosophy to objective-achieving decompositions means that the individual components should localise and encapsulate their own control. Thus, entities should have their own thread of control (i.e. they should be active) and they should have control over their own choices and actions (i.e. they should be autonomous).

For the active and autonomous components to fulfil both their individual and collective objectives, they need to interact with one another (recall complex systems are only nearly decomposable). However the system's inherent complexity means it is impossible to know *a priori* about all potential links: interactions will occur at unpredictable times, for unpredictable reasons, between unpredictable components. For this reason, it is futile to try and predict or analyse all the possibilities at design-time. It is more realistic to endow the components with the ability to make decisions about the nature and scope of their interactions at run-time. From this, it follows that components need the ability to initiate (and respond to) interactions in a flexible manner.

The policy of deferring to run-time decisions about component interactions facilitates the engineering of complex systems in two ways. Firstly, problems associated with the coupling of components are significantly reduced (by dealing with them in a flexible and declarative manner). Components are specifically designed to deal with unanticipated requests and they can spontaneously generate requests for assistance if they find themselves in difficulty. Moreover because these interactions are enacted through a high-level agent communication language, coupling becomes a knowledge-level issue. This, in turn, removes syntactic concerns from the types of errors caused by unexpected interactions. Secondly, the problem of managing control relationships between the software components (a task that bedevils traditional functional decompositions) is significantly reduced. All agents are continuously active and any coordination or synchronisation that is required is handled bottom-up through inter- agent interaction. Thus, the ordering of the system's top-level goals is no longer something that has to be rigidly prescribed at design time. Rather, it becomes something that is handled in a context-sensitive manner at run-time.

From this discussion, it is apparent that a natural way to modularise a complex system is in terms of multiple, interacting, autonomous components that have particular objectives to achieve. In short, agent-oriented decompositions aid the process of developing complex systems.

---

2 Indeed the view that decompositions based upon functions/actions/processes are more intuitive and easier to produce than those based upon data/objects is even acknowledged within the object-oriented community [7] pg. 44.

3.2 Appropriateness of Agent-Oriented Abstractions

A significant part of the design process is finding the right models for viewing the problem. In general, there will be multiple candidates and the difficult task is picking the most appropriate one. When designing software, the most powerful abstractions are those that minimise the semantic gap between the units of analysis that are intuitively used to conceptualise the problem and the constructs present in the solution paradigm. In the case of complex systems, the problem to be characterised consists of sub-systems, sub-system components, interactions and organisational relationships.

Taking each in turn:

- Sub-systems naturally correspond to agent organisations. They involve a number of constituent components that act and interact according to their role within the larger enterprise.
- The appropriateness of viewing sub-system components as agents has been made above.
- The interplay between the sub-systems and between their constituent components is most naturally viewed in terms of high-level social interactions: "at any given level of abstraction, we find meaningful collections of entities that collaborate to achieve some higher level view" [1] pg. 34. This view accords precisely with the knowledge-level treatment of interaction afforded by the agent-oriented approach. Agent systems are invariably described in terms of "cooperating to achieve common objectives", "coordinating their actions" or "negotiating to resolve conflicts".
- Complex systems involve changing webs of relationships between their various components. They also require collections of components to be treated as a single conceptual unit when viewed from a different level of abstraction. Here again the agent-oriented mindset provides suitable abstractions. A rich set of structures are typically available for explicitly representing and managing organisational relationships. Interaction protocols exist for forming new groupings and disbanding unwanted ones. Finally, structures are available for modelling collectives. The latter point is especially useful in relation to representing sub-systems since they are nothing more than a team of components working to achieve a collective goal.

3.3 Need for Flexible Management of Changing Organisational Structures

Organisational constructs are first-class entities in agent systems. Thus explicit representations are made of organisational relationships and structures. Moreover, agent-based systems have the concomitant computational mechanisms for flexibly forming, maintaining and disbanding organisations. This representational power enables agent-oriented systems to exploit two facets of the nature of complex systems. Firstly, the notion of a primitive component can be varied according to the needs of the observer. Thus at one level, entire sub-systems can be viewed as a singleton, alternatively teams or collections of agents can be viewed as primitive components, and so on until the system eventually bottoms out. Secondly, such structures provide a variety of stable intermediate forms, that, as already indicated, are essential for rapid development of complex systems. Their availability means that individual agents or organisational groupings can be developed in relative isolation and then added into the system in an incremental manner. This, in turn, ensures there is a smooth growth in functionality.

4 Conclusions and Future Work

This paper has sought to justify the claim that agent-based computing has the potential to provide a powerful suite of metaphors, concepts and techniques for conceptualising, designing and implementing complex (distributed) systems. However if this potential is to be fulfilled and agent-based systems are to reach the mainstream of software engineering, then the following limitations in the current state of the art need to be overcome. Firstly, a systematic methodology that enables developers to clearly analyse and design their applications as multi-agent systems needs to be devised. Secondly, there needs to be an increase in the number and sophistication of industrial-strength tools for building multi-agent systems. Finally, more flexible and scalable techniques need to be devised for enabling heterogeneous agents to inter-operate in open environments;

References

1. G. Booch (1994) "Object-oriented analysis and design with applications" Addison Wesley.
2. F. P. Brooks (1995) "The mythical man-month" Addison Wesley.
3. F. Buschmann, R. Meunier, H. Rohnert, P. Sommerlad, and M. Stahl (1998) "A System of Patterns" Wiley.
4. E. Gamma, R. Helm, R. Johnson and J. Vlissides (1995) "Design Patterns" Addison Wesley.
5. N. R. Jennings and M. Wooldridge (eds.) (1998) "Agent technology: foundations, applications and markets" Springer Verlag.
6. A. Newell, (1982) "The Knowledge Level" Artificial Intelligence 18 87-127.
7. B. Meyer (1988) "Object-oriented software construction" Prentice Hall.
8. H. A. Simon (1996) "The sciences of the artificial" MIT Press.
9. C. Szyperski (1998) "Component Software" Addison Wesley.
10. M. Wooldridge (1997) "Agent-based software engineering" IEE Proc Software Engineering 144 26-37.
11. M. Wooldridge and N. R. Jennings (1995) "Intelligent agents: theory and practice" The Knowledge Engineering Review 10 (2) 115-152.
12. M. J. Wooldridge and N. R. Jennings (1998) "Pitfalls of Agent-Oriented Development" Proc 2nd Int. Conf. on Autonomous Agents (Agents-98), Minneapolis, USA, 385-391.

Specification of Bahavioural Requirements within Compositional Multi-agent System Design

Daniela E. Herlea[1], Catholijn M. Jonker[2], Jan Treur[2], Niek J.E. Wijngaards[1,2]

1 University of Calgary, Software Engineering Research Network
2500 University Drive NW, Calgary, Alberta T2N 1N4, Canada
Email: danah@cpsc.ucalgary.ca
URL: http://www.cpsc.ucalgary/~danah

2 Vrije Universiteit Amsterdam, Department of Artificial Intelligence
De Boelelaan 1081a, 1081 HV, Amsterdam, The Netherlands
Email: {jonker, treur, niek}@cs.vu.nl
URL: http://www.cs.vu.nl/{~jonker, ~treur, ~niek}

Abstract. In this paper it is shown how informal and formal specification of behavioural requirements and scenarios for agents and multi-agent systems can be integrated within multi-agent system design. In particular, it is addressed how a compositional perspective both on design descriptions and specification of behavioural requirements can be exploited. The approach has been applied in a case study: the development of a mediating information agent. It is shown that compositional verification benefits from the integration of requirements engineering within the design process.

1 Introduction

Agent systems are among the most complex of systems to develop (cf. [20], [23]). The autonomy in the behaviour of the agents contributes inherently to this complexity. The tasks performed by the individual agents can be simple or complex in itself, but the agents' autonomy makes the emergent behaviour of the complete multi-agent system both hard to design and hard to verify. Nevertheless, in many applications it is required that the agents cooperate with each other and the users in a in some sense coordinated manner. Often it is essential to analyse requirements on the behaviour of the overall multi-agent system in relation to behavioural properties of the individual agents, in order to develop a system with the right properties.

Within multi-agent system development, the emphasis is often on specification of the system architecture that is designed, and on the implementation of this design. If requirements are considered, they are kept implicit or informal. In principle, the required behavioural properties play a heuristic role: the system design is made up in such a manner that the system behaviour does what is needed, although it is not explicitly specified what that means.

Requirements Engineering (cf. [5], [18], [21]) addresses the development and validation of methods for eliciting, representing, analysing, and confirming system requirements. Requirements express intended properties of the system, and scenarios specify use-cases of the intended system (i.e., examples of intended user interaction traces), usually employed to clarify requirements. Requirements and scenarios can be expressed in various degrees of formality, ranging from unstructured informal representations (usually during initial requirements acquisition) to more structured semi-formal representations and formal representations.

Requirements can be specified for a multi-agent system as a whole, but also for agents within a multi-agent system, and for components within agents. Starting from behavioural requirements for the *system as a whole*, by requirement refinement behavioural properties of *agents* can be identified, and, in a further step, for *components* within an agent. Such an approach fits quite well in compositional multi-agent system design, for example, as discussed in [3], and actually makes part of the heuristics of the design process explicit. One of the underlying assumptions is that such a compositional design method will lead to designs that are more transparent, better maintainable, and can be (partially) reused more easily within other designs. The process of requirements refinement defines the different *process abstraction levels* in more detail. On the basis of refinement of the requirements (and scenarios) for the entire system, system components are identified: agents, users and world components. For each of these components of the system, a specific sub-set of the refined requirements and scenarios is imposed to ensure that the system as a whole satisfies the overall requirements and scenarios. Also further refinement of the requirements and scenarios imposed on an agent leads to the identification of components within the agent, and their properties. The different refinement levels in requirements and scenarios are related to levels of process abstraction in the compositional design description being designed.

Within a compositional *verification* process, after a system has been designed, formalised behavioural requirements play a main role; cf. [17]. A verification process for an existing design often has a high complexity in two respects. On the one hand, the formal formulations of the properties at the different process abstraction levels have to be found. If no explicit requirements engineering has been performed, this can be very hard indeed, as the search space for requirement formulations is often not small and verification is only useful with respect to the appropriate requirements, and the properties and assumptions on which they depend. On the other hand, proofs have to be found. If, as part of the design process, requirements have been (formally) specified as well, these can be used as a starting point for a verification process, thus reducing the complexity of verification, by eliminating the search space for the requirement formulations at different process abstraction levels. If no requirements have been specified during the design process, during verification a form of reverse engineering has to be performed to obtain the (required) properties at the different process abstraction levels afterwards.

The methodological approach proposed results in the use of two (compositional) specification languages:

- a language to specify *design descriptions*
- a language to specify (behavioural) *requirements* and *scenarios*

Within the compositional multi-agent system development method DESIRE (cf. [3]; for a real-world case study see [2]), the first of these languages is already available;

the second is currently being added. Each of these languages fulfills its own purpose. A language to specify a (multi-agent) system architecture needs features different from a language to express properties of such a system. Therefore, in principle the two languages are different. The distinction between these specification languages follows the distinction made in the AI and Design community (cf. [13], [14]) between the *structure* of a design object on the one hand, and *function* or *behaviour* on the other hand. For both languages informal, semi-formal and formal variants are needed, to facilitate the step from informal to formal. Formal models specified in the two languages can be related in a formal manner: it is formally defined when a design description satisfies a requirement or scenario specification, and this formal relation is used to verify that the design description fulfills the requirements and scenarios.

In this paper it is shown how specification of behavioural requirements and scenarios from informal to formal can be integrated within multi-agent system design, in particular for a compositional design method with an underlying formal conceptual model for design descriptions: DESIRE. The approach has been applied in a case study: the development of a mediating information agent.

The example domain for the case study is the development of a multi-agent system that keeps its human users informed with respect to their interests and the rapidly changing available information on the World Wide Web. The task of the multi-agent system is to inform each of its users on information available (e.g., papers) on the World Wide Web that is within their scope of interest. The sources of information are the World Wide Web, but also information providing agents that operate on the World Wide Web, for example, agents related to Web sites of research groups, which announce new papers included in their web-site.

Different representations of requirements and scenarios from informal via semi-formal to formal are discussed in Section 2. The use of requirements and scenarios refinement across process abstraction levels is explained further in Section 3. The integration of the verification process and Requirements Engineering is the topic of Section 4. Section 5 concludes the paper with a discussion.

2   Informal and Formal Representation

In Requirements Engineering the role of scenarios, in addition to requirements, has gained more importance; e.g., see [11], [22]. Scenarios or use cases are examples of interaction sessions between the users and a system [22]; they are often used during the requirement elicitation, being regarded as effective ways of communicating with the stakeholders (i.e., domain experts, users, system customers, managers, and developers). Scenarios, for example, are also employed to formalise interactions among components within the system. Having both requirements and scenarios in a requirements engineering process provides the possibility of mutual comparison: the requirements can be verified against the scenarios, and the scenarios can be verified against the requirements. By this mutual verification process, ambiguities and inconsistencies within and between the existing requirements or scenarios may be identified, but also the lack of requirements or scenarios: scenarios may be identified for which no requirements were formulated yet, and requirements may be identified for which no scenarios were formulated yet.

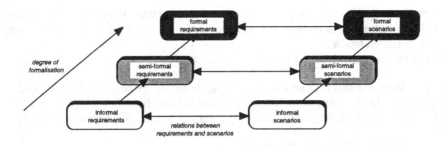

Fig. 1. Representations from informal to formal.

As stated above, requirements and scenarios are seen as effective ways of communicating with the stakeholders. This can only be true if requirements and scenarios are represented in a well-structured and easy to understand manner and are precise enough and detailed enough to support the development process of the system. Unfortunately, no standard language exists for the representation of requirements and scenarios. Formats of varying degrees of formality are used in different approaches. Informally represented requirements and scenarios are often best understood by the stakeholders (although approaches exist using formal representations of requirements in early stages as well: [9]). Therefore, continual participation of stakeholders in the process is possible. A drawback is that the informal descriptions are less appropriate when they are used as input to actually construct a system design. On the other hand, an advantage of using formal descriptions is that they can be manipulated automatically in a mathematical way, which enables verification and the detection of inconsistencies. Furthermore, the process of formalising the representations can be used as a way to disambiguate requirements and scenarios. At the same time however, a formal representation is less appropriate as a communication means with the stakeholders. Therefore, in our approach in the overall development process, different representations are used: informal and/or structured semi-formal representations (obtained during the process of formalisation) resulting from cooperation between stakeholders and designers of the system, and formal representations to be used by the designers during the construction of the design.

Independent of the measure of formality, each requirement and each scenario can be represented in a number of different ways, and/or using different representation languages, e.g., informally by way of use cases in UML. Examples are given below.

2.1 Informal Representations

Different informal representations can be used to express the same requirement or scenario. Representations can be made, for example, in a graphical representation language, or a natural language, or in combinations of these languages, as is done in UML's use cases (cf. [12], [15]). Scenarios, for instance, can be represented using a format that supports branching points in the process, or in a language that only takes linear structures into account.

For the example application, first a list of nine, rather imprecisely formulated initial requirements was elicited. As an example, the elicited requirement on 'keeping aware' is shown below.

Example of an informal initial top level requirement:

L0.R1   The user needs to be kept 'aware' of relevant new information on the World Wide Web.
Requirement L0.R1 is based on the information elicited from the interview with the stakeholder. The following scenario was elicited from the stakeholder as well:
L0.Sc1
1. user generates an **awareness scope** : AS1
2. user is waiting
3. **new information** is made available on the World Wide Web
4. user receives **results for awareness scope** AS1: ASR1

The requirement L0.R1 was analysed and reformulated into a more precise requirement. In the (reformulated) scenarios and requirements, terminology is identified, relevant for the construction of domain ontologies (words in bold-face are part of the domain ontologies being acquired).

Example of a reformulation of a requirement at top level:

L0.R1.1   The user will be notified of **new information** (on the World Wide Web) on an
awareness scope
after the user has expressed the **awareness scope** and
just after this **new information** becomes available on the World Wide Web,
unless the user has retracted the awareness scope (**awareness scope retraction**).

2.2   Structured Semi-formal Representations

Both requirements and scenarios can be reformulated to more structured and precise forms. To check requirements for ambiguities and inconsistencies, an analysis that seeks to identify the parts of a given requirement formulation that refer to input and to output of a process is useful. Such an analysis often provokes a reformulation of the requirement into a more structured form, in which the input and output references are made explicitly visible in the structure of the formulation. Moreover, during such an analysis process the concepts that relate to input can be identified and distinguished from the concepts that relate to output: *acquisition of a (domain) ontology* (cf. [19]) is integrated within requirements engineering. Possibly the requirement splits in a natural manner into two or more simpler requirements. This often leads to a number of new (representations of) requirements.

The ontology later facilitates the formalisation of requirements and scenarios, as the input and output concepts are already defined, at least at a semi-formal level. For nontrivial behavioural requirements a temporal structure has to be reflected in the representation. This entails that terms such as 'at any point in time', 'at an earlier point in time', 'after', 'before', 'since', 'until', and 'next' are used to clarify the temporal relationships between different fragments in the requirement.

For the informally specified requirement L0.R1.1, for example, the following reformulation steps can be made:
At any point in time
The user will receive on its input **results for awareness scope** , i.e., **new information**
on an **awareness scope**

after the user has generated on its output the **awareness scope** and
just after this **new information** becomes available as output of the World Wide Web ,
unless by this time the user has generated on its output an **awareness scope
retraction**.
At any point in time,
if at an earlier point in time the user has generated on its output an **awareness scope,**
and
since then the user has not generated on its output an **awareness scope retraction**
referring to this **awareness scope**, and
just before **new information** within this **awareness scope** becomes available as
output of the World Wide Web ,
then the user will receive on its input this **new information** within the **awareness
scope** .

Based on these reformulation steps the following semi-formal structured requirement can be specified:

L0.R1.2   At any point in time,
  if
      at an earlier point in time
          user output :   an **awareness scope,** and
      since then
          not user output :   **retraction** of this **awareness scope,** and
      just before
          World Wide Web output: **new information** within this **awareness scope**
  then
          user input: **new information** within this **awareness scope**

In summary, to obtain a structured semi-formal representation of a *requirement*, the following is to be performed:

- explicitly distinguish *input and output* concepts in the requirement formulation,
- define (domain) *ontologies* for the input and output information,
- make the *temporal structure* of the statement explicit using words like, 'at any point in time', 'at an earlier point in time', 'after', 'before', 'since', 'until', and 'next'.

For *scenarios*, a structured semi-formal representation is obtained by:

- explicitly distinguish *input and output* concepts in the scenario description,
- define (domain) *ontologies* for the input and output information,
- represent the temporal structure described implicitly in the sequence of events.

The interplay between requirements elicitation and analysis and scenario elicitation and analysis plays an important role. To be more specific, it is identified which requirements and scenarios relate to each other; for example, L0.R1.2 relates to L0.Sc1.2. If it is identified that for a requirement no related scenario is available yet (isolated requirement), then a new scenario can be acquired.

L0.Sc1.2
  1. user output: **awareness scope**
  2. user is waiting
  3. World Wide Web output: **new information**
  4. user input: **results for awareness scope**

2.3 Formal Representations

A formalisation of a scenario can be made by using formal ontologies for the input and output, and by formalising the sequence of events as a temporal trace. Thus a formal temporal model is obtained, for example as defined in [4] and [17]. Of course other formal languages can be chosen as well as long as they allow the formalisation of temporal dependencies that can occur within behavioural requirements without having to make further design choices first.

To obtain formal representations of requirements, the input and output ontologies have to be chosen as formal ontologies. The domain ontologies acquired during the reformulation process for the example application were formalised; part of the domain ontologies related to the focus on requirements and scenarios is shown below:

ontology element:	*explanation:*
SCOPE	a sort for the search scopes and awareness scopes
USER	a sort for the names of different users
PERSISTENCE_TYPE	a sort to distinguish between persistent and incidental scopes
INFO_ELEMENT	a sort for the result information
result_for_scope	a binary relation on INFO_ELEMENT and SCOPE
persistent, incidental	objects of sort PERSISTENCE_TYPE corresponding to the difference in persistence between an awareness scope and a search scope

input:

is_interested_in	a ternary relation on USER, SCOPE and PERSISTENCE_TYPE

output:

result_for_user	a ternary relation on INFO_ELEMENT, USER and SCOPE

In addition, the temporal structure, if present in a semi-formal representation, has to be expressed in a formal manner. Using the formal ontologies, and a formalisation of the temporal structure, a mathematical language is obtained to formulate formal requirement representations. The semantics are based on compositional information states which evolve over time. An *information state* M of a component D is an assignment of truth values {true, false, unknown} to the set of ground atoms that play a role within D. The compositional structure of D is reflected in the structure of the information state. A formal definition can be found in [4] and [17]. The set of all possible information states of D is denoted by IS(D). A *trace* M of a component D is a sequence of information states $(M^t)_{t \in \mathbf{N}}$ in IS(D). Given a trace M of component D, the information state of the input interface of component C at time point t of the component D is denoted by $state_D(M, t, input(C))$, where C is either D or a sub-component of D. Analogously, $state_D(M, t, output(C))$, denotes the information state of the output interface of component C at time point t of the component D. These formalised information states can be related to statements via the formally defined satisfaction relation $\models$. Behavioural properties can be formulated in a formal manner, using quantifiers over time and the usual logical connectives such as not, &, $\Rightarrow$. An alternative formal representation of temporal properties (using modal and temporal operators) within Temporal Multi-Epistemic Logic can be found in [10].

Examples of formal representations of top level requirements:

L0.R1.2 is formalised by L0.R1.3: The first part of this requirement addresses the case that information relating to an awareness scope is already present, whereas the second part addresses the case that the information becomes available later.

L0.R1.3:

∀M , t

  [$state_s$(M , t, output(U)) |= is_interested_in(U:USER, S:SCOPE, persistent)   &

    $state_s$(M , t, output(WWW)) |= result_for_scope(I:INFO_ELEMENT, S:SCOPE)]

  ⇒ ∃t' > t

    $state_s$(M , t', input(U)) |= result_for_user(I:INFO_ELEMENT, U:USER, S:SCOPE)

&

∀M , t1, t2>t1

    $state_s$(M , t1, output(U)) |= is_interested_in(U:USER, S:SCOPE, persistent) &

    $state_s$(M , t2, output(WWW)) |= result_for_scope(I:INFO_ELEMENT, S:SCOPE) &

    ∀t' [t1 < t' < t2   ⇒

    [not $state_s$(M , t', output(WWW))|= result_for_scope(I:INFO_ELEMENT, S:SCOPE) &

      not $state_s$(M , t', output(U)) |= not is_interested_in(U:USER, S:SCOPE, persistent)]

  ⇒ ∃t3 > t2

    $state_s$(M , t3, input(U)) |= result_for_user(I:INFO_ELEMENT, U:USER, S:SCOPE)

Example of a formal representation of a top level scenario

The following formal scenario representation relates to the second formal requirement representation expressed above. Note that point at time point 2 nothing happens, which corresponds to the waiting of the user, of course in another (but similar) scenario the waiting could take more time.

L0.Sc1.3:

    $state_S$(M , 1, output(U)) |= is_interested_in(U:USER, S:SCOPE, persistent)

    $state_S$(M , 3, output(WWW)) |= result_for_scope(I:INFO_ELEMENT, S:SCOPE)

    $state_S$(M , 4, input(U)) |= result_for_user(I:INFO_ELEMENT, U:USER,

    S:SCOPE)

To summarise, formalisation of a requirement or scenario on the basis of a structured semi-formal representation is achieved by:

- choosing *formal ontologies* for the input and output information
- formalisation of the *temporal structure* in a formal mathematical language

Checking a temporal formula F, which formally represents a requirement, against a temporal model M , formally representing a scenario, means that formal verification of requirements against scenarios can be done by model checking. A formal representation M of a scenario S and a formal representation F of a requirement are compatible if the temporal formula is true in the model. For example, the temporal formula L0.R1.3 is indeed true in scenario L0.Sc1.3: the result was available in the world at time point 4 in the scenario (after the user generated the persistent interest on its output at time point 1), at time point 5 (which is later than 4) the user has the information on its input.

3   Requirements at Different Process Abstraction Levels

In this section three levels of abstraction are discussed: requirements for the system as a whole, requirements for an agent within the system, and requirements for components within an agent. Example requirements at different levels of process abstraction for the example domain are used as illustration.

3.1   Requirements for the Multi-agent System as a Whole

First, the requirements for the multi-agent system as a whole, including interaction with users are considered. The requirements and scenarios in the previous sections are formulated with respect to the users and the World Wide Web, which is considered as the given environment. Otherwise no assumptions were made on the design of the multi-agent system that is to support the users. For example, no specific agents were assumed as yet. The requirements and scenarios as presented in Section 2 express the desired behaviour from a global perspective, and only refer to input and output of users and the environment (the World Wide Web). By refining these requirements and scenarios, more elementary units of behaviour can be identified (*behavioural refinement*); which units of behaviour are chosen is a specific design decision. For example, it can be postulated that on the basis of specific user outputs concerning its interest, an unpersonalized scope of interest is identified:

L0.R2   For each **search scope** of a user, an unpersonal **incidental need for information** on the scope of the search scope is generated.

L0.R3
    a. For each **awareness scope** of a user, an unpersonal **persistent need for information** on the scope of the awareness scope is generated.
    b. For each **awareness scope retraction** of a user, an unpersonal **persistent need for information retraction** on the scope of the awareness scope is generated.

Available new information is to be presented to those users interested in that information:

L0.R4   If **new information** is available , then each user with an **awareness scope** that has not been retracted by that user and that matches that information will receive that information.

L0.R5   If there is a **persistent need for information** that has not been retracted and information becomes newly available on the World Wide Web that matches this persistent need, then this information is identified as **new information**.

Note that new ontology elements are created that need not be part of the ontologies of a user input or output and are not meant to be part of these ontologies. In relation with the refinements L0.R2 to L0.R5 the design decision is made to identify at least two types of agents: Personal Assistant agents, that are in direct contact with users, and Information Provider agents, that only handle unpersonalized needs for information. Requirements L0.R2 and L0.R3 are imposed on the Personal Assistants, requirements L0.R4 and L0.R5 are imposed on the co-ordinated behaviour of both types of agents. The interfaces of the Personal Assistants and Information Providers will occur in semi-formal reformulations of the above requirements.

A global design of the multi-agent system is described in Fig. 2, in which two users, one Personal Assistant, two Information Providers, and the World Wide Web are depicted. The Personal Assistant has to co-operate with human agents (its users), and the Information Provider agents. The task of the Personal Assistant is to inform each of its users on information available (e.g., papers) on the World Wide Web that is within their scope of interest. Information on available papers is communicated to the Personal Assistant by Information Providers. The Personal Assistant is also capable itself of searching for information on the World Wide Web.

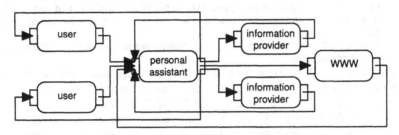

Fig. 2. Global multi-agent system description.

Given the design choice additional level L0 requirements can be formulated in terms of input and output of the agents and processes as identified:

L0.R6.2a /* Refinement of L0.R1.2 */
   At any point in time
   The user shall receive on its input **results for awareness scope**
   after the user has generated on its output that **awareness scope** and
   just after **new information** relevant for that awareness scope becomes available on the input of the Personal Assistant
   and the Personal Assistant did not receive on its input an **awareness scope**
   retraction before the **new information** was received on the Personal Assistants input.

L0.R6.2b /* Refinement of L0.R1.2 */
   At any point in time
   The Personal Assistant will generate on its output **results for awareness scope** for a user
   after it has received on its input an **awareness scope** of that user and
   just after **new information** relevant for that awareness scope becomes available on the output of the World Wide Web or on the output of one of the Information Providers
   and the Personal Assistant did not receive on its input an **awareness scope**
   retraction before the **new information** was received on the Personal Assistants input.

L0.R2.2   At any point in time
   If a user has generated on its output a **search scope** , then the Personal Assistant will generate on its output an unpersonal **incidental need for information** on the scope of the search scope.

L0.R3.2   At any point in time
   a.   If a user has generated on its output an **awareness scope**,
      then the Personal Assistant will generate on its output an unpersonal **persistent need for information** on the scope of the awareness scope is generated.
   b.   If a user has generated on its output an **awareness scope retraction**,
      and no other users have generated the same awareness scope without having it retracted,
      then the Personal Assistant will generate on its output an unpersonal **persistent need for information retraction** on the scope of the awareness scope is generated.

L0.R4.2 At any point in time
a. If the Personal Assistant receives **new information** on its input ,
then each user with an unretracted **awareness scope** matching that information will
receive that information on its input.
b. If an Information Provider receives on its input information that it identifies as **new information,**
and the **new information** matches an unretracted **persistent need for information**
that the Information Provider received on its input from the Personal Assistant,
then the Personal Assistant will receive this **new information** on its input.
L0.R5.2 At any point in time
If an Information Provider receives on its input a **persistent need for information** and
later information becomes newly available on the World Wide Web that matches this
persistent need, and this persistent need was not retracted before the new information
became available,
then this information is identified as **new information** and generated on the output of
the Information Provider.

In summary, for the current problem a design choice was made to design the system as a multi-agent system instead of as a single component system. The agents of the multi-agent system, the users, and the World Wide Web are all components of the system at the same level of process abstraction. For the top level, L0, the requirements pose constraints on more than one component of the multi-agent system. In other words the L0 requirements either specify the global purpose behaviour of the system (like L0.R1) or they specify the behaviour of the whole system in terms of relations between the behaviour of several of its components (L0.R2 to L0.R6). The latter are also requirements on the composition relation of the multi-agent system. Before the individual components can be designed, also requirements are to formulated on the behaviour of those individual agents and the component WWW.

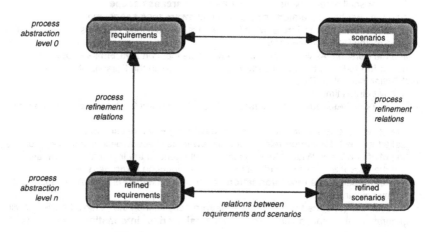

Fig. 3. Process abstraction level refinements.

3.2 Requirements for an Agent within the System

Requirements formulated on the behaviour of those individual agents and the component WWW are requirements of the next process abstraction level (see Fig. 3), in this case level L1. Again these requirements can be formulated informally, semi-formally, or formally. For example, the following requirements can be imposed on the Personal Assistant agent (abbreviated as PA):

L1.P1   For each incoming **search scope** of a user, the PA shall initiate an incidental quest for useful information on that scope by generating on its output:
    a. **communication** to Information Providers regarding an **incidental need for information** on the scope of the search scope.
    b. **observation to be performed** on the World Wide Web regarding the scope of the search scope.
L1.P2   For each incoming **awareness scope** of a user, the PA shall initiate an persistent quest for useful information on that scope by :
    a. only once generating on its output **communication** to Information Providers regarding a **persistent need for information** on the scope of the awareness scope.
    b. repeatedly generating on its output an **observation to be performed** on the World Wide Web regarding the scope of the awareness scope,
    until the PA receives on its input a corresponding **awareness scope retraction**.
L1.P3   At any point in time
    If the PA receives **new information**on its input ,
    then for each user with an **awareness scope** matching that information the PA will generate on its output an **awareness scope result** for that user,
    unless the PA received a corresponding **awareness scope retraction** before it received the **new information**.

Similarly, requirements (or assumed requirements) can be formulated for the other components of the multi-agent system. Again it is possible to define more elementary units of behaviour by refining some of the requirements. Whether it is desirable to do so depends on whether or not the constructed requirements are considered sufficiently elementary to serve as a starting point for a transparent design of each of the components. For some of the components the required behaviour might still be too complex for this aim. In that case, the requirements of those components can be refined in terms of their behaviour. For example, a possible behavioural refinement of L1.P3 includes the following three requirements:

L1.P4   The PA maintains a profile of its users that satisfies the following:
    a. contains the unretracted **awareness scopes** of that user.
    b. An **awareness scope** is added to the profile if it is received on PA's input.
    c. An **awareness scope** is removed from the profile if a corresponding **awareness scope retraction** is received on PA's input.
L1.P5   The PA is capable of matching **new information**received on its input with **awareness scopes** and determine the appropriateness of the information for the users that issued the **awareness scopes**.
L1.P6   The PA is capable of interpreting incoming communication information and generating communication information to other agents.

In relation to the behavioural refinements of requirements, a process refinement can be created if this is deemed appropriate. Furthermore, if a process refinement is deemed appropriate, then the choice still has to be made whether the current *process abstraction level is extended* with more processes (for example, whether the Personal Assistant agent is replaced by a number of agents at the same process abstraction level), or that an *additional process abstraction level* is created within one of the agents or processes (for example, composing the Personal Assistant of a number of sub-components). In this case, the latter alternative is chosen. For this choice a number of additional level L1 requirements have to be formulated to specify the behavioural properties of those sub-processes in their relation to each other (the behaviour of the sub-processes in relation to each other is global with respect to level

L1), and a number of L2 requirements have to be formulated to specify the behavioural properties of the individual sub-processes (this behaviour is local with respect to level L2). Before considering the requirements of level L2, first the sub-components must be identified and their global level L1 behaviour analyzed.

Based on the requirements L1.P4 to L1.P6 a design decision is made to identify at least three sub-components for the Personal Assistant: a component to maintain the user profiles (called Maintenance of Agent Information), a component capable of matching information with awareness scopes (called Proposal Determination), and a component that handles communication with other agents (called Agent Interaction Management). Requirement L1.P4 is imposed on component Maintenance of Agent Information (abbreviated by MAI), requirement L1.P5 on component Proposal Determination (PD), and L1.P6 is imposed on component Agent Interaction Management (AIM). For the other requirements of the Personal Assistant similar behavioural refinements can be made, this results in the addition of a few other sub-components. The next level of process abstraction of the design of the Personal Assistant is described in Fig. 4. Apart from the already mentioned components, the Personal Assistant also consist of a component called World Interaction Management (abbreviated by WIM, used for observing the World Wide Web and interpreting the observation results), a component called Maintenance of World Information (abbreviated by MWI, used to maintain information on the World Wide Web), and a component called Own Process Control (abbreviated by OPC, used to determine the strategies, goals, and plans of the agent).

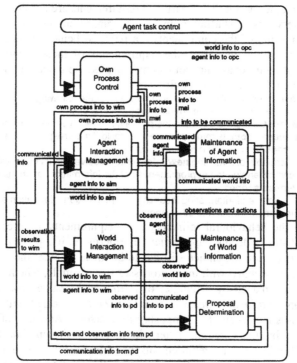

Fig. 4. Internal description of the Personal Assistant.

Given the above design choices, additional level L1 requirements can be formulated:

L1.P7   Incoming communication information received on the input of the PA is interpreted by AIM into **new information, awareness scopes, awareness scope retractions**, and **search scopes.**

    a.   AIM provides MAI with **awareness scopes** and **awareness scope retractions**.

    b.   AIM provides PD with **new information** and **search scopes**.

    c.   AIM provides MWI with **new information**.

L1.P8   PD provides AIM with **awareness scope results** and **search scope results** that are to be communicated to a user.

    L1.P9   MAI provides PD with the current awareness scopes **and** search scopes.

3.3   Requirements for a Component within an Agent

The individual behavioural properties of the components distinguished at process abstraction level L1 are specified by requirements at abstraction level L2. A few examples of level L2 requirements are:

L2.PD1   PD matches the current **awareness scopes** with **new information** it receives; if a match is found, then PD generates a corresponding **awareness scope result**.

L2.AIM1   If AIM receives an **awareness scope result**, then AIM generates an **outgoing communication** containing that result for the relevant user.

4   Requirements Specification and Verification

In this section some of the methodological aspects are summarized and discussed. In particular, the relation between requirements specification and compositional verification is addressed.

4.1   Methodological Aspects

Within the proposed methodology, during a design process, in relation to behavioural refinements of requirements, a process refinement is created if this is deemed appropriate.

A refinement of a behavioural requirement defines requirements on more elementary units of behaviour. Starting with behavioural requirements of the entire system, on the basis of requirement refinement it can be decided about the agents to use in the system, and in particular, which agent is meant to show which type of behaviour.

In a next step, for each of the agents it can be decided whether it is desirable to refine the requirements for the agent further, depending on whether or not the requirements constructed for the agent are elementary enough to serve as a starting point for a transparent design of the agent itself. For some of the agents the required individual behaviour may still be too complex to lead to a transparent design. In that case, the behavioural requirements of those agents can be refined. This can lead to the identification of requirements on more elementary units of behaviour within the agent and, in relation to this, to different components within the agent to perform this behaviour.

highest process abstraction level:
required behavioural properties of entire system

/ | \

next process abstraction level:
behavioural properties of agents

/ | \   / | \   / | \

next process abstraction level:
behavioural properties of components within agents

/ | \   / | \   / | \   / | \   / | \

.

(and so on)

.

Fig. 5. Behavioural properties at different process abstraction levels

This requirements refinement process can be iterated for some of the agent components, which, depending on the complexity of the agent, may lead to an arbitrary number of process abstraction levels within the agent (see Fig. 5). The result of this process is the identication of different process abstraction levels, from the level of the entire system, to the level of each of the agents separately, and further down to more specific processes within agents.

Sets of requirements at a lower level can be chosen in such a way that they realise a higher level requirement, in the following sense:

- given the *process composition* relation defined in the design description,
- if the chosen *refinements* of a given requirement *are satisfied*,
- then also the original *requirement is satisfied*.

This defines the logical aspect of a behavioural refinement relation between requirements. Based on this logical relation, refinement relationships can also be used to verify requirements: e.g., if the chosen refinements of a given requirement all hold for a given system description, then this requirement can be proven to hold for that system description. Similarly, scenarios can be refined to lower process abstraction levels by adding the interactions between the sub-processes. At each level of abstraction, requirements and scenarios employ the terminology defined in the ontology for that level.

4.2 Relation to Compositional Verification

The methodological approach to the creation of different process abstraction levels in relation to requirements refinement has a natural connection to the process of compositional verification (cf. [17]). The purpose of verification is to prove that, under a certain set of assumptions, a system will adhere to a certain set of properties, expressed as requirements and scenarios. In order to prove that a system is behaving as required, not only a complete specification of the system is necessary, but also the set of requirements and scenarios to verify the system against. If this set is not available, the verification process is hampered to a great extent, because formulating sufficiently precise requirements (and scenarios) for an existing system is nontrivial. For the purpose of verification it has turned out useful to exploit compositionality (cf. [17]).

Compositional verification as described in [17] takes the process abstraction levels used within the system and the related compositional structure of the system into account. The requirements and scenarios are formulated formally in terms of temporal semantics. During the verification process the requirements and scenarios of the system as a whole can be derived from properties of agents (one process abstraction level lower) and these agent properties, in turn, can be derived from properties of the agent components (again one abstraction level lower), and so on (see Fig. 5).

Primitive components (those components that are not composed of others) can be verified using more traditional verification methods. Verification of a (composed) component at a given process abstraction level is done using:

- *properties of the sub-components* it embeds
- a specification of the *process composition relation*
- *environmental properties* of the component (depending on the rest of the system, including the world).

This exploits the compositionality in the verification process: given a set of environmental properties, the proof that a certain component adheres to a set of behavioural properties depends on the (assumed) properties of its sub-components, and the composition relation: properties of the interactions between those sub-components, and the manner in which they are controlled. The assumptions under which the component functions properly, are the properties to be proven for its sub-components. This implies that properties at different levels of process abstraction play their own role in the verification process. A condition to apply a compositional verification method is the availability of an explicit specification of how the system description at an abstraction level is composed from the descriptions at the adjacent lower abstraction level.

Compositionality in verification reduces the search space for the properties to be identified, and the proofs, and supports reuse of agents and components. Complexity in a compositional verification process is two-fold: both the identification of the appropriate properties at different levels of abstraction and finding proofs for these properties can be complex. If the properties already are identified as part of the requirements engineering process, this means that the complexity of part of the verification process is reduced: 'only' the complexity of finding the proofs remains. Our experience in a number of case studies is that having the right properties reduces much more than half of the work for verification: due to the compositionality, at each process abstraction level the search space for the proofs is relatively small.

If no explicit requirements engineering has been performed, finding these properties for the different process abstraction levels can be very hard indeed, as even for a given process abstraction level the search space for possible behavioural requirement formulations can be nontrivial. If as part of the design process requirements have been (formally) specified as well at different levels of process abstraction, these can be used as a useful starting point for a verification process; they provide a detailed map for the verification process and thus reduce the complexity by eliminating the search space for the requirement formulations at different process abstraction levels.

Integration of the requirements engineering process within the system design process leads to system designs that are more appropriate for verification than arbitrary architectures. Moreover, reuse is supported; for example, replacing one component by another is possible without violating the overall requirements and scenarios, as long as the new component satisfies the same requirements and scenarios as the replaced component. In [16] a requirements engineering process model is described that can be used to support the requirements engineering process. Note that the idea of refinement is well-known in the area of (sequential) programs, e.g., [6]. The method of compositional requirements specification proposed here exploits a similar idea in the context of behavioural requirements.

5   Discussion

Requirements and scenarios describe the required properties of a system (this includes the functions of the system, structure of the system, static properties, and dynamic properties). In applications of agent systems, the dynamics or behaviour of the system plays an important role in description of the successful operation of the system. Requirements and scenarios specification has both to be informal or semi-formal (to be able to discuss them with stakeholders) and formal (to disambiguate and analyse them and establish whether or not a constructed model for a multi-agent system satisfies them).

As requirements and scenarios form the basis for communication among stakeholders (including the system developers), it is important to maintain a document in which the requirements and scenarios are organised and structured in a comprehensive way. This document is also important for maintenance of the system once it has been taken into operation. The different activities in requirements engineering lead to an often large number of inter-related representations of requirements and scenarios. The explicit representation of these *traceability relations* is useful in keeping track of the connections; traceability relationships can be made explicit (see Figs. 1 and 3): *reformulation* relations among *requirements* (resp., *scenarios*) at the same process abstraction level, *behavioural refinement* relations between *requirements* (resp., *scenarios*) at different process abstraction levels, and *satisfaction* relations between requirements and scenarios. For the case-study, these relationships have been specified using hyperlinks. This offers traceability; i.e., relating relevant requirements and scenarios as well as the possibility to 'jump' to definitions of relevant requirements and scenarios.

In summary, the main lessons learned from our case studies are:

- Integration of requirements and scenarios acquisition with *ontology acquisition* supports the conceptual and detailed design of the input and output interfaces of agents and agent components
- Refinement of requirements and scenarios in terms of requirements and scenarios on more elementary behaviours at the top level supports the identification of agents and the *allocation of behaviours to agents*
- Refinement of requirements and scenarios in terms of requirements and scenarios on more elementary behaviours within an agent supports the identification of agent components and the *allocation of functionality to agent components*
- A compositional approach to requirements and scenarios specification provides a basis for the *design rationale*: a documentation of the design choices made and the reasons for them
- A compositional approach to requirements and scenarios specification as an integral part of the multi-agent system design process strongly facilitates *compositional verification* of the designed system.
- The process of achieving an understanding of a requirement involves a large number of *different formulations and representations*, gradually evolving from informal to semi-formal and formal.
- *Scenarios* and their formalisation are, compared to requirements, of equal importance.
- Keeping track on the various relations between different representations of requirements, between requirements and scenarios, and many others, is supported by *hyperlink specifications* within a requirements document.
- As a result of these explorative studies it is proposed that a principled design method for multi-agent systems should include two specification languages:
- a language to specify *design descriptions*
- a language to specify (behavioural) *requirements* and *scenarios*

Each of these languages has its own chacteristics to fulfill its purpose. The distinction is similar to the one made in the AI and Design community [13], [14] between the *structure* of a design object on the one hand, and *function or behaviour* on the other hand. For both languages informal, semi-formal and formal variants have to be available to support the step from informal to formal, and, for example to support communication with stakeholders.

A formal specification language of the first type, and a semi-formal and graphical variant of this language, is already available in the compositional multi-agent system development method DESIRE, and is supported by the DESIRE software environment. This language was never meant to specify requirements or scenarios; a language to specify a (multi-agent) system architecture at a conceptual design level needs features different from a language to express properties of a system. In current research, further integration of the approach to requirements engineering as proposed in this paper in the compositional development method for multi-agent systems, DESIRE and, in particular, in its software environment is addressed.

The requirements and scenarios for agent systems often have to address complex behavioural properties. In comparison, it is not clear how, for example, in UML more complex behavioural requirements can be specified; use cases are informal, and activity diagrams seem too design specific and cannot express the necessary more complex temporal dependencies relevant to both requirements and scenarios. In the development of UML different representations of behavioural requirements and scenarios was not an issue [12], [15]. In [7], [8] an approach is presented in which more complex behavioural properties can be specified. A difference to our work is that no compositionality is exploited in requirements specification and verification. In recent research in knowledge engineering, identification and formalisation of properties of knowledge-intensive systems is addressed, usually in the context of verification or competence assessment of complex tasks; e.g., [1]. Such properties can be used as a basis for requirement specifications, and may play a role within specific agent compomenents.

References

1.   Benjamins, R., Fensel, D., and Straatman, R., Assumptions of problem-solving methods and their role in knowledge engineering. In: W. Wahlster (Ed.), Proceedings of the Twelfth European Conference on Artificial Intelligence, ECAI'96, John Wiley and Sons, 1996, pp. 408-412.

2.   Brazier, F.M.T. , Dunin-Keplicz, B., Jennings, N.R. and Treur, J. Formal specification of Multi-Agent Systems: a real World Case. In: Lesser, V. (ed.), Proceedings of the First International Conference on Multi-Agent Systems, ICMAS'95, MIT Press, Menlo Park, VS, 1995, pp. 25-32. Extended version in: International Journal of Cooperative Information Systems, M. Huhns, M. Singh, (eds.), special issue on Formal Methods in Cooperative Information Systems: Multi-Agent Systems, vol. 6, 1997, pp. 67-94.

3.   Brazier, F.M.T., Jonker, C.M., and Treur, J., Principles of Compositional Multi-agent System Development. In: J. Cuena (ed.), Proceedings of the 15th IFIP World Computer Congress, WCC'98, Conference on Information Technology and Knowledge Systems, IT&KNOWS'98, 1998, pp. 347-360.

4.   Brazier, F.M.T., Treur, J., Wijngaards, N.J.E. and Willems, M., Temporal semantics of compositional task models and problem solving methods. Data and Knowledge Engineering, vol. 29(1), 1999, pp. 17-42.

5.   Davis, A. M., Software requirements: Objects, Functions, and States, Prentice Hall, New Jersey, 1993.

6.   Dijkstra, E.W., A discipline of programming. Prentice Hall, 1976.

7.   Dubois, E. (1998). ALBERT: a Formal Language and its supporting Tools for Requirements Engineering.

8.   Dubois, E., Du Bois, P., and Zeippen, J.M., A Formal Requirements Engineering Method for Real-Time, Concvurrent, and Distributed Systems. In: Proceedings of the Real-Time Systems Conference, RTS'95, 1995.

9.   Dubois, E., Yu, E., Petit, M., From Early to Late Formal Requirements. In: Proceedings IWSSD'98. IEEE Computer Society Press, 1998.

10. Engelfriet, J., Jonker, C.M. and Treur, J., Compositional Verification of Multi-Agent Systems in Temporal Multi-Epistemic Logic. In: J.P. Mueller, M.P. Singh, A.S. Rao (eds.), Pre-proc. of the Fifth International Workshop on Agent Theories, Architectures and Languages, ATAL'98, 1998, pp. 91-106. To appear in: J.P. Mueller, M.P. Singh, A.S. Rao (eds.), Intelligent Agents V. Lecture Notes in AI, Springer Verlag. In press, 1999

11. Erdmann, M. and Studer, R., Use-Cases and Scenarios for Developing Knowledge-based Systems. In: Proceedings of the 15th IFIP World Computer Congress, WCC'98, Conference on Information Technologies and Knowledge Systems, IT&KNOWS (J. Cuena, ed.), 1998, pp. 259-272.

12. Eriksson, H. E., and Penker, M., UML Toolkit. Wiley Computer Publishing, John Wiley and Sons, Inc., New York, 1998.

13. Gero, J.S., and Sudweeks, F., (eds.), Artificial Intelligence in Design '96, Kluwer Academic Publishers, Dordrecht, 1996.

14. Gero, J.S., and Sudweeks, F., (eds.), Artificial Intelligence in Design '98, Kluwer Academic Publishers, Dordrecht, 1998.

15. Harmon, P., and Watson, M., Understanding UML, the Developer's Guide. Morgan Kaufmann Publishers, San Francisco, 1998.

16. Herlea, D.E., Jonker, C.M., Treur, J., and Wijngaards, N.J.E. A Formal Knowledge Level Process Model of Requirements Engineering. In: Proceedings of the 12th International Conference on Industrial and Engineering Applications of AI and Expert Systems, IEA/AIE'99. Lecture Notes in AI, Springer Verlag, 1999, To appear.

17. Jonker, C.M. and Treur, J., Compositional Verification of Multi-Agent Systems: a Formal Analysis of Pro-activeness and Reactiveness. In: W.P. de Roever, H. Langmaack, A. Pnueli (eds.), Proceedings of the International Workshop on Compositionality, COMPOS'97. Lecture Notes in Computer Science, vol. 1536, Springer Verlag, 1998, pp. 350-380

18. Kontonya, G., and Sommerville, I., Requirements Engineering: Processes and Techniques. John Wiley and Sons, New York, 1998.

19. Musen, M., Ontology Oriented Design and Programming: a New Kind of OO. In: J. Cuena (ed.), Proceedings of the 15th IFIP World Computer Congress, WCC'98, Conference on Information Technology and Knowledge Systems, IT&KNOWS'98, 1998, pp. 17-20.

20. Nwana, H.S., and Ndumu, D.T., A Brief Introduction to Software Agent Technology. In Jennings, N.R., and Wooldridge, M. (eds.), Agent Technology: Foundations, Applications, and Markets. Springer Verlag, Berlin, 1998, pp. 29-47.

21. Sommerville, I., and Sawyer P., Requirements Engineering: a good practice guide. John Wiley & Sons, Chicester, England, 1997.

22. Weidenhaupt, K., Pohl, M., Jarke, M. and Haumer, P., Scenarios in system development: current practice, in IEEE Software, pp. 34-45, March/April, 1998.

23. Wooldridge, M., and Jennings, N.R., Agent Theories, Architectures, and Languages: a survey. In: Wooldridge, M., and Jennings, N.R. (eds.) Intelligent Agents, Lecture Notes in Artificial Intelligence, vol. 890, Springer Verlag, Berlin, 1995, pp. 1-39.

Agent-Oriented Design

K. S. Barber, T. H. Liu, D. C. Han

The University of Texas at Austin
Department of Electrical and Computer Engineering
24th and Speedway, ENS 240
barber@mail.utexas.edu

Abstract. Recent development in the field of Multi-Agent Systems (MAS) has attracted researchers from various fields with new techniques rapidly emerging. Due to its multi-disciplinary nature, it is not surprising that proposed theories and research results in the field are not coherent and hard to integrate. In this paper we propose a functional decomposition of problem solving activities to serve as a framework to assist MAS designers in their selection and integration of different techniques and existing research results according to their system requirements. The basic phases include agent organization construction, plan generation, task allocation, plan integration, and plan execution. An example usage of the proposed model for the domain of naval radar frequency management is also presented.

1 Introduction

Multi-agent systems (MAS) may be regarded as a group of intelligent entities called agents, interacting with one another to collectively achieve their goals. By drawing on other agents' knowledge and capabilities, agents can overcome their inherent bounds of intelligence. A generic agent has a set of goals (or intentions), certain capabilities to perform actions, and some knowledge (or beliefs) about its environment [10]. To achieve its goals, an agent needs to reason about its environment (as well as behaviors of other agents), to generate plans and to execute these plans. Many real-world systems are naturally distributed by spatial, functional, or temporal differences, therefore, MAS can easily fit into such distributed environments. An agent's responsibilities are often specified a-priori by assigning domain specific goals to the agent.

Modeling operational requirements of the specific domain is necessary to assist design decisions for the definition of agents in the particular application. Similar to the object class definition in objected oriented analysis and design (OOA/OOD), formal analysis should be performed in order to scope the required functionality and responsibilities of an agent. Questions like how many agents exist in the system and what each of those agents should "do" cannot be answered without such domain knowledge and requirement analysis.

In addition to assign domain-specific functionality, there exist a set of inherent functionality for each agent. Specifically, agents must operate to solve problems by cooperating with a group of agents. Each agent must 1) operate within an organization of agents whether that organization is specified at design time or during

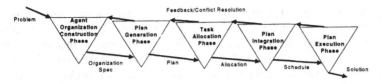

Fig. 1. A decomposition of MAS problem solving activities.

run-time, 2) generate plans under that organization structure, 3) allocate tasks to proper agents, 4) integrate agent individual plans and schedules, and 5) execute the plans to solve the problem(Figure 1). Multiple types of strategies exist for each phase and will be discussed in the context of the phases which capabilities they satisfy.

Actions at each phase are dictated by the strategy selected. By actions, we mean agents' behaviors including those that are not externally observable. For example, if a Contract Net is selected for the distribution of tasks, then in the task allocation phase the actions would include announce, bid, award, and so on. The strategies and actions chosen for each problem solving phase dictate the solution space for the subsequent phases as shown in Figure 1. If the result from agent organization construction is a centralized structure, then plan generation (both the actions and strategy) is determined by the centralized master agent.

MAS researchers have developed strategies with impressive results offering agents capabilities for many types of problem domains as in the examples described above. General methodologies to integrate existing techniques for agent oriented analysis and design are still under investigation. Drogoul and Collinot proposed an approach for agent oriented design, named Cassiopeia, which specifies and designs MAS around the notion of organization [11]. The major design steps of Cassiopeia are to design an agent's elementary behaviors, relation behaviors, and organizational behaviors. Elementary behaviors, relation behaviors, and organizational behaviors can help to classify agents' behaviors, but such classification does not really help MAS designers design the above listed problem solving activities. In addition, the elementary behaviors include only agents' external behaviors that can be observed from outside. Internal agent activities are also important and should be considered in the design procedures. Such activities include reasoning about behaviors, planning, resolving conflicts, and strategy selection, which cannot be observed directly as explicit actions.

In order to combine strategies, the system designers of MAS must determine 1) the strategy for use during each phase (what is the best or most appropriate strategy to use), and 2) dependencies among strategies across problem solving phases (are the chosen strategies for each phase compatible). The difficulties of integration arise from the interdependencies between phases performed by the agent and the associated strategies selected to perform those functions. For example, how organizations are designed really depends what kind of tasks the agents are involved in. When agents generate plans to solve a problem, they must consider their relationship with other agents and how the problem can be decomposed, which agent should do which tasks and when to do the tasks. To assign tasks to agents, the group needs to consider resource distribution and agents capabilities as well as load balancing. How agents can efficiently fulfill their jobs depend on how these agents are organized. We propose a framework and methodology for describing the interactions among the above stated problem solving activities and the integration of techniques.

This paper is organized as the following. An introduction and discussion of our methodology for domain independent agent oriented design is presented in Section 2. Although domain dependent design is not the main focus of this paper, domain specific agent specification is briefed in Section 3 for completeness. The Sensible Agent Testbed is presented as a case study of our methodology allowing the integration of heterogeneous techniques selected by an MAS designer in Section 4. Section 5 concludes the paper.

2 Domain Independent Agent Oriented Design

Agent-oriented design involves the selection and integration of problem solving activities. A two-staged design paradigm is proposed: 1) selection and integration of strategies tied to core agent problem solving functionality, and 2) selection and integration of system- and agent-wide infrastructure to support the core agent problem solving functionality.

The basic core agent functionality is composed of five distinct phases as shown in Figure 1. Agent organization construction (AOC) specifies how the agents should interact with one another. Plan generation (PG) determines how the agents decide on the actions that need to be executed. Task allocation (TA) is the assignment of tasks/goals to specific agents for execution. Plan integration (PI) is the integration of individual plans and schedules. Plan execution (PE) is the execution and monitoring of the actions. Selection and integration of problem solving activities for each of the five phases occurs in the first stage.

The second stage is to design the agent system infrastructure to support problem solving activities based on the requirements of the domain and constraints established by the first design stage. The infrastructure to support the problem solving activities includes mechanisms for communication, coordination, conflict resolution, and belief maintenance.

2.1 Strategic Decision Making

A strategy is a decision making mechanism which provides long-term consideration for selecting actions toward specific goals [13]. Each strategy "attacks" a solution space in a different manner. Strategic decision making [15] helps to select the appropriate strategy. Whether performed on-line or off-line by the MAS designer, decisions must be made with regard to which strategies are most appropriate for: AOC, PG, TA, PI, and PE. The selected strategy serves as a long-term guideline to assist selecting feasible and appropriate actions to take. Through executing actions, agents can provide the solutions to the problems that triggered the decision-making process. Figure 2 shows the relations among actions, strategies, and strategic decision making.

In order to accomplish a specific goal, agents must perform an action or a sequence of actions that trigger events and change certain states. Researchers have developed several process models (or action theories) to represent and reason about actions, including sequencing, selection, non-determinism, iteration, and concurrency [14]. Usually the term action refers to agents' activities that can be observed as their

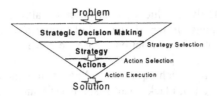

Fig. 2. Relationships between Actions, Strategies, and Strategic Decision Making.

external behaviors. When we model the whole problem solving activity, there are certain activities that cannot be observed from outside. Therefore, we extend the definition of action to include those that will also change agents' internal states or mental attitudes, for example the selection of actions to take.

A strategy can help agents to observe the environment, evaluate alternatives, and prescribe and schedule actions. In addition, strategies can be formulated and implemented not only within an agent, but also among a group of agents. For any given problem, various strategies may be available. Although a strategy may help to achieve success, it does not guarantee success. Therefore strategic decision making is needed for strategy selection. At this level, various styles have been developed to evaluate strategies, for example, based on utility calculations, priority, heuristic rules, or preference [3].

2.2 Core Agent Functionality Design: Evaluation of Available Strategies

Problem solving activities consist of five distinct phases: agent organization construction (AOC), plan generation (PG), task allocation (TA), plan integration (PI), and plan execution (PE). The basic interactions among each of these tasks are characterized by the structure shown in Figure 1. Each triangle in Figure 1 represents the three layers described in Figure 2, applied to that phase: actions, strategies, and strategic decision making.

Agent Organization Construction Phase (AOC). Upon considering goals that the agent wishes to achieve, the agent (or the system designers) must decide the manner in which it will interact with other agents. The result could be static or dynamic organizational structures which are designed for each goal an agent processes or for all goals for all agents. This phase can be viewed as directing how agents should perform the tasks.

Major approaches of organizational design can be classified as functional, divisional, matrix, teach, and network [8]. Available research results for MAS include Self-organization Design [18], Dynamic Adaptive Autonomy [23], and teamwork models [28], and so on.

Plan Generation Phase (PG). Many strategies have been developed for action selection, such as hierarchical planning [7], or operator based search methods [24]. In this phase, agents will decompose the goal and develop available plans with the planning strategies available under the current organizational structure (selected in phase 1, AOC) – either for the agent itself, or for other agents. Coordination at this phase will determine how plans are generated. For example, blackboard systems let agents contribute voluntarily, and hierarchical structures allow agents to plan only for those parts they are responsible for. If agents fail to develop plans, they need to go back to agent organization construction phase re-considering how they should generate plans.

Example plan generation techniques including traditional planning approaches [24], multi-agent planning [7], black board systems [16], and Partial Global Planning (PGP) [9;12] and so on. This phase may be tightly coupled with the next phases (i.e. task allocation and plan integration). For example, in PGP, each iteration of planning may include plan generation, task allocation and plan integration.

Task Allocation Phase (TA). Allocated goals or plans must match the assigned agents' capabilities, knowledge distribution, and resources distribution. This phase could be viewed as deciding which agent should take what actions with what resources. If agents fails to allocate tasks within these constraints, they must return back to previous levels (i.e. plan generation and agent organization construction for different levels of goals). The task allocation phase could be strictly after or integrated with the plan generation phase. If task allocation is part of plan generation, then agents generate plans concurrently with the consideration of which agents are allocated which actions.

Example techniques developed for task allocation include the Contract Net protocols and its derivatives [25;26], and the organization approach [22]. Different strategies of task allocation can be implemented, e.g. based on resource consideration, knowledge distribution, execution cost comparison, or load balancing.

Plan Integration Phase (PI). Agents must integrate partial plans for all goals and generate a system level schedule as well as each agent's local level schedule. Coordination at this phase specifies how partial plans can be merged together without clobbering each other and finalizing agent execution schedules. Conflicts among agents' goals and plans can be detected at this phase. When a conflict happens, there are multiple potential choices available for conflict resolution. For example, agents may deal with the conflict during plan integration or return to previous phases. This phase can be viewed as the phase that decides when agents should do what. If agents fail to find appropriate schedules, they need go back to previous levels (including task allocations, plan generation, and agent organization construction for different levels of goals) to relax the constraints.

Various techniques are available for this phase. Examples for merging agents' plans include Partial Global Planning, multi-agent planning, and so on. Examples for conflict resolution are negotiation (and various styles of negotiation), arbitration, voting, self-modification, social law, and so on.

Plan Execution Phase (PE). In dynamic and uncertain environments, a well integrated plan is not guaranteed to achieve its goals (since there could exist unknown actors or contingencies that may interfere the plan). Agents must monitor 1) the execution of their chosen actions to insure that the intended effects are achieved, and 2) the states of the environment (as well as behaviors of other agents) to ensure that resources are available and cooperation (if there is any) is still working. When certain planned actions are not available or portions of the plan are no longer achievable, the agent may return to earlier phases to re-start planning activities. To handle unexpected

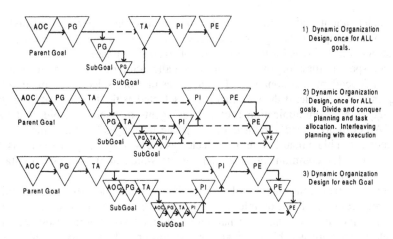

Fig. 3. Examples of various styles of interaction among Agent Organization Construction (AOC), Plan Generation (PG), Task Allocation (TA), Plan Integration (PI), and Plan Execution (PE).

events, techniques like Jennings's commitment and convention model [19] can be applied.

Interactions Among Phases. The flow of problem solving activities could be recursive and iterative among phases. How the loops will be formed depends on the algorithms selected and the domain requirements. For example, in Figure 3 (1), Agent Organization Construction may be performed for all goals that the agent holds (e.g. selection of one static organization). Plan Generation phase is performed recursively for all sub-goals. Task Allocation is performed for the final plan generated. Figure 3 (2) shows Plan Generation and Task Allocation closely coupled with Plan Integration. The plans for each agent for each sub-goal are integrated while allocation is performed. Figure 3 (3) shows a more complicated design style that for each goal, agents will reason about the suitable agent organization construction, generate plans and allocate tasks. The exact order of these phases may also be subject to the technology the system designer selects to implement. Phases that have only a single strategy implemented can be viewed as having the strategic decision making process executed by the system designer, such as systems with a static organizational structure.

2.3 Infrastructure Design: Requirements Analysis for Selected Strategies

The next design task is to design a system and agent architecture to support the requirements of the core agent functionality. According to the source of requirements, the requirements can be domain-specific or technique-specific. Two types of requirements must be considered: system and agent level requirements:

System Level Requirements. System level requirements are derived from an agent's need to support interactions among agents. Communication and resource distribution are classical system requirements and depend on 1) if all agents processes the same domain-independent and domain-specific functionality (homogeneous agents) or if the system is composed of agents of different functionality (heterogeneous agents), and 2) selected techniques for the various problem solving phases.

Domain specific functionality is based on the allocation of domain goals to agents. Domain independent functionality differences result from selected problem solving techniques. For example, if the Contract Net is selected as the task allocation method, then it requires a communication protocol for agents to announce, bid, and award tasks. MAS designers need to consider appropriate languages for this communication requirement. If a blackboard system is selected as the way agents generate plans, then there is a need for communication among agents which allows access to data in a public repository.

Resource distribution may involve with both domain-specific and technique-specific requirements. For example, if a certain radar on a ship is allowed a wider frequency range, then the agent is naturally equipped with more resources. If the organization structure is a hierarchical one, the resource distribution should support such an organization structure (i.e. the agents higher in the hierarchy need more decision making resources than the agents at the bottom).

Agent Level Requirements. Agent level requirements are tied to the internal operation of an agent. Domain-specific-requirements may impose constraints on agent architecture design. For example, if specific agents are equipped with actuators, those agents must process corresponding modules/objects/layers for control.

Technology wise, different approaches of agent architecture design may provide different features. The MAS designer may select from many agent architectures [20], including: layered (either horizontal layering or vertical layering), sub-sumption architecture, practical reasoning agent architecture (like belief-desire-intention model), or the Sensible Agent Architecture [1]. In addition, MAS designers must consider how an agent can represent and maintain its mental attitudes. For example, an intelligent agent need to represent its goal (so as plans, beliefs, intention, commitment, responsibility, and so on) to support problem solving activities. A counter-example would be the design approach that agents are simple, like ants which do not require the representation of complex mental attitudes.

Another design requirement is how agents make decisions. If game theory-based utility is the major decision making mechanism, then the ability to calculate attribute values must exist. If agents can select among strategies (for planning, conflict resolution, or other tasks), then a strategic decision making mechanism should be supported in the agent architecture.

3 Domain Specific Agent Specification

Section 2 describes core agent functionality design and MAS infrastructure design, which are independent of the domain and can be reused across various applications. The definitions for "What is an agent ?" differ, it is the position of the authors that the core agent functionality and infrastructure requirements discussed in Section 2 are fundamental capabilities setting agents apart from just any software module.

While not the main focus of this paper, this section briefly introduces the domain specific agent specification process for completeness. When specifying agents comprising a system to operate and solve problems in a particular application domain, modeling domain-specific, application-driven operational requirements is necessary to determine 1) how many agents will reside in the system, and 2) the domain-specific characteristic of the agent (i.e. domain-specific goals, data, and states.) In this regard, the objectives of agent specification are similar to object class definition in object oriented analysis and design (OOA/OOD). Such formal analysis scopes the required domain-specific functionality.

Methodologies such as the Systems Engineering Process Activities (SEPA)[2] provide the designer with a systematic process from requirements gathering, through domain modeling, to responsibility decomposition[29]. The information captured in the requirements gathering process must be synthesized to ascertain the operational and data requirements of the system. These requirements (operational functions and data) must then be distributed/allocation to constitute "parts" of the system. In OOA/OOD, these parts are object class and modules. For MAS, these "parts" are agents.

Several Agent Oriented (AO) methodologies could be applied and incorporated with the proposed approach in Section 2. For example, MAS-commonKADS [17] (which extends CommonKADS for MAS with added techniques from software engineering) defines seven models in the development process: agent model, task model, expertise model, organization model, coordination model, communication model, and design model. Similarly, the three models (agent model, organizational model, and cooperation model) Burmeister developed can also be used to build supporting representation mechanisms in our approach [6]. DESIRE [5] is another formal framework for MAS modeling which can provide rich syntax for implementation of our approach as well as domain-specific specification of agent functionality.

4 Case Study

In this section, a case study of designing a MAS in the domain of naval radar frequency management by following the proposed framework will be presented. The objective of this section is to demonstrate the interactions among different phases and illustrate the motivation for an agent-oriented design framework rather than to give the details of implementation.

4.1 Naval Radar Frequency Management Domain

The problem domain is naval radar frequency management. Naval ships are geographically and functionally distributed; each ship has its own radar(s) associated with certain frequency ranges. Radar frequencies are resources for each radar. Improper assignment of radar frequencies may cause radar interference and impair detection ability. Ships in a region may form groups: friends (those who are willing to help each other), enemies (those who are hostile to our group), and neutral 3rd parties (those who are not related and exhibit arbitrary behavior). In an open and dynamic system: ship radars may join a group, leave a group, perform tasks, and so on. Interested readers can find more detailed problem description in [27].

Assignment of radar frequencies must be coordinated among the ships. Due to the open nature of the system, ships in different groups may hold different attitudes about eliminating radar interference, ranging from cooperative to hostile (e.g. enemies may try to trigger interference on purpose). Each agent controls the radars of a single ship with the goal of maintaining a radar interference free state.

4.2   MAS Design for Naval Radar Frequency Management

Following the problem solving decomposition proposed in Figure 1, we will introduce how each phase interacts with each other. For simplicity, let us assume that there are two agents in the system, agent1 and agent2, both planning for a single goal, to maintain an interference free state. AND/OR goal trees developed in [21] are used to represent potential goal decomposition and combinations as well as their interactions.

For the implementation of the naval radar frequency management problems, we selected the Sensible Agent Architecture [1]. Each phase of problem solving activities is assigned to specific modules. A module called the Autonomy Reasoner is responsible for agent organization construction. Plan generation, task allocation, and plan integration are assigned to a module called the Action Planner which implements hierarchical methods in conjunction with domain specific frequency selection algorithms. Since the selection of frequencies is dependent upon which agent the assignment will be given, the plan generation phase and the task allocation phase are tightly coupled together. A module called the Conflict Resolution Advisor is responsible for detecting and providing solutions for both goal conflicts and plan conflicts in the plan integration phase.

Agent Organization Construction Phase. Since the environment of the problem domain is highly dynamic and uncertain, we chose Dynamic Adaptive Autonomy (DAA) operating in the Autonomy Reasoner module of the Sensible Agent Architecture developed in [23] as the major approach for organizational structure design. The basic idea is that agents are equipped with the reasoning capabilities on autonomy levels (planning interaction framework) for each of their goals, ranging from command-driven, to consensus, to local autonomous and master, based on the characteristics of the problem, the environment, available resources and so on. When agents modify their autonomy levels, the organizational structure will also be modified.

When considering a goal the agent wishes to achieve, the first item the agent must decide upon is the manner in which it will interact with other agents for solving this goal. This may result in the agent being the master of other agents, peers of other agent, command driven by other agents, or independent and work alone. Since both agents hold the same goal in the case study example, they choose to work on this goal together and form a consensus group. The result of this phase is an Autonomy Level Agreement (ALA) describing the organization under which the agents agree to plan for goal1. Based on the chosen ALA, these two agents begin their coordinated planning effort: plan generation, task allocation, and plan integration.

Plan Generation Phase. For the plan generation phase, these two agents follow a "divide and conquer" methodology and decompose the goal. For simplicity, we assume these two agents agree with the goal decomposition. If they do not agree with each other, certain coordination efforts need to occur – the coordination of the way goal1 should be decomposed can be implemented with different strategies, for example, negotiation or voting (of course, not valid for the case of two agents). The choice of strategies in this phase is limited by their ALA – they must agree to reach consensus.

Task Allocation Phase. After plan generation, an abstract plan is generated which includes goal2 and goal3. For task allocation, we have selected the Goal and Responsibility Allocation Protocol and Language (GRAPL) [4] as the protocol to coordinate agents. If we assume that both agents agree, through GRAPL, that goal2 is assigned to agent1 and goal3 is assigned to agent2, then agent1 and agent2 will work on the subgoals starting from the first phase (since we selected DAA as the agent organization construction technique, which assigns autonomy levels for each goal). Before these two agents can jump into the plan integration phase for goal1, they must finish planning activities (including the phases of agent organization construction, plan generation, task allocation, and plan integration) for all the subgoals of goal1.

Figure 4 shows how the recursive process happens. Agent1 starts agent organization construction for goal2, and in this scenario, we assume it chooses to do it alone (i.e. in a locally autonomous manner and forming a group consisting of a single agent). Then agent1 choose goal4 (instead of the other choice of goal5) as the subgoal of goal2 during plan generation phase. For simplicity, again, we assume agent1 assigns goal4 to itself. Planning continues in a similar manner by agent1 for goal4, and by agent2 for its subgoal, goal3.

Plan Integration Phase. Before the plan integration phase of goals at each level proceeds, all of the sub-plans of involved sub-goals need to be integrated. In our case study example, agent1 and agent2 need to merge the partial plan for goal2 {action3, action4} and goal3 {action1, action2}. If plan conflicts happen (i.e. these two partial plans may clobber with each other), techniques like promotion, demotion, white knight, and separation can be applied to eliminate the conflict [24]. If goal conflicts

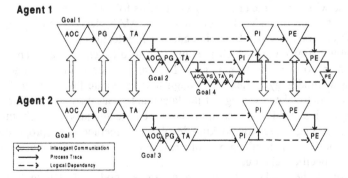

Fig. 4. Recursive problem solving activities based on goal tree. Agents perform agent organization construction for each sub-goal. Until all the sub-goals have passed the plan integration phase, *goal1* cannot enter its own plan integration phase.

happen between goal3 and goal4, one of the solutions is to trace back goal4 to the plan generation phase of goal2 and agent1 can choose goal5 to resolve the conflict. After conflicts are resolved, agents continue or restart (if new goals or actions are added) the planning activities. When finally returning to the top level, an integrated plan is finished and ready for execution. This plan should include both a verified organization-wise schedule and each agents' verified local schedule.

Plan Execution Phase. We simulate the agents' plan execution in a distributed simulation environment. The actions that each agent plan to perform are placed on a totally ordered queue with a time stamp for when to execute the action. After execution, the agents monitor the environment to check if they have successfully removed radar interference from the system. If they have not, they must return to the previous phases to re-plan.

The simulation results show that there are significant performance differences between various agent organizations based on such factors as time to solution, average interference, and number of frequencies tried in cases with and without communication. Due to the varying performance abilities of the different organizations during runtime, Dynamic Adaptive Autonomy (DAA) is necessary to allow the agents to adjust their organizations with the environment.

5 Conclusions

In this paper, we describe and illustrate the need for strategic design of multi-agent systems focusing on both the core domain-independent problem solving activities expected of agents and the selection of technologies to deliver that core agent functionality. The proposed design framework highlights strategic decision making for the selection and integration of technology addressing one of the five problem solving phases required by agents: organization construction, plan generation, task allocation, plan integration, and plan execution. For each phase, design considerations evaluating 1) actions to be executed by the agent, 2) strategies to help agents select actions based on long term considerations, 3) and strategic decision making to help choose appropriate strategies. MAS designer's selection of strategies at one problem solving phase will impact the decision making of its following phases.

Our contributions include: 1) guidelines for MAS design which consider the needed problem solving capabilities first and the architecture second, and 2) a flexible problem solving framework which is applicable to different domains and considers implementations of various techniques. In addition, technology changes rapidly. This design methodology is flexible enough to incorporate these changes, allowing system engineers to take advantage of the latest and greatest strategies. Our approach acknowledges this need and accommodates new techniques through the use of strategy and strategic decision making levels. The methodology proposed in this paper promotes cross-fertilization of research efforts and re-use of agent functionality-specific techniques.

While use of the methods in this paper are a good first step in generating a comprehensive agent oriented design methodology, outstanding research issues remain. Future work includes expanding this methodology to include: 1) a domain analysis methodology guiding the decomposition and assignment of domain-specific functionality across a system of agents, 2) a representation specifying techniques for problem solving phases and agent architecture designs to support automation assistance, and 3) verification mechanisms for the evaluation of design completeness.

References

1. Barber, K. S.: The Architecture for Sensible Agents. In Proceedings of International Multidisciplinary Conference, Intelligent Systems: A Semiotic Perspective (Gaithersburg, MD, 1996) National Institute of Standards and Technology, 49-54.
2. Barber, K. S., Graser, T. J., Jernigan, S. R., McGiverin, B. J., and Silva, J.: Application of the SEPA Methodology and Tool Suite to the
3. National Cancer Institute. In Proceedings of 32nd Hawai'i International Conference on System Sciences (HICSS32) (Maui, Hawaii, 1999)
4. Barber, K. S., Liu, T. H., Goel, A., and Ramaswamy, S.: Flexible Reasoning Using Sensible Agent-based Systems: A Case Study in Job Flow Scheduling. Special issue of Production Planning and Control, (1999) .
5. Barber, K. S. and McKay, R. M.: Allocating Goals and Planning Responsibility in Dynamic Sensible Agent Organizations. In Proceedings of IEEE International Conference on Systems, Man, and Cybernetics (San Diego, CA, USA, 1998) IEEE, 405-410.
6. Brazier, F. M. T., Dunin-Keplicz, B., Jennings, N. R., and Treur, J.: DESIRE: Modelling Multiagent systems in a Compositional Formal Framework. International Journal of Cooperative Information Systems, 6, 1 (1997) 67-94.
7. Burmeister, B.: Models and Methodology for Agent-Oriented Analysis and Design. In Proceedings of Working Notes of the KI'96 Workshop on Agent-Oriented Programming and Distributed Systems (Saarbrücken, Germany, 1996)
8. Corkill, D. D.: Hierarchical Planning in a Distributed Environment. In Proceedings of Sixth International Joint Conference on Artificial Intelligence (1979) 168-175.
9. Daft, R. L. and Marcic, D. Understanding Management, Second edition. The Dryden Press, Fort Worth, TX, 1998.
10. Decker, K. S. TÆMS: A Framework for Environment Centered Analysis and Design of Coordination Mechanisms (ch16). In Foundations of Distributed Artificial Intelligence. Sixth-Generation Computer Technology Series, O'Hare, G. M. P. and Jennings, N. R., (eds.). John Wiley & Sons, Inc., New York, (1996) 429-448.
11. Demazeau, Y. and Müller, J.-P.: Decentralized Artificial Intelligence. In Proceedings of Decentralized A.I., Proceedings of the 1st European Workshop on Modelling Autonomous Agents in a Multi-Agents World (Cambridge, England, 1989) Elsevier Science, 3-13.
12. Drogoul, A. and Collinot, A.: Applying an Agent-Oriented Methodology to the Design of Artificial Organizations: a Case Study in Robotic soccer. Autonomous Agents and Multi-agent systems, vol.1, 1 (1998) 113-129.
13. Durfee, E. H. and Lesser, V. R.: Using Partial Global Plans to Coordinate Distributed Problem Solvers. In Proceedings of Tenth International Joint Conference on Artificial Intelligence (1987) International Joint Conferences on Artificial Intelligence, Inc., 875-883.
14. Findler, N. V. Contributions to a Computer-Based Theory of Strategies. Springer-Verlag, New York, NY, 1990.
15. Georgeff, M. P.: A Theory of Action for Multi-Agents Planning. In Proceedings of Proceedings of 1984 Conference of the American Association for Artificial Intelligence (1984) 121-125.
16. Grant, R. M. Contemporary Strategy Analysis. Blackwell Publishers Inc, Oxford, UK, 1995.
17. Hayes-Roth, B. A.: Blackboard Architecture for Control. Artificial Intelligence, 26, 3 (1985) 251-321.

18.Iglesias, C. A., Garijo, M., Gonzalez, J. C., and Velasco, J. R.: Analysis and Design of Multiagent Systems Using MAS-CommonKASD. In Proceedings of 4th International Workshop, ATAL'97 (Providence, Rhode Island, USA, 1997) 313-327.

19.Ishida, T., Gasser, L., and Yokoo, M.: Organization Self-Design of Distributed Production Systems. IEEE Transactions on Knowledge and Data Engineering, 4, 2 (1992) 123-134.

20.Jennings, N. R.: Commitments and Conventions: The Foundation of Coordination in Multi-Agents Systems. The Knowledge Engineering Review, 8, 3 (1993) 223-250.

21.Jennings, N. R., Sycara, K., and Wooldridge, M.: A Roadmap of Agent Research and Development. Autonomous Agents and Multi-agent systems, vol.1, 1 (1998) 7-38.

22.Lesser, V. R.: A Retrospective View of FA/C Distributed Problem Solving. IEEE Transactions on Systems, Man, and Cybernetics, 21, 6 (1991) 1347-1362.

23.Malville, E. and Bourdon, F.: Task Allocation: a Group Self-Design Approach. In Proceedings of Third International Conference on Multi-Agent Systems (Paris, France, 1998) 166-173.

24.Martin, C. E., Macfadzean, R. H., and Barber, K. S.: Supporting Dynamic Adaptive Autonomy for Agent-based Systems. In Proceedings of 1996 Artificial Intelligence and Manufacturing Research Planning Workshop (Albuquerque, NM, 1996) AAAI Press, 112-120.

25.Penberthy, J. S. and Weld, D. S.: UCPOP: A Sound, Complete, Partial Order Planner for ADL. In Proceedings of Proceedings of the 3rd International Conference on Principles of Knowledge Representation and Reasoning (1992) 103-114.

26.Sandholm, T. and Lesser, V. R.: Issues in Automated Negotiation and Electronic Commerce: Extending the Contract Net Framework. In Proceedings of First International Conference on Multi-Agents Systems (San Francisco, CA, 1995) 328-335.

27.[26] Smith, R. G.: The Contract Net Protocol: High-level Communication and Control in a Distributed Problem-Solver. IEEE Transactions on Computers, 29, 12 (1980) 1104-1113.

28.[27] Suraj, A., Ramaswamy, S., and Barber, K. S.: Behavioral Specification of Sensible Agents. In Proceedings of International Multidisciplinary Conference, Intelligent Systems: A Semiotic Perspective (Gaithersburg, MD, 1996)

29.[28] Tambe, M.: Towards Flexible Teamwork. Journal of Artificial Intelligence Research, 7 (1997) 83-124.

30.[29] Tracz, W. Domain-Specific Software Architectures, Frequently Asked Questions, Loral Federal Systems Company, 1996.

A Developer's Perspective on Multi-agent System Design

P. Charlton and E. Mamdani

Imperial College of Science Technology and Medicine
Department of Electrical and Electronic Engineering
Exhibition Road, London, UK
p.charlton@ic.ac.uk

Abstract. This paper draws upon the practical experience gained in the development of software agents for the deployment of intelligent distributed services and information access. We review a set of multi-agent architectures starting from the communication and co-ordination requirements of such systems. The aim is to illustrate the common components in current designs and implementations of MAS which are often based on the communication nature of these systems. Further to this we show some benefits and drawbacks of these systems that are developed form this aspect. Part of the limitations of these systems is due to basing their communication semantic interpretation on the belief desire and intention model (BDI) which is a mental agency. The mental agency is used for the internal reasoning part of the agent and places implicit assumptions on the communication behaviour. We examine this limitation and report on how two MASs overcome some of the constraints. In light of these practical solutions we outline some pragmatic design concepts in reducing potential constraints of the BDI model on the communication layer. The result is a discussion about how to bridge between mental agency dependencies and the role of social agency when developing multi-agent systems.

1 Introduction

A common software development gap is the discrepancies between theory and practice. Practical developments of multi-agent systems often take from theory features which appear important and have computational interpretation. The process may result in different interpretations of a theory no matter how well defined it is.

Central to any multi-agent system is the communication language which must capture implicitly or explicitly cooperation and domain requirements of an application in some way. The literature has a number of formal representations and models about agent communication languages and cooperation requirements [18, 27, 22, 24]. There are also a number of implemented systems. A selection of these systems will be reviewed in the next section.

The paper is organised as follows: a review of a set of agent architectures and their communication support for co-ordination. From this analysis of a set of architectures we provide a common set of components which are often part of implemented MASs. The benefits from a software engineering view are considered. The drawbacks of basing the communication semantics on BDI model are discussed along with other the co-ordination and communication issues. Finally this work concludes by briefly examining how social agency and commitments may be, in the future, included when designing and developing agents for MAS.

2 Architectures, communication and co-ordination

To build an agent system, we must be able to break down an agent system into several components and may have to define explicitly some computational components' interfaces. This exercise is clearly dependent for its ultimate success on the co-operation of procedural protocols and conceptual modelling expertise, along with clearly defining the role of co-ordination. Many MAS systems place the emphasis on a rich communication language to communicate *high level concepts* about information to distributed reasoning processes. We start from the communication language requirements in a MAS system to illustrate the common software components that are often involved in supporting the communication part.

The communication part in agent systems is used to some extent to co-ordinate and share information and services. It is the main way an agent externalises its requests or solutions to the rest of the community. Being able to communicate in a rich manner offers a potential infrastructure of openness, autonomy, robustness, scaleability and flexibility. The trade off in order to reach these potential benefits is the complexity in maintaining coherence of distributed information through co-ordination. The main cost is how to co-ordinate these different services without placing too many restrictions on the communication language and the internal reasoning of the agent. There will inevitably be some restriction due to the modelling of complex application domains. The co-ordination feature of a MAS architecture is often distributed over four aspects of the communication language:

1. Protocols handled by the outer language (the content language is classed as an inner language). In knowledge query manipulation language (KQML [10]) is partly supported by a performative and FIPA ACL [9] is supported by communicative act, FIPA protocol and linked to the content via an action definition.
2. Content part contains the expressions of encoded information and service details in a sharable way (via the language parameter and ontology model) for other agents to interpret syntactically.
3. Language used to express the syntax of the content expressions, e.g., Prolog
4. Ontology model which provides the explicit model of an application domain to allow an agent to apply an intended meaning to the content to be shared.

The actual reasoning about these aspects of a message, which is communicated from an external source (agent), needs to be internalised so the reasoning behaviour of an agent can deal with the intended meaning of the content. The receiving agent must take into account the protocol and its own belief model and current behaviour status of a set of current interactions.

2.1 Current MAS Architectures

We have made some statements about MAS and how they may support co-ordination through their communication language. In order to substantiate this statement we review five MAS architectures. Table 1 summarises an evaluation of a sample set of architectures.

Architecture Supports/ Understands	KAoS	InteRRap	InfoSleuth	KIMSAC	FACTS
Performative/Action (outer language first– level protocol)	Yes	Yes	Yes	Yes	Yes
Language	Yes	No	Yes	Yes	Yes
Ontology	no	No	Yes	Yes	Yes
Content expressions	Yes	Yes	Yes	Yes	Yes

Table 1: *Summary of the aspects of agent communication language supporting co-ordination in a sample set of architectures.*

KAoS
The KAoS (Knowledgeable Agent-oriented System) [2] architecture was developed with a view to addressing the problems with agent communication languages, and addressing infrastructural, architectural, security and scaleability issues. It focuses on the issue of agent interoperability and defines agent characteristics as their ability to serve as universal mediators, tying together loosely-coupled, heterogeneous components.

InteRRaP
An architecture providing BDI (belief, desire and intention) infrastructure is the InteRRaP architecture [12]. This architecture's design is based on using a layered model approach and a BDI representation that provides different abstraction models in each of the architecture's layers. The InteRRaP architecture has three main components to describe the agent world: world interface, a control unit and a knowledge base. The control unit has a behaviour-based layer (BBL), a local plan layer (LPL) and a co-operative planning layer. Relationships exist between the layers to allow exchange of information through the knowledge-base hierarchy.

InfoSleuth
Agent-Based Semantic Integration of Information in Open and Dynamic Environments [3]. The InfoSleuth architecture is used to integrate information in open and dynamic environments. The design is concerned with combining information rich systems, such as databases with the Web infrastructure. Hence, the need to support an open infrastructure, as information may be added, modified or removed at any time. This constraint means that the architecture must operate in a dynamic environment. The merging of database access with distributed technology aims to support the user with access to heterogeneous information in a co-ordinated and coherent way.

   IntoSleuth supports explicit co-ordination at the language level, passing analysis and translation of the content to various agents. There is however, no explicit component for an agent to use, which defines how an agent, might on a general level, behave in a co-operative manner. These features are supported in CooperA platform [26] and Martial architecture [20]. However these architectures make other assumptions, which cause limitations (similar to InterRap they have no explicit ontology or language reference – see table 1). KAoS supports an infrastructure, and capabilities models but does not offer anything further in defining co-operative behaviour within a multi-agent architecture. InteRRap models explicitly many of the features of co-ordination to provide co-operative behaviour. However, there is no explicit ontology model, which implies supporting co-ordination across a domain is done internally by the agent.

KIMSAC

The KIMSAC (acts 030 -- Kiosk-based Integrated Multimedia System Access to Citizens [6]) architecture is similar to InfoSlueth by supporting four aspects of a communication language to provide the external semantics of the co-ordination requirements of the domain. The domain application used to deploy the KIMSAC architecture was public information and services, specifically social welfare services and job searching. The architecture, similar to KAos, used CORBA to support heterogeneity across languages and platforms. The communication language used between agents was based on KQML and KIF [15]. The end user requirements and the PSA approach meant that the information and service delivery had to support a rich interactive medium. This last requirement of a rich visualisation model actually presented an orthogonal requirement of integrating multimedia in a flexible way.

It is the KIMSAC's use of an asset description language [7,1,21] as a template that grounds four important aspects of information sharing between the agents and the end user. The aspects defined to allow the sharing of content across a distributed system and facilitate scaleable service provision are:

- **Media content:** defines properties, types and values to be understood by the presentation system that will render the media content by interpreting these property values.
- **(Service) Domain model:** defines intended use of the content, that is, which service is this intended for. This is used as one level of integration between the service agents and the asset manager and another level between the content description and the presentation system.
- **Task model:** this is used by the agents and can be used by the presentation end to support navigation
- **Action model:** supports the understanding of what should happen when the media object is interacted with. This action model is supported by a scripting language. Certain actions are dynamic and are replaceable. This allows the agents to specialise the type of actions that should be executed when the user interacts with a media object. Some actions are static and are directly related to visual changes, which will occur. The actions specialised by an agent usually specify the type of return information about the current event that the agent is interested in.

The asset description structure was often used within the agent communication language as the content language itself. There where other types of communication between the agents which where not asset description templates but task requests and information sharing between the agents. However, when an agent would offer a service, set of services or information to an end user the agent would call upon the help of the asset manager which would select an appropriate asset template to fulfil the task of providing services and interaction to the end user (for more details see [21]). The interesting result of such an approach was that agents did not need to understand multimedia but could request at a semantic level via task details. They could specialise the type of information returned to them via an action language which essentially translated to a KQML type message with content encoded in the appropriate way. The presentation system [6] was specialised in understanding asset description content and would synchronise the domain information with the appropriate multimedia object exactly. To summarise, asset description language (ADL) offered the following:

- A structured way of co-ordinating multimedia content and domain data for agents.
- Automate the process of returning information and results to agents in the language the agent understood. This is set in the **action** part of the asset description structure.
- Provides a content language in its own right as it holds rich information. The template provides an expected co-ordination of information. The asset description language allows this process to be automated. Everything in the structure is explicit so an agent can select the aspects which are important to it. The asset manager offers the service to update and select new templates. However, an agent could use the structure to communicate and share information with other agents through the action language, the domain and the task (the multimedia objects would perhaps not be of interest if the agent was not communicating in a visual way).

AVEB-FACTS application

The AVEB-FACTS (FIPA Agent Communication Technologies and Services -- acts AC317 [8]) architecture is similar to KIMSAC by supporting four aspects of a communication language to provide the external semantics of the co-ordination requirements of the domain. The domain application used to deploy this multi-agent architecture is to assist the user at home in selecting and filtering incoming program offers. This is done through a set of user centred agents which facilitates negotiations in order to purchase and subscribe to interesting programs. Software support for this complex application has been built using a community of agents which have different skills and goals.

Interoperability and agent development is supported by a platform called JADE (JADE Java Agent DEvelopment framework, [8]). JADE provides a framework which supports FIPA compliant agents [9]. The communication interactions within the AVEB-FACTS architecture use FIPA protocols. From a developers perspective it is these protocols which provide the main development advantages. The FIPA protocols offer co-ordination support and constrains the actual system. They do not limit the system as a developer can always use the communicative acts primitives. However, by using a set of protocols then the designers and developers know the expected dialogues between agents. The developer(s) is (are) left with mapping the domain requirements into a content language to meet the application objectives.

2.2 Common components in MAS

To summarise, most implemented MAS will have a set of software components that provide:
- A communication protocol, like KQML (Knowledge Query Manipulation Language) [10] and/or ACL (agent communication language) [22];
- a syntax for the protocol (e.g. KQML);
- a content language specialised to handle current applications/services, one that is also extensible;
- a general[1] interface (from a formal view this is the base ontological level) which binds the application to the understanding and use of content [21];

In order to support the communication language a MAS will have at least one communication channel (TCP/IP or CORBA are examples of these). Most MASs will support a standard[2] way of registering agents' roles and requesting information about other agents (referred to as a facilitator or broker). Another component that is commonly defined is a dialogue manager which manages some general protocols for an agent to interpret content and communication in context. This should be extensible to permit an agent to specialise dialogues, which are unique to certain communicating agents. Also, most agents in a MAS system will keep track of interactions with other agents and their own internal reasoning state hence a belief database store may also be a general component in the system.

This common set of components found repeatedly in a number of agent architectures provide a set of software abstractions that are now deemed essential for most agent systems. These components start to define the re-usable software patterns in agent oriented development. The agent-oriented approach extends the common set of object patterns but most importantly to make these patterns reusable they have a defined semantics which provides the developer with the necessary constraints. This is key to understanding a fundamental role of agents as a development paradigm shift in software.

One of the main claims about object oriented approach to software engineering was code re-use. This has only been minimally achieved but not strictly through code re-use but code compression [3](see [13]). Gabriel gives a good account of the software engineering problems inherent in the object-oriented approach. There are both advantages and disadvantages (object patterns see [14] and anti-patterns see [4]). Purely from an agent software engineering approach agent technology moves closer to code re-use. Agent code re-use is seen in practice today as the developers use *agent*

---

[1] General in an architecture sense to permit extensibility and automation

[2] This can only be standard within the architecture being developed as the agent community only has informal standards at this point. However, groups such as FIPA [9] have certain documents and recommendations available.

[3] [13] "Compression in object-oriented languages is created when the definition of a subclass bases a great deal of its meaning on the definitions of its superclasses. If you make a subclass of a class which adds one instance variable and two methods for it, the expression of the new class will be simply the new variable, two method, and a reference to the existing class. To some, the programmer writing this subclass is reusing code in the superclass, but a better way to look at it is that the programmer is writing a compressed definition, the bulk of whose details are taken from the context in which the superclass already exists" pg 5.

platforms in order to build intelligent agent systems that supply some set of services. The functionality that an agent platform supports will vary from one system to another. Most of these platforms will support many of the common software components, such as, a communication language, content language and communication channel. The platform should be extensible, in that an agent developer can add new content language parsers, ontology objects etc. To summarise, central to getting code re-use on such a large scale via an agent platform is the "formal semantics" that pins down the agent software components. Key to MAS systems is the communication language. However, as discussed in the next section the semantics used to define a communication language used by a number of MAS systems is based on a belief desire and intention model which has some limitations.

3 Discussion of co-ordination and communication in agent systems

A recent view of agent communication languages provided by Singh (see [25]) illustrates the problems encountered when using KQML and ACL semantics. The main criticism is the communication language focuses on the internal agent view of the world making interoperability between MAS systems almost impossible. This is due to the co-operative behaviour of an agent system relying heavily on the implicit reasoning of an agent which is devised carefully by the developers. It is possible to overcome some of these restriction within KQML and ACL. For example in the KIMSAC architecture a cooperative framework was defined through the asset description language. This content language has an explicit representation which means other agents from other developing vendors could use this language to interact with agents on the KIMSAC architecture. The services would be delivered to the user having both visual and service coherence preserved through the use of the asset description language. However, very little attention was paid to the outer language performatives. This makes dialogue interactions defined implicitly by the agent's interpretation of the application.

In the AVEB application co-operation relies upon FIPA protocols. An extension by the application was made to improve error handling when using the protocols. Also, the current content language is not SL as proposed by FIPA. A number of interpretation problems where encountered with the language and to pursue development a simpler content language was supported by JADE. The ambiguity of the language semantics is well illustrated by Wooldridge (see [28]).

Both KQML and FIPA ACL semantics is based on speech acts [23]. These communication languages encourage mental agency of belief desire and intention model. However, this model does not provide the means to interpret the beliefs and intentions of a random agent [25]. Further to this we encounter other problems with BDI models [11]. Fisher observed that a BDI architecture, in practice, has little fundamental difference between desires and intentions. Also, while practical systems incorporate elements termed beliefs and intentions, these are distinct from the formally defined beliefs and intentions model. Further to this most languages used for implementing agents do not provide an obvious representation for linking beliefs to intentions. This needs to be programmed by the developer.

To summarise, there are three key interrelated problems:

- the key communication languages' semantics used in agent architectures are based on this mental agency which represents the private context of an agent,
- the BDI formal semantics often suffers from only a tenuous link to the systems that are implemented and
- A limited distinction between intentions and desires for an implementation.

Essentially, a developer often treats the communication language as a software interface. The interactions, dialogues or protocols are a set of calls to a particular program. Often an internal model of an agent interprets the input from a message, using both its current beliefs and the message to create a context in which to determine what to do next. The agent developer, like with most software development, will have a knowledge of the expected input (communications received) and the expected output (communications sent). Protocols, communicative acts and content definitions are driven by the application requirements. Certain degree of separation can be achieved e.g. through the use of FIPA protocols to obtain a level of *architectural* openness. But much is still tied implicitly to the internal reasoning of the agent community to ensure coherence of interaction and service delivery. This limits interoperability and flexibility of an implementation.

4. Summary: Social Agency and commitments

Singh [25] proposes a shift from this mental agency model to a social agency model in order to develop a framework of interoperability. As discussed in the previous section there are current limitations when using current languages, such as, KQML or FIPA ACL. Part of the solution to creating flexibility but co-ordinated systems is the use of protocols. However, much of the MAS' social behaviour and an agent's commitments are based on the application/domain specifics. The design of a multi-agent system which supports social agency and commitments through protocols will separate out domain independent concerns from domain specific concerns.

The approach is to achieve cooperation of a set of agents which have committed to achieving a joint goal. There are number of approaches to reasoning about the communication and cooperation in agent systems (see [16,17,19]). Haddadi proposes incorporating cooperation with reasoning about actions. Jennings' solution is based on negotiation as an approach to generalise the cooperative process and Lesser illustrates the inclusion of organisation design into an agent framework.

There exist a number of pre-defined high level protocols, such as, contract net protocol [5] for negotiation. These naturally require some form of commitment agreement. Haddadi defines pre-commitment rules to establish a potential commitment. In order to establish commitments among a set of agents the agents will have to announce their role(s) which must be interpreted into what an agent will commit to. This mapping from roles to commitments essentially establishes a set of cooperative policies, which can be implemented as a set of protocols.

It is worth noting that natural conceptual clustering occurs in the design of agent systems even when an explicit model of social agency does not exist. However, without an explicit model of cooperative policies then interoperability between agent architectures is at best only at the sending and receiving of messages. In order to support these cooperative policies means representing an agent with both an internal organisation and an external organisational view. An agent's belief database must hold two sets of belief states: (a) about itself and (b) the organisation. The representation of the internal reasoning model of an agent appears to favour a belief and intentional model (and perhaps desires). The organisational representation seems to favour the explicit modelling of roles, commitments and cooperative policies.

The organisational model explicitly represents the social agency. As a minimum this agency defines a possible team or cluster of agents explicitly that are involved in an overall service delivery/access. Currently, in many systems most of the social agency is implicit, that is the agents are assumed to cooperate as the explicit computational behaviour of a MAS is defined by the set of services it supports. It is deemed successful if the behaviour exhibited provides the desired functional support of these services. Hence the social agency has a dependency on the application or service it is supporting. However, as we have seen some common software patterns in current MAS already emerging. It is quite possible that another common component would be the explicit support of the organisational model that represents this concept of social agency. Already mentioned in this paper are a few approaches to achieving cooperation explicitly which is the first step to gaining social agency. However, there is not, currently, an accepted standard (formal or otherwise) to including such a concept into computational MAS. This limits the potential for scaleablility, robustness, autonomy and flexibility to the implicit assumptions made by the development of each agent acting in a particular MAS making interoperability between MAS dependent on these implicit assumptions.

In order to incorporate a set of software patterns that can express the social agency of each agent explicitly requires a language in which to describe the terms and a way of communicating these terms. There are a number of ways that a developer can extend the current set of components in order to gain a more explicit model of the social agency. An obvious point in which to include this explicit model is in the agent's communication language. Potentially the outer language parameters could be extended to include a specific attribute called for example **social-policies**. The content property in the communication language can be used to express a particular instance of a policy that the agent is agreeing to. Another feature which can be extended is the set of communicative acts and/or protocols to convey the social policy of a particular communication.

Just as there are ontology models, which define objects, such as a user model object which implements the user model ontology, there are social policy models which define a set of objects that can be implemented. These sets of objects define the social policy ontology. The explicitness of the ontology depends on how much assumption is placed on understanding the meaning of a single term representing the policies. For example, there may be a set of social policies that defines the way a team of agents operate when a new user logs on to a particular MAS. A policy could, for example be given the label **new-user-policy**. This might be the limit to the policy definition in the run time system. To actually understand the meaning of this policy the developer of a new agent, which would like the agent to participate in the policy, would refer to the specifications or implementation details of this policy to find out what the attribute values are and their meaning. However, it is possible to make more aspects about this new-user-policy explicit. We can define the attribute values of such a policy. These attributes might be, simply, size of team (number of agents allowed to participate to limit the group size), language of the agents communicate in, the location of the agents, supports a friendly interface, has on-line help etc. An agent can commit to a particular new-user-policy by stating that it only works with agents that operate on a particular platform and/or there are other agents that can support on-line help etc. An agent can register its policies and in what context it will commit to these policies just as it registers its service support. Another aspect to consider is the relationship between the policies and the protocols supported in the communication language. Do different policies demand different sets of protocols?

To summarise, in order to address some of the limitations discussed, we need to establish a set of cooperative policies that can be formulated as protocols. Roles and commitments need to be defined which support the cooperative policies. Finally, these two orthogonal views of an internal agent's reasoning behaviour and an external organisational model need to be integrated in a structured way. Part of the expected result of extending the communication layer by designing and developing a social agency component explicitly is a set of software patterns that enriches the agent engineering paradigm through further affective code re-use. This may lead to an approach to evaluating the effect of different policies on the behaviour of individual agents and the system as a whole. This will enable developers to examine appropriate policies in relation to the service they are supporting.

References

1. Y. Arafa, P. Charlton, E. Mamdani & P. Fehin: "Designing & Building PSAs with Personality: From Metaphor to Implementation", *1ˢᵗ International Workshop on Embodies Conversational Characters*, pp 12-15, 1998.
2. J. Bradshaw, S. Dutfield, S.; P. Benoit, & J. Woolley, "KaoS: Toward An Industrial-Strength Open Agent Architecture",. pp 375-418, Chapter 17. 1997.
3. R. J. Bayardo, *et al.*. InfoSleuth: Agent-Based Semantic Integration of Information in Open and Dynamic Environments. In *Readings in Agents*, Ed: M. Huhns & M. Singh, pages 205-216, 1997.
4. W.J.Brown, R.C. Malveau, H. W.S. McCormick III & T.J. mowbray "Anti Patterns:Refactoring Software, Architectures and Projects in Crisis" Wiley Computer Publishing, 1998
5. B. Burmeister, A. Haddadi & K. Sundermeyer "Generic, Configurable, Cooperation Protocols for Multi-Agent Systems", In LNAI, From Reaction to Cognition, MAAMAW 93, pg 157-171, 1993
6. P. Charlton, E. Mamdani, O. Olsson, J. Pitt, F. Somers, A. Waern. An Open Agent Architecture Supporting Multimedia Services on Public Information Kiosks. In Proc. 2nd Int. Conf Practical Application of Intelligent Agents & Multi-Agent Technology, pp 445-465, 1997.
7. P. Charlton, E. Mamdani, O. Olsson, J. Pitt, F. Somers & A. Waern, Using an Asset Model for Integration of Agents & Multimedia to Provide an Open Service Architecture, Multimedia Applications, Services & Techniques, *Lecture Notes in Computer Science, (ECMAST '97)*, pp 635-650, 1997.
8. F. Bellifemine, A. Poggi, G. Rimassa. JADE – A FIPA-compliant Agent Framework. In Proc. 4ᵗʰ Int. Conf Practical Application of Intelligent Agents & Multi-Agent Technology, pp 97-109, 1999.

9. FIPA - Foundations for Intelligent Physical Agents, www.fipa.org

10. T. Finin & R. Fritzson; KQML: A Language & Protocol for Knowledge & Information Exchange, In *Proc. of 19th Intl. Distributed Artificial Intelligence Workshop*, pages 127–136. Seatle, USA, 1994.

11. M. Fisher "Implementing BDI-like Systems by Direct Execution" In IJCAI 97, Japan, pg. 316-321, 1997

12. K. Fischer, J. Muller, and M. Markus,. A pragmatic BDI Architecture. *In Readings in Agents*, Ed: M. Huhns & M. Singh, pages 217–231, 1997.

13. R. Gabriel "Patterns of Software: Tails from the software community", Oxford University Press, 1996.

14. E. Gamma, R. Helm, R. Johnson & J. Vlissides "Design Patterns: Elements of Reusable Object-Oriented Software", Addison-Wesley Professional Computing Series, 1995.

15. M. Genesereth and R. Fikes. Knowledge Interchange Format, Version 3.0. Reference manual, Technical Report, Computer Science Department, Stanford University. 1992.

16. A Haddadi "Communication and Cooperation in Agent Systems: A Pragmatic Theory" In Springer-Verlag, Berlin, 1996.

17. N. Jennings "Co-ordination Techniques for Distributed Artificial Intelligence" In *Foundations of Distributed Artificial Intelligence*, Wiley Interscience, pp. 187-229

18. Y. Labrou & T. Finin, "Semantics and Conversations for an Agent Communication Language," *In Readings in Agents*, Ed: M. Huhns & M. Singh, pages 235-242, 1997

19. V. Lesser "Reflections on the Nature of Multi-Agent Co-ordination and Its Implications for an Agent Architecture" In Autonomous Agents and Multi-Agent Systems vol 1. No.1, pg 89-111, 1998.

20. F. von Martial. *Coordinating Plans of Autonomous Agents*. PhD Thesis, Lecture Notes In Artificial Intelligence, Springer-Verlag, 1992

21. R. McGuigan, P. Delorme, J. Grimson, P. Charlton, & Y. Arafa, The Reuse of Multimedia Objects by Software in the KIMSAC System, In *proceedings of Object Oriented Information Systems, OOIS'98*. 1998

22. P. Breiter and M. D. Sadek "A Rational Agent as a Kernel of a Cooperative Dialogue System: Implementing a Logical Theory of Interaction," in Proc. ECAI-96 *Workshop Agent Theories, Architectures and Languages*, Springer-Verlag, Berlin, pp 261-276

23. J. R. Searle. *Speech Acts*. Cambridge University Press Cambridge, UK, 1969.

24. M. Singh "A Semantics of Speech Acts*", *In Readings in Agents*, Ed: M. Huhns & M. Singh, pages 458-470. 1997

25. Munindar p. Singh, "Agent Communication Languages: Rethinking the Principles", In *IEEE Computer*, November 1998, Pages 40-47

26. L. Sommaruga, N. Avouris, & M Van Liedekerke,.The Evolution of the CooperA Platform. In *Foundations of Distributed Artificial Intelligence*, Wiley Interscience, pp.365-400, 1997.

27. Wooldridge, M and Jennings, N. 1997 Formalizing the Cooperative Problem Solving Process. In *Readings in Agents*. Pages 430-432 , 1997.

28. M. Wooldridge, "Verifiable Semantics for Agent Communication Languages" in Proceedings ICMAS 98, pg 349-356, 1998

A Development Environment for the Realization of Open and Scalable Multi-agent Systems

Federico Bergenti and Agostino Poggi

Dipartimento di Ingegneria dell'Informazione, Università degli Studi di Parma
Parco Area delle Scienze 181A, I – 43100 Parma, Italy
{bergenti, poggi}@CE.UniPR.IT

Abstract. This paper presents a development environment suitable for the design and implementation of multi-agent systems. This environment is designed following the guidelines found in FIPA specifications. Therefore, it offers the management agents and services necessary to realize a FIPA-compliant open system. An agent prototype is also provided in order to ease the implementation of domain-specific agents. Even if the development environment mainly supports the C++ language, the resulting architectures are heavily based on the concept of roaming agent through a distributed environment. Interoperability with other systems, supporting other languages such as Java, is guaranteed by FIPA specifications. The presented environment has been used to develop a multi-agent system that should integrate the different software modules performing sensory data interpretation, planning and faults diagnosis of a robot working in a space station.

1 Introduction

Nowadays, the complexity and dynamics of organizations, and the growth in networked information resources require information systems that can be distributed on a network and interoperate with other systems. Such systems can not be easily realized with traditional software technologies because of the limits of these technologies to cope with distribution and interoperability. The emergence of agent-based technologies seems to be a promising answer to facilitate the realization of such systems as they were designed to cope with distribution and interoperability [10]. In fact, two recent market surveys have concluded that agents will be the most important computing paradigm in the next ten years. In particular, it is claimed that by the year 2000 every significant application will have some form of agent functionality [13] and that the total value of agent-related markets in the States and in Europe could be worth 1.2 billion pounds by the same year [11].

Agent technologies are still immature and few truly agent-based systems have been realized. The FIPA standardization effort is in the direction to allow an easy interoperability between agent systems because FIPA, beyond the agent communication language, specifies also the key agents necessary for the management of an agent system, the ontology necessary for the interaction between systems and the protocol transport level.

This paper presents a development environment that can be used to design and implement dynamic agent architectures following FIPA [3] recommendations. The system provides a set of building blocks and services supporting the creation of flexible agent architectures within a distributed environment. The system reference language is C++, but the interoperability required by FIPA specifications should enable agents implemented with any other system to integrate into the designed architectures.

The rest of this paper is organized as follows: section 2 introduces FIPA agent standard as a mean to design interoperable and flexible agent architectures. Section 3 describes the platform architecture as a compile-time library supported by a run-time environment. Section 4 briefly outline a robotic application developed with the presented system while section 5 points some differences between the presented system and what can be found in the literature. Finally, sections 6 and 7 present the main outcomes and the planned future directions of the work.

2   FIPA Agent Standard

The *Foundation for Intelligent Physical Agents (FIPA)* is an international non-profit association of companies and organizations sharing the effort for designing specifications for agent technologies [3]. FIPA current direction is to investigate the possibility to define a set of basic technologies that can be integrated by developers in order to make complex systems with a high degree of interoperability.

FIPA has been formally established on September '96. It adopts a standardization process based on work items. Each work item lasts one year and is composed of a *Call for Proposals for new Agent Technologies and Applications*, a phase of selection and refinement of the received proposals and, finally, the public release of a set of specifications. The subsequent year is instead devoted to the validation of these specifications via field trials.

The first set of specifications, called FIPA 97, has been approved at the 7th meeting in Munich in October '97 [6]. This consists of seven parts: the first three concern the normative specifications of some generic agent technologies. The other four concern the informative description of how the normative items can be applied to four applications which can take benefit from the specified agent technologies: personal travel assistance, personal assistant, audio-visual entertainment and broadcasting, network management and provisioning.

As the main characteristic of agents is their social ability, it should not cause surprise that FIPA gave priority to specify the rules to allow a society of agents to effectively exist, operate and be managed. It specifies the minimum amount of technology deemed necessary for the management of agents in an open agent system, including agent roles, agent-management content languages and ontologies.

Three key mandatory roles have been identified into an agent platform; all these roles are played by agents. The *Agent Management System (AMS)* is the agent that exerts supervisory control over access to and use of the platform; it is responsible for authentication of resident agents and control of registrations. The *Agent Communication Channel (ACC)* is the agent that provides a mean for the basic contact between agents inside and outside the platform. It is the default communication method which offers a reliable, orderly and accurate message routine service; it supports IIOP protocol [15] for interoperability between different agent platforms. The *Directory Facilitator (DF)* is the agent that provides a yellow pages service to the agent platform. It is worth noting that no restriction is given to the actual technology used for the platform implementation: e-mail based platforms, CORBA based platforms and Java multi-thread applications could all be FIPA compliant implementations.

FIPA 97 also specifies the *Agent Communication Language (ACL)*. It is based on a societal view of computation where agents are able to interoperate and reach goals by exchanging information and services with their peers. As a consequence, the content of communication must be unambiguous and universally shared by all FIPA-compliant agents. The agent interaction is here at a higher abstraction level than communication methods, such as CORBA or Java RMI. As a matter of fact, some systems could decide to implement agent communication on one of those message transportation mechanisms. The ACL is based on the *speech-act theory* [1], where messages are communicative actions, in just the sense that physical actions are: messages are sent with the intention of obtaining a desired change in the world. This part of the standard is then a catalogue of communicative acts, their formal semantics and a set of high-level interaction protocols that allow complex negotiations among agents, such as several kinds of auctions, contract-net, ordering or requesting actions.

Part 3 of FIPA 97 applies to any other non-agentized software with which agents could need to connect. Such systems include legacy software, conventional databases, middleware for all manners of interaction including hardware drivers. Because it is expected that in most significant applications, non-agentized software may dominate software agents, FIPA defines a single tool by which agents may connect to software.

Those *wrapper* agents are specified by FIPA through the wrapper ontology and the software dynamic registration mechanism. The *Agent Resource Broker (ARB)* service is also defined allowing advertisement of non-agent services in the agent domain and management of their use by other agents during negotiation of parameters, evaluation of cost and priority, authentication and permission.

3   Platform Architecture

The presented system is a development environment that can be used to design and implement dynamic agent architectures following the FIPA specifications. FIPA specifications give the minimum amount of technology deemed necessary for the management of agents in an open agent system, including agent roles, an agent communication language, an agent management content language and a standard way to interact with non-agentized software.

In particular, the flexible architecture described below and the platform services introduced in section 3.2 should enable the creation of flexible agent architectures, as

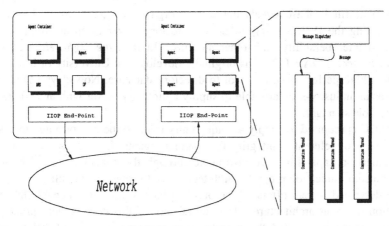

Fig. 1. Platform architecture.

depicted in figure 1. The described system implements agents as multi-thread entities running within an *agent container*. Agent containers are the fundamental environment in which agents run; those containers are the only responsible for agent creation and offer the basic communication capabilities and management facilities needed by an agent to execute.

A container provides connectivity between agent implementing an IIOP end-point and ensures a life-cycle management being able to start, stop, suspend and resume agents execution.

The IIOP end-point allows the interaction between agents of different containers. When an agent needs to send a message, it appends a request to the IIOP end-point message queue, thus asking for delivery. If the destination agent is in the same container, the IIOP end-point appends the message in its input queue, else the IIOP end-point dispatches the message to the IIOP end-point of the other container that appends the message to the input queue of the destination agent.

An agent architecture is a set of agent containers communicating through a network, but some special-purpose agents are also needed to enable the implementation of real-world applications.

An AMS is required to ensure high flexibility in the platform architecture. In fact, the AMS is the agent responsible for all agents' life cycle. An agent is created within the platform, asking the AMS to request for the creation to the desired agent container. The agent container responds to this request by loading the agent executable code, as a special form of DLL, and allocating all required resources within its scope. Once the agent acknowledges the AMS of its creation, the agent is made visible to all the system and its data are placed into the platform database. Destruction and mobility of agents through the containers are implemented in a similar fashion.

The platform database is managed by the AMS and by the DF. The AMS is responsible for locating a roaming agent keeping a trace of all agents move providing a white-pages service, while the DF provides a yellow pages service. Both the DF and the AMS have direct access to the database and play the role of agent wrapper to the DBMS. A detailed analysis of the relationships between the data that should be stored into the platform database reveals that they are organized as a directory. This suggests implementing the DBMS using an *LDAP* directory server to ensure high performances and interoperability with other systems. In fact, *the Lightweight Directory Access Protocol*, LDAP [12], was originally developed at University of Michigan to provide a high-performance protocol to directory database. Nowadays LDAP is accepted as an industry-standard able to supply a directory server with an efficient and interoperable standard.

An ACC is required to supply a unique entry point to the platform and to ease the enforcement of referential integrity for roaming agents. In fact, as the basic agent communication capabilities are distributed through the containers, there is no real need of a communication proxy for architectures not supporting mobility.

The described system offers all the building blocks that should enable the implementation of agent architectures. The central tool of this development process is a *platform metaservice* called the *architecture manager*. This visual tool is used to define an agent architecture by selecting which containers, agents and platform-services should be part of the architecture. In fact, the user is able to create an agent architecture by choosing a set of agent containers distributed though the network and allocating agents and platform services within them. This approach should enable fast architecture prototyping and should also support for some sophisticated load balancing policies at the architecture level.

3.1 Agent Model

The described system offers a multi-thread agent model implemented through a compile-time support, enabling for the creation of a suitable agent executable code, and a run-time support, in the form of agent containers. Once compiled into a suitable form of DLL, the agent can be loaded by a container and executed as a thread pool within the container process.

This multi-thread architecture allows an agent to manage different conversations in parallel. In fact, the idea is to introduce an agent thread for every conversation: the *conversation-id* of every incoming message discriminates to which thread the message should be dispatched. This architecture is implemented by a message-dispatching thread receiving messages from the IIOP end-point. This thread simply loops parsing the incoming ACL messages: information such as the content language, ontology and the conversation-id of the message are thus acquired. For every parsed message, the message-dispatching thread:

- dispatches the message to the appropriate conversation thread, if the message belongs to an active conversation;
- creates a new conversation thread if the message starts a new conversation;
- processes the message, if the message does not belong to an active conversation and does not start a conversation. This could happen, for example, when a message is incorrect or the required ontology is not supported by the destination agent.

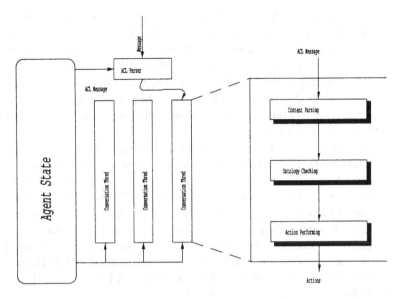

Fig. 2. Agent processing an incoming message.

An ACL message reaches a conversation thread in the form of an object containing a reference to the message content string. The standard behavior of a conversation thread is to choose an *ontology-driven parser* on the base of the specified content language and to use it to parse the message.

An agent has a different parser for each content language it supports: the parser receives as parameters an ACL-content message and an *ontology descriptor*. The purpose of the ontology descriptor is to constraint the set of language objects and actions belonging to the ontology and to supply the corresponding semantic actions.

The current implementation supports KIF [9] and SL [6], as content languages, and the FIPA management ontologies [7]: the user is requested to develop the application-specific ontologies. This approach offers great flexibility to agent design as the user is required only to concentrate on the particular ontology rules. Figure 2 depicts the process of message handling within an agent.

3.2 Platform Services

An agent architecture can support common-use services by means of special-purpose agents. The AMS is the central manager of an architecture as it is the agent responsible for all other agents life cycle. This service plays a central role within an agent architecture and it is the architecture manager referee. Once a new agent architecture is created by the architecture manager, an AMS is started within a chosen container in order to support for the following configuration.

The AMS is the only agent that can send command to the agent containers and thus it is the final responsible for agent mobility. Agent mobility is supported by the described system by means of a multi-step protocol. First the roaming agent is requested to serialize its state and send it to the AMS, here acting as a transient storage; then the agent executable code is removed from the container. This code removal corresponds to a code loading by the target container. In order to deal with distributed environments where a uniform access to disk files is not supported, such as open networks, the code is loaded through the HTTP protocol. Once loaded, the agent is instantiated by a constructor method supplied with the serialized form of the agent state.

The final step in this protocol is the database update that should support the referential integrity of the moving process.

The agent-mobility implies the need of locating an agent by means of some position-independent name. This name-virtualization scheme is enabled by the presence of the AMS and the ACC. Once an agent is created by the AMS, it is registered with a *platform unique name (PUN)* within the platform DBMS. The main role of the AMS is to associate a PUN to the actual IIOP address of the agent. If the target of a communicative act is supposed to be roaming, an agent should query the AMS before actually sending a message. Sometimes it is more efficient, in term of communication overhead, to use the ACC as a message proxy. In fact, as ACC and AMS are usually placed into the same agent container, ACC can resolve a PUN into an IIOP address without sending requests through the network.

When an agent is created, it is requested to supply a brief textual description of its capabilities within a chosen ontology. This description is fundamental in dynamic environments where agents need a capabilities-based collaboration. In fact, it is quite common for an agent to feel the need to collaborate with some other unknown agent that could fulfill its requirements. The easiest way to retrieve the PUN of an agent with certain capabilities is to query the DF supplying some keywords. In fact, what the DF is responsible for is the retrieval of an agent PUN once supplied with some keyword in the scope of an ontology. This simple search scheme is powerful enough to cope with many real-world applications as dynamic collaborations are usually quite simple and mechanical.

4 The JERICO System

We are using the presented development environment for the implementation of a multi-agent architecture [8] that will control the activities of the JERICO system [4]. JERICO is a robotic manipulator with a set of sensors and cameras; its objective is to establish a powerful and versatile robotically tended exposure payload infrastructure on the Russian Service Module of the International Space Station.

This robot control system is being developed by a consortium of seven Italian research centers: the planned activity is to realize six software modules performing the control system activities, and a middleware layer for their integration.

In order to ease the integration of the different modules and to make the system extensible to new required functionality, agent technology has been chosen to support modules interactions. Therefore, following FIPA specifications, each software module is encapsulated into a wrapper agent. One wrapper agent is supplied for each

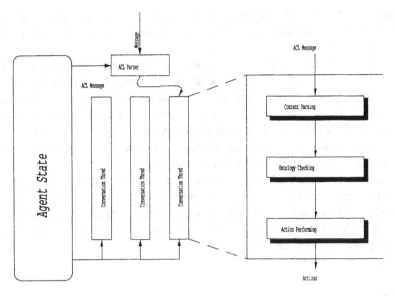

Fig. 2. Agent processing an incoming message.

software module: supervision, diagnosis, man-machine interface, planning, sensory data interpretation and plan execution.

The operator, who may be either the specialist on board or the scientist monitoring the experiment from station or from the Earth, may interact with the robotic system at a high abstraction level through the man-machine interface agent, by providing only the goals to be achieved.

The planning agent generates the action plan necessary to satisfy the goals required by the operator: a plan is built by one or more task sequences, where a task is a collection of basic activities such as "move to", "grapple", "unlock". Then, the plan execution agent executes the generated plan.

If some problems arise during the execution, the plan execution agent sends a message to the planning agent in order to replan or refine the previous plan. During the plan execution, the sensory data interpretation agent acquires and aggregates data coming from the sensors of the robotic system. These sensors provide kinetic, dynamic and telemetric data parameters of the manipulator during its motion, and the image sequences acquired by cameras during the manipulator operations. These data are processed to provide a symbolic representation in terms of logic assertions describing the system state and the expectations about possible system evolutions. This representation is sent to the diagnosis agent. The aim of this agent is to formulate hypotheses about failures and malfunctions responsible for deviation from the nominal behavior of the monitoring apparatus. In particular, the results of the diagnosis agent indicate to the operator that some components can not be used because they are faulty, or they suggest that other components must not be solicited because their behavior is not exactly nominal. This agent may also suggest to the supervision module the actions to be performed in order to better discriminate among several possible diagnostic hypotheses. The supervision agent assures the correct functioning of the system in different operation modes: it should be noted that this module interfaces with all other agent.

At the moment, the different software modules are under development; however, starting from their specification documents, we are using the development environment described in this paper to realize the agents that will encapsulate the different software modules. In particular, a first prototype of the agent architecture for the control robot system has been realized implementing all the goal system interaction protocols and simulating the behavior of the encapsulated software modules. Figure 3 shows the agent architecture of the control robot system.

At this prototyping stage, wrapper agents implement the basic features required to make the different modules interoperate, but they do not yet perform sophisticated negotiations or brokerage for the lacking of the driving intelligence. In particular, the benefits provided by the multiple-conversation agent model are not yet evident as not complex protocol is fully implemented.

5 Related Work

Agents technologies seem to be still immature and not practicable for real applications, however a lot of people is working for the standardization of such technologies [16][15][3] and in the realization of development environments to build agent systems (see, for example, RETSINA [18], MOLE [17], ZEUS [14] and JADE [2]). Such environments provide some predefined agent models and tools to ease the development of multi-agent systems. Moreover, some of them try to allow interoperability with other agent systems through the use of a well-known agent communication language such as KQML [5] or FIPA ACL [6].

The FIPA agent standard has not yet been intensively used as a guideline to design agent platforms as it is still considered new and immature for real applications. For this reason, just a few FIPA-compliant agent platform can be found in the literature and, as far as compliance is concerned, JADE is probably the most remarkable. JADE claims to be a fully FIPA-compliant platform providing all the services required by the standard, in fact all the special-purpose agents such as the ACC and the AMS are implemented both in terms of functionality and supported protocols. From the developer point of view, JADE is a set of Java APIs and services designed to provide some basic agent mechanisms such as the required communication capabilities and a behavior abstraction. When compared to the presented platform, some deep differences can be found as far as the described robotic application is concerned. In particular, the choice of Java as the programming language is not well suited when time performance is an important characteristic of the system. Moreover, JADE implements a sophisticated thread mechanism based on its behavior abstraction which seems to be too restrictive when trying to integrate existing engines just like in the Jerico project.

6 Future Work

As described in the previous sections, the platform can deal with the problem of providing an open environment for the development of distributed robotic applications. The limitations of the proposed approach, when compared to other more specifically robotic-oriented architectures, are found mainly in the poor support for time-dependent applications. To cope with this problem, we are planning system extensions both in the in-process and network architectures. In fact, the lack of real-time multi-threading could be a problem when dealing with event-driven time-critical applications. From the network architecture point of view, the use of a general-purpose protocol, such as IIOP, can not support fundamental concepts such as quality of service and statically allocated paths.

Long-term plans include: the extension of the system to support all new features introduced by FIPA 98 specifications [7], the specialization of the agent architecture for supporting rule-based programming and BDI models, and to continue the development and experimentation of systems in the fields of robotics.

7 Conclusions

This paper presents a development environment suitable for the implementation of FIPA-compliant agent architectures. The platform allows to efficiently distribute the agents on different machines and to realize systems in C++ beyond offering FIPA special-purpose agents and a model to define new agents.

When applied to the described robot control system, the platform exploited its FIPA-orientation showing to be suitable for the integration of non-agentized software modules. In fact, the integration required just few days of work while keeping the performance overhead limited.

Acknowledgments

The work has been partially supported by the Italian Space Agency through the grant "Un Sistema Intelligente per la Supervisione di Robot Autonomi nello Spazio".

References

1. J. L. Austin. *How to Do Things with Words*. Harvard University Press, Cambridge, 1962.
2. F. Bellifemine, A. Poggi and G. Rimassa. JADE - A FIPA-compliant Agent Framework. In *Proceedings of the Fourth International Conference on the Practical Application of Intelligent Agent and Multi Agent Technology (PAAM99)*, pp. 97-108, London, 1999.

3. L. Chiariglione. Helping agent technologies get across to the market place. In *CSELT Documenti Tecnici*. CSELT, Torino, 1996.
available at `http://www.cselt.it/fipa/general agents.htm`.

4. ESA/ASI. JERICO system description. In *ESA/ASIRCS Energia*. ASI, Noordwijk, The Netherlands, 1997.

5. T. Finin and Y. Labrou. KQML as an agent communication language. In Brashaw, editor, *Software Agents*, pages 291-316. 1997.

6. FIPA. FIPA 97 specication.
available at `http://www.cselt.it/fipa/spec/fipa97/fipa97.htm`.

7. FIPA. FIPA 98 specication.
available at `http://www.cselt.it/fipa/spec/fi pa98/fipa98.h tm`.

8. S. Gaglio. Un sistema intelligente per la supervisione di robot autonomi nello spazio.
available at `http://www.unipa.it/~asi-proj/`.

9. M. R. Genesereth and R. E. Fikes. *Knowledge Interchange Format - Version 3 - Reference Manual*. Stanford University, Stanford, 1992.

10. M. R. Genesereth and S. P. Ketchpel. Software agents. *Communication of ACM*, 37(7):48-53, 1994.

11. C. Guilfoyle and E. Warner. Intelligent agents: the new revolution in software. *Ovum Report*, 1994.

12. IETF. RFC 2251.
available at `ftp://ftp.isi.net/in-notes/rfc2251.txt`.

13. P. C. Janca. Pragmatic applications of information agents. In *BIS Strategic Decisions*. 1995.

14. H. S. Nwana, D. T. Ndumu and L. C. Lee. ZEUS: An advanced tool-kit for engineering distributed multi-agent systems. In *Proceedings of the Fourth International Conference on the Practical Application of Intelligent Agent and Multi Agent Technology (PAAM98)*, pages 377-391, London, 1998.

15. OMG. 95-11-03: Common facilities RFP3 final draft, 1995.
available at `http://www.omg.org/docs/1995/95-11-03.ps`.

16. R. S. Patil, R. E. Fikes, P. F. Patel-Scheneider, D. McKay, T. Finin, T. Gruber and R. Neches. The DARPA knowledge sharing effort: Progress report. In *Proceedigns of the Third Conference on Principles of Knowledge Representation and Reasoning*, pages 103-114, Cambridge, 1992.

17. M. Straßer, J. Baumann and F. Hohl. MOLE - A Java based mobile agent system. In M. Mühlhäuser, editor, *Special Issues in Object Oriented Programming*, pages 301-308. Verlag, 1997.

18. K. Sycara, A. Pannu, M. Williamson and D. Zeng. Distributed intelligent agents. *IEEE Expert*, 11(6):36-46, 1996.

Modelling Agents in Hard Real-Time Environments[1]

V. Botti, C. Carrascosa, V. Julian, J. Soler

Departamento de Sistemas Informáticos y Computación
Universidad Politécnica de Valencia
Camino de Vera s/n
46020 Valencia
☎ 96 387 73 50   Fax: 96 387 73 59
E-mail: {vbotti, carrasco, vinglada, jsoler}@ dsic.upv.es

Abstract. Over the last few years more complex techniques have been used to develop hard real-time systems, and the multi-agent system paradigm seems to be an appropriate approach to be applied in this area. The temporal restrictions of these systems made necessary to build agents architectures that satisfy these restrictions. A formal Agent architecture to model hard-real time systems is proposed in this paper. A prototype that follows this agent architecture and works in a hard real-time environment has been implemented. Finally, a study case is described to show the design agent process.

1   Introduction

Over the last few years the use of the agent/multi-agent system paradigm has increased sharply as an important field of research within the Artificial Intelligence area. This paradigm has been applied to different fields, such us control processes, mobile robots, commercial applications, etc. Concurrently, Real-Time Systems, and more specifically Real-Time Artificial Intelligence Systems (RTAIS) have emerged as useful techniques for solving complex problems which require intelligence and real-time response times. In new hard real-time systems, flexible, adaptive and intelligence behaviours are some of the most important ones. Thus, the agent/multi-agent system paradigm seems especially appropriate for developing hard real-time systems in hard real-time environments. A real-time environment may have different features which affect the design of the agent architecture. Two of the main features of a real-time environment are:

- Non-deterministic: the next state of the environment cannot be determined by the current state and the selected action to be executed.
- Dynamic: the environment can change while the system is deliberating.

Different environment classes require different agent structures. Therefore, it is necessary to define an appropriate structure in order to use agent methodology on a hard real-time environment.

---

[1] This work has been funded by grants number TAP97-1164-C03-01 and TAP98-0333-C03-01 of the Spanish government.

A real-time system is defined as a system in which the correctness of the system depends not only on the logical result of computation, but also on the time at which the results are produced [28, 27]. In a real-time system, some tasks have deadlines. A deadline defines the greatest time interval in which the system can provide an answer. If the answer is obtained after this time, it will not probably be useful, and the system can produce catastrophic effects. Another temporal characteristic in a typical real-time system is its periodic behaviour as determined by its period. The period determines the activation frequency of the tasks in the system. This period is needed due to the external environment's own dynamic. This means that the system has to satisfy aperiodic temporal restrictions, to deal with non deterministic environments, and to respond to internal and external sporadic events (events associated to changes in the problem data). Therefore, it is impossible to guarantee the CPU time allocation to a critical task for an unknown period as in the case of asynchronous systems. It is not adequate for real-time systems. One way of solving this problem is by using the concept of maximal occurrence frequency of an event (period). With this concept, it is possible to off-line schedule the most relevant events. With this method, it is possible to determine the moment at which each component of the system must be activated.

A hard real-time system is a real-time system where the execution of a task after its deadline has no value. On the other hand, a soft real-time is characterised by the fact that the execution of a task after its deadline only decreases the value of the task [29]. Different techniques are needed for hard and soft real-time systems. In this paper we consider only hard real-time systems. Systems of this kind are critical systems, and severe consequences will result if the timing responses are not satisfied. Satisfying the temporal restrictions requires the scheduling of the system according to an off-line test (schedulability analysis), which guarantees that all deadlines will be met. The periodic behaviour of these systems makes the schedulability analysis possible.

On the part of AI systems, the task of solving a specific problem may involve searching in large search spaces. Hence, hard real-time AI systems must accomplish complex and critical processes under a, probably dynamic, environment with temporal restrictions [22].

Previous approaches to RTAIS can be found in the literature. Anytime algorithms [9] and approximate processing [13] are the most promising. One line of research in RTAI has been in building large applications or architectures that embody real-time concerns in many components [13], such as Guardian [14], Phoenix [15], PRS [17] and CIRCA [23]. Recent work in this area has incorporated the CELLO agent model [25] presented as an integrative answer for reactive and deliberative capabilities of a RTAI system. Almost all the above architectures are designed for soft real-time systems (without critical temporal restrictions).

In this paper, we propose an agent architecture for hard real-time systems which critical timing requirements are 100% guaranteed by means of an off-line schedulability analysis as detailed in [12]. The agent must control an environment through a set of sensors. After this, the system must compute and transmit a response to the environment using a set of effectors. The response can be obtained after a reflex process or a cognitive process. Furthermore, the agent must work with hard temporal restrictions in dynamic environments. On the other hand, the agent architecture presented can be integrated into a multi-agent system. To do this, the proposed architecture must be extended to at least include inter-agent communication. The rest of this paper is structured as follows: section 2 presents an overview of the terms agent and agent architectures. Section 3 extends our ARTIS agent architecture to hard real-time environments. Section 4 gives an example of the application of the proposed system. Some conclusions are presented in section 5.

2 Agent Definition

A great number of definitions of the concept *agent* have been proposed in the literature. We describe an agent as an entity that perceives an environment and acts on this environment. This simple definition is basically the Russell definition [26]. We adopt this general definition because it includes many kinds of agents, we think that an agent can be characterised through its attributes (which define its behaviour) according to a particular problem. Then, we can talk about a social agent, an adaptive agent, etc. according to the attributes that it has. In fact, there are similar reflections about the term agent in other works. Franklin [11] formalises an agent as a *system situated within and a part of an environment that senses that environment and acts on it, over time, in pursuit of its own agenda and so as to effect what it senses in the future*. It is important to point out that Franklin defines an agent with an autonomy attribute. Another similar definition is mentioned by Huhns [16], *agents are active, persistent components that perceive, reason, act, and communicate*. In this case, we believe that some of the properties in this definition are added to the agent concept.

The objective of this paper is not to start an open discussion about what an agent is. We only want to explain our point of view in order to establish what we consider an agent to be.

2.1 Agent attributes

When we study the attributes to be reached by an agent for a particular problem, we can describe a lot of properties and the degree to which the agent has these properties. Some of the generalised attributes described by authors such as Franklin and Graesser [11], and Nwana [24] are:

- Temporal continuity: we consider an agent a process without end, continuously running and developing its functions.
- Autonomy: an agent is completely autonomous if it is able to act based on its experience. The agent is able to continue although the environment changes severely. On the other hand, a soft definition of autonomy is when the agent can perceive the environment.
- Sociability: this attribute allows an agent to communicate with other agents or even with other entities.
- Rationality: the agent is able to reason about the data that it perceives in order to calculate the best suitable answer.
- Reactivity: an agent acts as a result of changes on its environment. In this case, an agent perceives the environment and these changes direct the agent's behaviour.
- Proactivity: an agent is proactive when it is able to control its own objectives in spite of changes in the environment. This definition does not contradict reactivity.

The agent behaviour is a result of two types of behaviours, the *receiving behaviour* and the *discovering behaviour*. In a receiving behaviour, the agent is guided by the environment. The discovering behaviour gathers internal processes of the agent to obtain its own objectives. The agent behaviour must be close to the middle of the two behaviours. The agent must to have a degree of receiving behaviour (reactivity attribute) and a degree of discovering behaviour (proactivity attribute).

RECEIVING   DISCOVERING
BEHAVIOUR   BEHAVIOUR

AGENT BEHAVIOUR

Fig. 1. Situation of the agent behaviour.

- Adaptivity: we relate adaptive with learning when an agent is able to learn and it changes its behaviour based on that learning.

At this moment no consensus has been reached about the degree of importance of each one of these properties in an agent. We can say, and we think that there is consensus that these properties distinguish agents from mere programs.

2.2 Agent Architectures

The area of agent architectures considers the issues related to the construction of computer systems that satisfy agent theory properties. We can consider that an agent architecture is a particular methodology for building agents [20]. Three types of architectures are distinguished according to the agent paradigm:

- Deliberative architectures: in which the agent is built according to the symbolic AI paradigm. Some examples of architectures of this kind are IRMA [3] and GRATE* [18].
- Reactive architectures: in which the agent does not include a central symbolic world model and does not use complex symbolic reasoning. Examples of these are Subsumption architecture [4], PENGI [1] and ANA [20].
- Hybrid architectures: in this approach, the agent is built in two or more subsystems. One is deliberative, containing a symbolic world model, and the other is reactive. TouringMachines [10], COSY [5], INTERRAP [21] are the most representative.

3 Overview of ARTIS Architecture

The ARTIS architecture [8, 12] is an extension of the *blackboard* model adapted to work in hard real-time environments. The main purpose of this point is to present an agent architecture based upon the ARTIS architecture. This new vision of the ARTIS architecture allows us to build agents that follow the above-mentioned agent definition with some additional features.

This agent architecture comprises two levels of agents, the so–called ARTIS Agent (AA) and a set of agents (in-agent –Internal Agent-) within it – both of which are explained in the next two sections-. In accordance with the agent architectures mentioned above, the ARTIS architecture could be labelled as a hybrid architecture that works in a hard real–time environment.

One of the main features of this agent architecture is its hard real-time behaviour that guarantees the execution of the whole system's specification by means of an off-line analysis of the specification. This analysis is based on well-known predictability analysis techniques in the real-time systems community. More specifically, these techniques are based on the Rate Monotonic algorithm [19].

3.1   ARTIS Agent (AA)

An ARTIS Agent (AA) is (according to the Russell's definition) an agent that is also autonomous, reactive, proactive and has temporal continuity.

In an optional way, an ARTIS Agent (AA) may include even more features. Though the basic **AA** is designed to work properly under hard real-time restrictions, some of the optional features (such as communication with other agents or a social behaviour) may avoid this real-time behaviour due to the unpredictable actions they involve. Therefore, it is the agent's designer decision to choose which features (and therefore which behaviours) the agent is going to have.

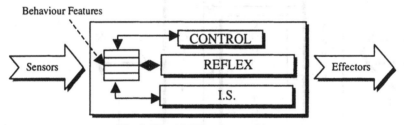

Fig. 2. The ARTIS Agent architecture.

An **AA** is formed from the following elements:

- A set of sensors and effectors to be able to interact with the environment.
- A control module that is responsible for the real–time execution of each component that belongs to the **AA**. This module has some *behaviour features* that allow it to give the agent some specific attributes.
- A reflex level: assures an answer to any critical environment event. It is formed from the reflex levels of the different **in-agents** that form the **AA**.
- An Intelligent Server (IS) which is used for higher quality answers if there is enough time for it (calculated by the cognitive levels of the different **in-agents**) and which handles non-critical sporadic environment events. Thereby, it is in charge of all the non-critical cognition of the **AA**.

The agent may or may not need different attributes depending on the kind of problem it has to solve. Some of these attributes are: sociability, communication, adaptivity, user interface, mobility, etc. Each one of these optional attributes may be implemented inside the AA architecture as a **behaviour feature** that would be added or not depending on the problem to be solved.

3.1.1   Formalisation

From a formal point of view, an ARTIS Agent can be seen as the following tuple:
$$AA = (U_{AIA}, f_{AIA}, B)$$
where:
- U_{AIA} = A set of internal agents (*in-agents*) –defined in the following section-.
- f_{AIA} = A function of selection of internal agents (implemented by the Control module along with the Intelligent Server).
- B = A set of believes representing the environment and internal states of the agent. This set is composed of the beliefs of all the **in-agents** and a set of global beliefs.

3.2   Internal Agent or In-Agent

An **in-agent** is an ARTIS internal entity that has the necessary knowledge to solve a particular problem (this knowledge can incorporate IA techniques that provide "intelligence" for solving the problem). This entity periodically performs a specific task (which may or may not be complex).

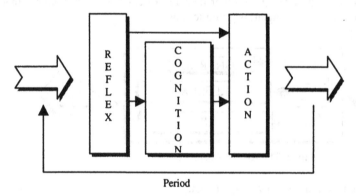

Period

Fig. 3. In-agent's behaviour.

This **in-agent** is also an agent according to the agent definition, with the additional features of:
- Reactivity: periodically looks for changes in its environment.
- Collaborative performance: each **in-agent** has to solve a particular subproblem, but all the **in-agents** of a particular **AA** cooperate to control the entire problem, and an **in-agent** may use information provided by other **in-agents**. The communication among **in-agents** is based on the blackboard model.
- Hard real-time activity: according to this characteristic, each in-agent must have a deadline and a period that enable it to work in environments of this kind.
  To provide this behaviour, each **in-agent** consists of:
- A Reflex level: assures a minimum answer (low quality answer in a bounded time) to the particular problem it is applied to.

- An Intelligent or Cognitive level: calculates a reasoned answer through a deliberative process (usually in an unbounded computation time).
- An Action level: carries out the corresponding answer, no matter what level it was calculated in.

At each period, the **in-agent** must decide between a reflex answer (provided directly by the reflex level that is always executed until completion) and a more detailed answer provided by the cognition level. This decision depends first on the time available to improve the answer, that is, if it is possible to calculate a better answer before the deadline.

An **in-agent** lives within a real-time system with other **in-agents** and other tasks.

3.2.1 Life Cycle of an in-agent

The life cycle of an **in-agent** can be seen as a phase sequence that is repeated each time it is executed (whenever its time period expires).

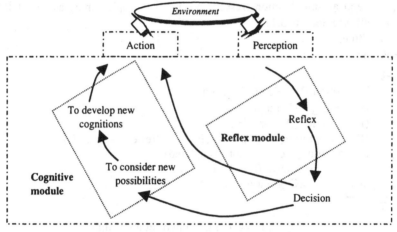

Fig. 4. Graphical representation of the in-agent phases sequence.

Therefore, the perception phase is the initial phase in which the **in-agent** falls. In this phase, the **in-agent** gets all the information it is interested in from its environment. After this, the **in-agent** passes to the second phase, the reflex one. In the reflex phase, the **in-agent** calculates an answer to the problem in a bounded time, and then evolves to a decision phase. In this new phase, it has to decide whether it must act at that moment or whether it has enough time to calculate a better answer (a refinement or an alternative one). If it decides to act, then it passes to an act phase where it executes the action it has calculated at the reflex phase. On the other hand, if it decides to consider new possibilities, it selects the appropriate cognitive process from the whole set of possibilities. It then passes to executing the cognitive process, where it calculates a new action to be executed in the action phase.

3.2.2   Formalisation

Formally, an **in-agent** can be seen as a belief set, a reflex operations list, a cognition operations list, a selection function for each one of the preceding lists, a deadline and a period.

IN-AGENT = $(B_{AIA}, L_r, f_r, L_c, f_c, D, T)$
where:

- B_{AIA} = A set of beliefs representing the internal state and environment of the **in-agent**. As mentioned above, these beliefs are part of the belief set (B) of the **AA** that the **in-agent** belongs to. All the data in this set are time stamped[2] using a temporal logic as explained in [13].
- L_r = A list of all the possible reflex actions that are known by the **in-agent**.
- f_r = A selection function of a reflex action from the L_r according to the current B_{AIA}.
- L_c = A list of all the possible cognition actions that are known by the **in-agent**.
- f_c = A selection function of a cognition action from the L_c according to the actual B_{AIA}, D, and an initial action (result from f_r). It is implemented as an Intelligent Server call (see Section 3.1).
- D = Deadline.
- T = Period.

> Perception(t) ← Read(Environment, t)
> B_{AIA} ← B_{AIA} ∪ Perception(t)
> $(B_{AIA}$, Reflex_Action) ← $f_r(B_{AIA}, L_r)$
> $(B_{AIA}$, Cognition_Action) ← $f_c(B_{AIA}, L_c$, Reflex_Action, D)
> if (Cognition_Action = not_completed)
>   Execute(Reflex_Action)
> else Execute(Cognition_Action)
>
> T

Fig. 5. In-agent main interpret algorithm:

As seen in fig. 5, at each period (T), the in-agent reads the new incoming values of the data (perceptions) that it is interested in from the environment (*Read* function). These new values are added to the existing belief set (B_{AIA}) stamped with the time of the beginning of the period. This set is used by the f_r function to select, in a bounded computation time, an appropriate reflex action from the L_r. Next, the f_c function attempts to compute a better action than the reflex one. If there is not enough computation time to calculate a better action, the f_c function returns "not_completed", and so the reflex action will be executed; otherwise the action returned by the f_c will be executed. When there are no significant changes between the perception of two consecutive periods, the f_c function can continue to improve the solution calculated at the previous period without computing the previous work again. Both f_r and f_c can modify the in-agent's internal state that is part of the B_{AIA} set.

According to the off-line schedulability analysis, reflex actions from all the in-agents are guaranteed a priori [8, 12]. That is, the selection of a reflex action and the

---

[2] There is a temporal validity window for each piece of data in the set.

execution of this action are guaranteed. However, there is no temporal guarantee that a better action than the reflex one will be obtained in the cognition phase. As this cognition phase is only an improvement process, its execution is not necessary for the correct working of the system (it does not have hard real-time restrictions) but it is convenient because it improves the quality of the answer. The cognition phase execution will not avoid the fulfilment of the system hard real-time restrictions.

4 Implementation

There exists a prototype of an AA running under a Solaris 2.5 operating system. As it has been commented, an AA includes its own operating system (prepared to work in a hard real-time environment) that will control one processor.

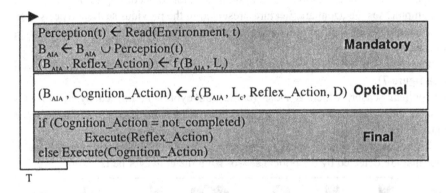

Fig. 6. Correspondence between the in-agent and the low-level task model.

In this way, we can translate an AA to a run-time entity that consists of a RTOS (Real-Time Operating System) module, a global memory, and a low-level task set [12]:

1. RTOS module: it provides the necessary real-time operating system services to create, communicate and synchronise internal processes. RTOS also includes the necessary functions to schedule these internal processes using a real-time scheduler (first-level scheduler) based on pre-emptive fixed priorities [12]. This RTOS module coincides with the Control module of the **AA**.

2. A global memory: it is implemented based on the blackboard model. It is a time stamped database that is based on the frame paradigm. Each one of its facts has only one temporal window in which it is valid [13].

3. The low-level task set: it is based in a low-level task model in which a task is divided into three parts: mandatory, optional and final. Only the mandatory and final parts of a task are critical.

Each in-agent of the AA is translated to one of these low-level tasks. This task has the same period and deadline as the in-agent and the following correspondence (fig. 6):

- Mandatory part: includes the processes of perception, the update of the belief set (B_{AIA}) and the selection of the reflex action (f_r).
- Optional part: corresponds to the process of selection of the cognition action (f_c).
- Final part: coincides with the action level.

There is a high-level environment language that allows the user to specify an AA along with its corresponding in-agents [6].

5   Example

ARTIS application prototypes have been developed to control simulated processes. In this paper, we present a prototype of a system, developed according to our approach, which emphasises the agent architecture presented in the previous section. The system we present allows the control of a conveyor belt in a glazed tile factory. The system is composed by:

- A conveyor belt, which is moving glazed tiles from left to right at a specific speed (see figure 7).
- An optical sensor, which is close to the conveyor belt, formed by an infrared system and a video camera. The optical sensor allows the detection of faults in the glazed tiles.
- And a robot arm, which is next to the optical sensor. The arm removes the faulty tiles that are detected by the optical sensor from the conveyor belt.

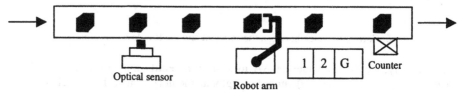

Fig. 7. The conveyor belt system.

The main goal of the system is the analysis and the evaluation of the glazed tiles. The analysis may be done before the glazed tiles are packed for storage. We can describe the whole process as follows:

1. The glazed tiles arrive to the conveyor belt from the corresponding kiln.
2. The pieces are moved along the conveyor belt in a sequential manner.
3. When a piece passes in front of the optical sensor, its surface is analysed. The analysis allows for the detection of different colours, irregularities, etc.
4. When a piece is considered faulty, the system must be able to eliminate the piece. The robot arm takes away the bad piece and throws it into the corresponding container.

5. On the contrary, if the piece is accepted, it passes along the conveyor belt and it arrives to a packer, which distributes the glazed tiles in different boxes for their subsequent storage. The control of the process explained above takes different aspects and features of the system into account. We identify the following main features:

- The pieces pass along the conveyor belt at a determined speed and a specified separation between pieces. The system control must allow for changes in these parameters.
- The optical sensor has a temporal restriction to do its job. It must determine the product quality before another glazed tile passes in front of it.
- The robot arm has the same temporal problem. It must remove a bad piece in a restricted period of time (before another bad piece arrives to the robot arm). It also has to classify the faulty pieces into different categories (first quality, second quality, or garbage).
- The system has a counter that knows the number of analysed pieces. The system must control this counter in order to maintain a minimum number of analysed pieces per period of time.
- In order to meet production needs, the system may increase or decrease the speed of the conveyor belt. The separation between pieces can also be reduced or increased.
- To illustrate, we consider someone who puts the pieces on the conveyor belt and someone who picks up the pieces at the end.

According to these characteristics we can say that the system is a real-time system; temporal restrictions direct the system behaviour in the optical sensor and the robot arm. On the other hand, we are talking about a dynamic system with sporadic events.

5.1 Design

Based on our approach, we designed an AA to control the entire process, that is, the work on the conveyor belt. The AA can take into account all the features mentioned above. We identified two main tasks to be carried out in the problem:

- To get a pattern of the glazed tiles by the optical sensor
- To analyse the glazed tiles removing the faulty ones

To control each one of the main tasks, we designed an in-agent. The AA must mainly control these processes in a dynamic and real time scenario. It will respond to sporadic events and it must adapt its behaviour depending on the environment status. As we explained in the previous section, an in-agent must be characterised by a set of temporal restrictions. These restrictions are evaluated at the system design time and must be guaranteed by an off-line schedulability test in order to guarantee that both in-agents meet their timeline restrictions. The two in-agents that forms the AA are:

- *The optical sensor in-agent*: it is in charge of examining the pieces and creating a pattern for each one. When a piece passes in front of the optical sensor, the in-agent must analyse it until a new piece arrives. As this occurs at a constant velocity and the distance between pieces is also constant, a periodic behaviour can be observed in this process. The possible actions are calculated in the following way:

– Reflex Action: based on infrared, it determines a basic pattern of the piece.
– Cognitive Action: by means of a video camera, it gets a more detailed pattern than the reflex one.

The pattern obtained is stored in a data structure in the shared memory area.

- *The robot arm in-agent*: in addition to the control of the robot arm, this in-agent is in charge of the evaluation of the piece's quality and its validity (using the pattern obtained by the other in-agent). In this case, the in-agent has temporal restrictions that are similar to those of the other in-agent, because it must remove the bad pieces until a new bad piece arrives. The possible actions are calculated in the following way:

    – Reflex Action: determines the quality of the piece based on basic pattern recognition, and rejects the pieces that do not match patterns (sending them to the garbage container).
    – Cognitive Action: refines the reflex response, which in the case that the piece is not a perfect one, determines the degree of quality (first quality, second quality or useless).

If the piece must be removed, then the in-agent orders the robot arm to pick up the piece from the conveyor belt.

5.2   Extensions

We are working on several improvements to our architecture. The sociability attribute is one of the behaviour features we are trying to add. Let us suppose the process of putting pieces on the conveyor belt and the process of picking up at the end. We consider that an autonomous robot puts pieces in a determined way and another autonomous robot picks up the accepted pieces from the conveyor belt. Each robot is controlled by an AA. Therefore, this scenario is composed of three AA, each one controlling a specific part of the whole system (the conveyor belt and the two robots). When the system is working, we identify some conflictive points of interaction between agents. For instance, if the conveyor belt Agent changes its behaviour (decreasing the speed of the conveyor belt because it is not able to evaluate the pieces), the two robot agents must be alerted to change their behaviour as well (adapting their movements to the new conveyor belt speed).

This new approach gives us a multi-agent scenario, where the agents have a common goal (to maintain production guidelines and to optimise the process) that they are not able to reach individually, due to their limited capabilities or knowledge of the problem in its entirety.

6   Conclusions

A formalisation of the ARTIS agent architecture that is suitable for solving real-time problems has been presented in this paper. This agent architecture comprises two levels of agents, the ARTIS Agent (AA) and a set of agents (in-agent) within it.

This architecture is being evaluated through some application prototypes to control simulated systems. For instance, the conveyor belt system (exposed at the present paper) and a purifier plant system (as seen in [2]).

An agent toolkit for designing, developing and debugging AAs is being developed. This new toolkit allows the programmer to do the off-line schedulability analysis of the hard temporal restrictions of the new AA, as is necessary when a real-time system is designed.

Further investigation is necessary to add new behaviour features to the AA. Initial work has begun on the inter-agent communication as a social behaviour of an AA. This new feature is being developed adding a communication language (KQML-like). There are plans to incorporate other behaviour features to the AA in the near future.

References

1. Agre, P., Chapman, D.: An implementation of a theory of activity. In Proceeding of the Sixth National Conference on Artificial Intelligence (AAAI-87). (1987)
2. Botti, V., Hernández, L.: Control in Real-Time Multiagent Systems. In: Garijo, F., Lemaitre, C. (eds.): Proceedings of the Second Iberoamerican Workshop on DAI and MAS. Toledo, Spain (1998) 137-148.
3. Bratman, M. E., Israel, D. J., Pollack, M. E.: Toward an architecture for resource-bounded agents. Technical report CSLI-87-104. Center for the Study of Language and Informations, SRI and Stanford University, (1987).
4. Brooks, R. A.: A robust layered control system for a mobile robot. IEE Journal of Robotics and Automation, 2(1):14-23. (1986)
5. Burmeister, B., Sundermeyer, K.: Cooperative problem solving guided by intentions and perceptions. Decentalized AI 3, pages 77-79 Elsevier Science Publisher B.V.: Amsterdam, The Netherlands.(1992)
6. Carrascosa, C., Julian, V. J., García-Fornes, A., Espinosa, A.: Un lenguaje para el desarrollo y prototipado rápido de sistemas de tiempo real inteligentes. Actas de la CAEPIA97, 685-694 (1997).
7. Crespo, A., Barber, F., Botti, V., Gallardo, D., Onaindía, E.: A Temporal Blackboard model for process control. Selected Papers from the International Symposium on Artificial Intelligence in Real-Time Control (1993) 459-465.
8. Crespo, A., Botti, V., Barber, F., Gallardo, D., Onaindia, E.: A Temporal Blackboard for Real-Time Process Control. Engineering Applications of Artificial Intelligence. Pregamon Press Ltd. (1994) 225-256.
9. Dean, T., Boddy, M.: An analysis of time-dependent planning. Proceedings of the seventh National Conference on Artificial Intelligence, 49-54, St. Paul, Minessota, August (1988).
10. Ferguson, I. A.: TouringMachines: An architecture for Dynamic, Rational, Mobile Agents. PhD thesis, Clare Hall, University of Cambridge, UK. 1992
11. Franklin, S., Graesser, A.: Is it an Agent, or just a Program?: A Taxonomy for Autonomous Agents. Proceedings of the Third International Workshop on Agent Theories, Architectures, and Languages. Springer-Verlag (1996).

12. García-Fornes, A., Terrasa, A., Botti, V., Crespo, A.: Analyzing the Schedulability of Hard Real-Time Artificial Intelligence Systems. Engineering Applications of Artificial Intelligence. Pregamon Press Ltd. (1997) 369-377.

13. Garvey, A., Lesser, V.: A survey of research in deliberative Real-Time Artificial Intelligence. The Journal of Real-Time Systems, 6, 317-347, (1994).

14. Hayes-Roth, B., Washington, R., Ash, D., Collinot, A., Vina, A., and Seiver, A.: Guardian: A prototype intensive-care monitoring agent. Artificial Intelligence in Medicine, 4:165-185, (1992).

15. Howe, A. E., Hart, D. M., and Cohen, P. R.: Addressing real-time constraints in the design of autonomous agents. The Journal of Real-Time Systems, 2: 81-97, (1990).

16. Huhns, M., Singh, M. P.: Readings in Agents. Readings in Agents. Chapter 1, 1-24.

17. Ingrand, F., Georgeff, M. P., and Rao, A.: An architecture for real-time reasoning and system control. IEEE Expert, 34-44, December (1992).

18. Jennings, N. R.: Specifications and implementation of a belief desire joint-intention architecture for collaborative problem solving. Journal of Intelligent and Cooperative Information System, 2(3):289-318. (1993).

19. Lehoczky, J., Sha, L., Ding, Y.: The Rate-Monotonic Scheduling Algorithm: Exact Characterization and Average Case Behaviour. Proceedings IEEE Real-Time Systems Symposium (1989).

20. Maes, P: The agent network architecture (ANA). SIGART bulletin, 2(4) (1991)115-120.

21. Muller, J. P.: A conceptual model for agent interaction. In Deen, S. M. Editor, Proceedings of the second International Working Conference on Co-operating Knowledge Base Systems, pages 213-234, DAKE Centre, University of Keel. (1994)

22. Musliner, D. J., Hendler, J. A., Agrakala, A. K., Durfee, E. H., Strosnider, J. K., Paul, C. J.: The Challenges of Real-Time AI. Computer IEEE January (1995) 58-66.

23. Musliner, D., Durfee, E., Shin, K.: CIRCA: a co-operative intelligent real-time control architecture. IEEE Transactions on Systems, Man and Cybernetics, 23(6), (1993).

24. Nwana, H. S.: Software Agents: An Overview. Intelligent Systems Research. AA&T, BT Laboratories, Ipswich, United Kingdom (1996).

25. Occello, M., Demazeau, Y.: Modelling decision making systems using agents satisfying real time constraints, IFAC Proceedings of 3rd IFAC Symposium on Intelligent Autonomous Vehicles, 51-56, Vol. 1, March (1998).

26. Russell, S., Norvig, P.: Artificial Intelligence: A Modern Approach. Prentice Hall International Editions (1995) chapter 2, 31-50.

27. Stankovic, J. A.: Distributed Real-Time Computing: The Next Generation. Journal of the Society of Instrument and Control Engineers of Japan (1992).

28. Stankovic, J. A.: Misconceptions About Real-Time Computing. IEEE Computer, vol. 12, no. 10 (1988) 10-19.

29. Stankovic, J. A., Ramamritham, Krithi: What is predictability for Real-Time Systems?. Real-Time Systems, vol. 2 (1990) 247-254.

Multi-agent Systems on the Internet: Extending the Scope of Coordination towards Security and Topology

Marco Cremonini[1], Andrea Omicini[1], and Franco Zambonelli[2]

[1] LIA - DEIS - Università di Bologna
Viale Risorgimento, 2 40136 – Bologna, Italy
Ph.: +39 051 6443087- Fax: +39 051 6443073
{mcremonini, aomicini}@deis.unibo.it
[2] DSI - Università di Modena
Via Campi 213b 41100 – Modena, Italy
Ph.: +39 059 376735- Fax: +39 059 376799
franco.zambonelli@unimo.it

Abstract. The Internet is rapidly becoming the privileged environment for today's Multi-Agent Systems. This introduces new issues in MAS' design and development, from both a conceptual and a technological viewpoint. In particular, the dichotomy between the openness of the execution environment and the need for secure execution models makes governing agents' interaction a really complex matter, especially when *mobile agents* are involved. If *coordination* is managing the interaction, then the issue of agent coordination is strictly related with the issues of *topology* (how the space where agents live and possibly move is modelled and represented), *authentication* (how agents are identified), and *authorisation* (what agents are allowed to do). To this end, we first discuss the TuCSoN model for the coordination of Internet agents, then show how it can be extended to model the space where agents live and interact as a hierarchical collection of locality domains, where programmable coordination media are exploited to rule agent interaction and to support intelligent agent exploration. This makes TuCSoN result in a single coherent framework for the design and development of Internet-based MAS, which takes coordination as the basis for dealing with network topology, authentication and authorisation in a uniform way.

Keywords: Coordination, Multi-Agent Systems, Internet Agents, Agent Mobility, Security

1   Introduction

Multi-Agent Systems (MAS henceforth) are spreading all over the Internet: more and more, multi-agent metaphors and technologies are exploited to build complex Internet applications. In this context, we see the Internet as a multiplicity of agent execution environments, heterogeneous and physically distributed. Since these environments are typically under decentralised control and often highly dynamic, the Internet is usually an unpredictable space, unlikely to be completely known *a-priori* by agents.

As an agent space, the Internet is then the environment where agents live and possibly move, and where they interact with other agents and with resources, too. *Coordination* generally deals with managing the interaction among components [18]: so, in the context of MAS, it addresses the issue of how agents interact. Like agent architectures and languages support in designing, engineering and experimenting agents [23], *coordination languages* and *models* [11] are meant to provide for the abstractions and tools required to get agents together and build a multi-agent system [3].

However, coordination models alone cannot face the complexity intrinsically related with Internet-based MAS. First, the dichotomy between the need for open application environments and the ever-growing requirement of safe and reliable execution models makes coordination and security two dual and strictly connected topics. Then, agents exploring the heterogeneous and unpredictable space of the Internet put network topology and coordination in relation. More precisely, when defining an effective framework for the design and development of Internet-based MAS, the issue of coordination turns out to be in strict relation with the issues of *(i)* how agents are identified (*authentication*), *(ii)* what they are allowed to do (*authorisation*), and *(iii)* how the space where agents live and possibly move is modelled (*topology)*.

From this perspective, this paper discusses and extends the TuCSoN model for the coordination of Internet agents [20]. Here, coordination is exploited as the conceptual basis where all the abstractions and mechanisms for modelling the Internet and managing security are rooted, providing for a uniform approach for the authentication, authorisation and topology issues.

Interaction within Internet nodes is ruled by the TuCSoN *tuple centres* [7] working as the core of the whole framework. From a coordination viewpoint, tuple centres are *programmable coordination media* [6] whose behaviour can be defined in order to rule component interaction. From a security viewpoint, tuple centres mediate between agents and resources, so that they can be exploited to restrict interaction and implement access control policies. From a topology viewpoint, tuple centres are exploited as knowledge repositories for agents, containing information about network topology, which is modelled by means of the *place*, *domain*, and *gateway* abstractions.

2 Coordination in Context

Coordination is concerned with managing the interaction among software components [11]. Coordination models and languages [3] aim at providing the abstractions and mechanisms which are most suitable for the effective design and development of multi-component software systems, like MAS, where active components (e.g., agents) communicate, synchronise, cooperate and compete within an execution framework.

Choosing the Internet as the environment for MAS extends the scope of agent coordination beyond the conceptual boundaries set up by the current research on coordination [5, 21]. Since agents live and possibly move through a collection of heterogeneous and physically distributed execution environments, and there interact with both protected resources and other agents, both *topology* and *security* strictly relate to coordination, as discussed in the following subsections.

2.1 Coordination and Topology

Two main problems have to be addressed in the coordination of network-aware agents: *(i)* how the space where agents live is modelled (*network modelling*), and *(ii)* how the knowledge about the structure of that space is made available to the agents (*network knowledge*).

The problem of network modelling is particularly evident when dealing with intrinsically structured domains, as Internet environments frequently are. In fact, Internet nodes are often grouped in clusters, subject to highly coordinated management policies and possibly protected by a firewall. Moreover, large clusters can be further characterised by the presence of enclosed sub-clusters, in a hierarchical structure of protected administrative domains. A typical example can be found in most academic environments, where a single large cluster enclose all the academic nodes and defines basic management policies. Different enclosed clusters, such as the one of the single research laboratories, provide protected domains with their own policies, typically under the administration of a single system manager.

As far as network knowledge is concerned, agents may either have an *a-priori* knowledge of the space they live in, or acquire it dynamically by need. The former choice would not affect the agent interaction protocol, which could simply exploit the topological information that agents are statically provided with. However, this approach is unsatisfactory, since it makes difficult to deal with the typical dynamicity and unpredictability of Internet-based domains. With the latter approach, instead, an agent first acquires information about the structure and properties of the agent space, then interacts and possibly moves through that space according to the knowledge gained. This actually affects the coordination protocol, since part of the agent interaction concerns the acquisition of information about topology, and makes network knowledge a coordination-related issue.

2.2 Coordination and Security

While the Internet intrinsically promotes the openness of the application environments, its exploitation in domains where safe and reliable execution models are required is growing quite fast. Roughly speaking, while coordination technology for the Internet is typically concerned with enabling interaction and making it fruitful, security technology is typically meant to bound interaction so as to make it harmless. This makes coordination and security two strictly related topics, even though somehow dual. More precisely, while coordination deals with how agents interact, security (according to the interpretation of the term adopted in this paper, which includes access control models) deals with *(i)* how agent are identified (*authentication*), and *(ii)* what they are allowed to do (*authorisation*).

The absence of a centralised control for both the MAS and the Internet nodes raises the issue of authentication: before accepting an incoming agent, or a query from a remote agent, a node should verify its identity. So, the first interaction between an agent and an execution environment always concerns agent authentication. A coordination framework should then endorse a global agent naming scheme and support an identification protocol, univocally mapping agents onto names. Coherently, a coordination model should embody a suitable notion of agent identity, by allowing any communication operation to be associated to the proper agent identifier. Even more, a broader notion of identity should be supported, which enables a MAS to be denoted as a whole, and single agents to be characterised by both their MAS' identity and their *role* in the MAS.

Authorisation is what more directly concerns interaction, and may somehow be seen as the conceptual security counterpart of coordination. While a coordination language may allow an agent to perform a communication primitive, an authorisation policy may instead limit the agent interaction protocol, by forbidding, for instance, its access to some resources, or by preventing some communication operations to be performed. According to that, a coordination framework should enable authorisation policies to be defined over the coordination language, so as to make it possible to achieve the best compromise between expressive power and safety in the interaction.

Finally, in a distributed environment like the Internet, security policies may be either completely decentralised (every node defines and implements its own authentication and authorisation patterns), or partially/totally structured according to the network model, by exploiting some form of (either implicit or explicit) delegation. The latter choice, by relating the network structure to both authentication and authorisation, relates security to topology, too.

3 Coordination of Internet Agents in TuCSoN

3.1 Communication in TuCSoN

TuCSoN is a model for the coordination of Internet agents [20], where agents interact through a multiplicity of independent coordination media, called *tuple centres*, spread over Internet nodes. Agents exchange tuples via tuple centres by means of a small set of communication primitives (out, in, rd, inp, rdp) having basically the same semantics of Linda ones. In short, out puts a tuple in the tuple centre, while the *query primitives* (in, rd, inp, rdp) send a tuple template (in their *pre phase*) and expect a matching tuple back from the tuple centre (in their *post phase*). More in detail, in and inp delete the matching tuple from the tuple centre, while rd and rdp leave it there; in and rd wait until a suited tuple becomes available, while inp and rdp fail if no such a tuple is found.

Each tuple centre is associated to a node and has a unique name: in particular, a tuple centre can be denoted either by its full Internet (*absolute*) name or by its local (*relative*) name. More precisely, tuple centre *tc* provided by the Internet node *node* can be referred to by means of its absolute name *tc@node* from everywhere in the Internet, and by means of its relative name *tc* in the context of node *node*. Correspondingly, the TuCSoN interaction space can be seen either as a *global interaction space*, featuring a collection of uniquely denoted tuple centres (when considering absolute names), or as a collection of *local interaction spaces*, replicating the name space on each node (when considering relative names).

The general form for any admissible TuCSoN communication operation performed by an agent is *tc?op(tuple)* asking tuple centre *tc* to perform operation *op* using *tuple*. Since *tc* can be either an absolute or a relative tuple centre's name, agents can adopt two different forms of primitive invocation, according to their contingent needs: the *network* and the *local* one, respectively. The network communication form *tc@node?op(tuple)* is used by agents when behaving as network-aware entities, by denoting tuple centres by their absolute names in the global TuCSoN interaction space. In its turn, the local communication form *tc?op(tuple)*, which refers by definition to the local tuple centre's implementation of the current execution node of an agent, is used by agents when behaving as local components of their current hosting environment. As shown in [20], the availability of both forms particularly suits mobile agents.

3.2 TuCSoN Tuple Centres

TuCSoN tuple centres are tuple spaces enhanced with the notion of *behaviour specification*: the behaviour in response to communication events of every tuple centre can be defined according to the system requirements. The interaction space provided by a TuCSoN node relies on a multiplicity of tuple centres: so, TuCSoN shares the advantages of models based on multiple tuple spaces and goes beyond, since different coordination media can encapsulate different coordination laws, providing system designers with a finer granularity for the implementation of global coordination policies.

The behaviour of a stateful coordination media like a tuple centre is naturally defined as the observable state transition following a communication event. Correspondingly, defining a new behaviour for a tuple centre basically amounts to specifying a new state transition in response to a standard communication event. This is achieved by allowing any admissible TuCSoN communication event to be associated to specific computations, called *reactions*. In particular, a *specification tuple* reaction(*Op,R*) associates the event generated by an incoming communication operation *Op* to the reaction *R*.

A reaction is defined as a sequence of *reaction goals*, which may access the properties of the communication event triggering the reaction, perform simple term operations, and manipulate tuples in the tuple centre. In particular, operations on the tuple space (out_r, in_r, rd_r, no_r) work similarly to communication operations, and can trigger further reactions in a chain. Reaction goals are executed sequentially, each with a success/failure semantics, and a reaction as a whole is either a *successful* or a *failed* one depending on whether *all* its reaction goals succeed or not. Each reaction is executed with a transactional semantics:

a successful reaction can atomically modify the tuple centre state, a failed reaction yields no result at all. Moreover, all the reactions triggered by a given
communication event are executed before taking into account serving any other
communication event, so as to ensure that agents perceive only the final result of
the execution of the communication event *and* the set of all the triggered reactions. (More details on the reaction specification language and execution model
can be found in [7].)

As a consequence, the result of the invocation of a communication primitive
from the agent's viewpoint is the sum of the effects of the primitive itself and of
all the reactions it triggered, perceived altogether as a single-step transition of
the tuple centre state. This makes it possible to uncouple the agent's view of the
tuple centre (which is perceived as a standard tuple space) from the tuple centre
actual state, and to connect them so as to embed the laws of coordination. Since
the reaction specification language is Turing-equivalent [7], any computable coordination law can be encapsulated into the coordination medium. In particular,
as shown in [20], this enable TuCSoN to address some of the typical issues in the
design and development of Internet-based MAS, such as the heterogeneity of the
agent execution environments, the support of incremental system development,
and the definition and enforcement of security policies.

Since each TuCSoN tuple centre stores both its data (ordinary tuples) and
its behaviour specifications (specification tuples) locally, coherently with the
distributed nature of component-based systems, coordination intelligence can
be spread where needed all over the agent space. Furthermore, thanks to their
uniform representation, agents can manipulate data tuples and behaviour specification tuples adopting the same conceptual protocol. So, in principle, intelligent agents may modify/integrate the behaviour of a TuCSoN MAS in the same
straightforward way as they communicate with other agents, that is, by adding,
removing, and reading (specification) tuples.

3.3 Security in TuCSoN

The TuCSoN security model defines neither a naming scheme nor an authentication mechanism, instead it simply assumes that it is somehow possible to
authenticate an agent and to denote it with a suitable identifier. Given that,
TuCSoN provides a simple yet expressive authorisation scheme, based on the
definition of an access control model over tuples. Each tuple centre may be
made either visible or invisible, and its tuples (both ordinary and specification
ones) readable/writable/removable, to any (class of) agent(s). Both tuples and
specification tuples (that is, those defining reactions) are marked with the owner
identity, that is, the identifier of the agent who put the tuple in the tuple centre. Then, *(i)* any communication operation on a tuple centre performed by an
agent may either succeed or fail also according to the rights granted to the agent
itself, and *(ii)* any reaction associated to the operation may either succeed or
fail also according to the rights granted to the agent owning the corresponding
specification tuple.

Thus, the effect of a communication primitive is defined by the joint effects of both the coordination and authorisation policies: for instance, the effect of an **out** operation performed by agent **a** on tuple centre **tc** depends on *(i)* the default operation's semantics, *(ii)* the reactions possibly associated to it by the **tc**'s behaviour specification, and *(iii)* the access rights of **a** with respect to **tc**.

4   Extending TuCSoN

4.1   Concepts and Terminology

In order to enable it to effectively deal with the security and topology issues, we extend TuCSoN with new *locality abstractions* which enable it to model the Internet as a hierarchical collection of *places*, *domains*, and *gateways*, as well as with a notion of *agent identity* rooted in standard Internet security mechanisms.

The *place* provides the abstraction for the agent execution environment. The *domain* concept is used to group places sharing common policies and privileges. Each domain is associated to a *gateway*, which is the place in charge of agent authentication on behalf of domain's places, as well as of inter-domain routing for both incoming and outgoing agents. Domains can be nested, so that a place of a domain can be the gateway for a sub-domain. As a result, the collection of the Internet nodes hosting a TuCSoN MAS can be represented with a hierarchical structure: a TuCSoN *tree*. Places are the leaves of a TuCSoN tree, and gateways are the nodes whose children are the associated domain's places, so each sub-domain is represented by a sub-tree. The tree root is the most external gateway, which works as a bridge with the Internet and possibly connects different TuCSoN domains.

All parties associated with a TuCSoN MAS are known via *principals* [15], that is, identities (unique names) that can be authenticated. Thus, agents and places are identified via the *Developer*, *User*, and *Node* principals, exploiting X.509 certificates issued by a certified authority of a PKIX infrastructure: the *Developer* represents the responsible for the agent class, the *User* is the responsible of the agent instantiation, and the *Node* is the responsible for the agent execution environments. Attribute certificates [9] enable both the definition of a global notion of MAS' identity, and the association of a *role* to each agent, representing its specific task within the MAS. So, authentication in TuCSoN associates to each agent both the global identity of the agent's MAS and the specific agent's role within the MAS. This notion of agent identity can then be exploited for agent authorisation, that is, to provide the agent with the *permissions* needed to access and modify tuples in the tuple centre.

4.2   Understanding TuCSoN

In order to help understanding the extended TuCSoN model and its features, we presents a simple example of a TuCSoN MAS – the **bookreader** MAS – where some of the agents are mobile and roam the Internet nodes of a University

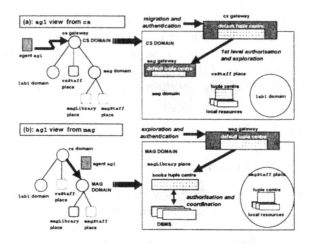

Fig. 1. An example of a TuCSoN framework.

looking for book references. The University has one central library and several departmental libraries, along with a bunch of book collections owned by single research groups. Actually, this represents a typical application context suitable to be addressed by multi-agent technology, as well as an ideal scenario for our framework, due to *(i)* the hierarchical organisation of the structure, *(ii)* the decentralisation of control, *(iii)* the need for global policies, *(iv)* the cooperation required to each domain, and *(v)* the intrinsic heterogeneity of resources.

The topology aspect is obviously addressed by exploiting the locality abstractions introduced above so as to model the Internet agent space. As an example, Fig. 1 depicts a University department network modelled as a TuCSoN tree: the root is the Computer Science department gateway (**cs**), associated to the **cs** domain, which contains as its children nodes places like **csStaff** and gateways for both laboratories (such as **lab1**) and research groups, such as the Multi-Agent Group one (**mag**). In its turn, the **mag** sub-domain contains the **magLibrary** and **magStaff** places. In particular, as a TuCSoN node, **magLibrary** provides for the **books** tuple centre, representing the catalogued books of the Multi-Agent Group. Mobile agents of the application **bookreader**, in charge of finding book references, will then explore all the **books** tuple centres available in the **cs** domain and in its sub-domains, including the one provided by the **magLibrary** place.

In TuCSoN, the role of gateways is fundamental to support and control the execution of the agents moving along the network or remotely accessing places. Each gateway can authenticate agents on behalf of its associated domain, by verifying agents' identity and by propagating it by default to all domain's places and sub-gateways. More precisely, agent authentication must be performed by each gateway receiving an agent request from an external source, as usual in Internet applications with security requirements. Since the information about the agent identity is propagated to the sub-tree, deeper gateways could decide to trust the authentication already performed by the higher gateway, and perform only a weaker form of authentication: for example, by simply verifying that the agent comes from the higher gateway. Even though any gateway is left free to fully authenticate an agent autonomously, wherever the agent comes from, authentication delegation between gateways permits to gain in performance and to reduce the complexity of security requirements for mobile agent applications. For instance, in Fig. 1, once authenticated by the cs gateway, the bookreader agent ag1 recognises the presence of an inner gateway, the mag one, which it may be interested to explore. Then, as ag1 comes to mag, it needs not to be re-authenticated, but is instead recognised as a bookreader agent coming from cs, since mag trusts on cs authentication.

Besides acting as centralised points for authentication, TuCSoN gateways work as *knowledge repositories*, providing agents with a multi-layered description of the agent space. For this purpose, the default tuple centre of any gateway (the one accessed when no tuple centre identifier is specified in the invocation of a communication primitive) contains knowledge about its associated domain, and is programmed to make that information available based on agent's identity and role. Thus, an agent can dynamically retrieve from a gateway the set of the accessible places and sub-domains in the domain, as well as the set of the tuple centres made visible to it by each place of the domain. In this context, TuCSoN tuple centres work not only as a mere coordination media, but are exploited also as authorisation engines, given that authorisation policies can be charged upon both the behaviour specification and the access control model of a tuple centre. Moreover, this supports intelligent agent exploration, since agents are not supposed to have a complete, *a-priori* knowledge of the agent space, but can instead gain information about the agent space incrementally, by need.

For example, according to Fig. 1(a), agent ag1 accesses the default tuple centre of the cs gateway, and discovers what places are in the domain and which tuple centres are accessible to it. By providing the corresponding knowledge in form of tuples (see also Fig. 2), cs authorises ag1 to access the mag gateway and the csStaff place (grey in figure) but forbids it to access to the lab1 domain (white in figure), whose existence is hidden to ag1. When ag1 moves to the mag gateway, as shown in Fig. 1(b), it can access the magLibrary place only, because the existence of magStaff is kept hidden to it by the behaviour specification of the default tuple centre of mag. As a result, both authorisation and dynamic acquisition of knowledge about the agent space are achieved by gateways in a uniform way by exploiting the coordination media, *i.e.*, the tuple centres.

4.3 Impact on Agent Design

As shown in [8], the adoption of tuple centres as the coordination media has a positive impact on the way in which agents of a MAS are designed. Since the behaviour of a tuple centre can be programmed so as to embody any computable coordination law, agents can be freed of the load of coordination, and designed around very straightforward interaction protocols, where single agent computation is kept cleanly separate from multi-agent coordination.

```
– agent exploration –
<goto d>                         migration to gateway d
<identify>                       gateway d authenticates the agent on behalf of all the places
                                 of its associated domain
?rd(subdomlist)                  access the default tuple centre of gateway d to obtain infor-
?rd(placelist)                   mation about domain structure, in terms of accessible sub-
?rd(commspace)                   domains (subdomlist), places (placelist), and tuple centres
                                 (commspace), filtered according to agent's identity and role
<for pl in placelist do>         exploration of the accessible places of the domain d
  <goto pl>                      migration to place pl
– agent interaction –
  <for tc in commspace do>       for any visible tuple centre tc of place pl
    tc?op(tuple)                 ask tuple centre tc of place pl to execute op(tuple)
– agent exploration (sub-domains) –
<for sd in subdomlist do>        exploration of the accessible subdomains
  <goto sd>                      migration to gateway sd
  <...>                          keep on exploration and access, in a recursive fashion
```

Fig. 2. A possible interaction protocol for a mobile agent in TuCSoN.

In addition, extending the scope of the TuCSoN coordination model towards topology and security has further advantages, as pointed out by Fig. 2, which shows the scheme of a possible exploration protocol of an agent roaming an environment modelled as a TuCSoN tree. On the one hand, the example emphasises the clear distinction between the exploration of the agent space (*agent exploration* in Fig. 2) and the management of the agent interaction within the execution environment (*agent interaction* in Fig. 2). On the other hand, it shows how the same interaction protocol is adopted for the definition of both authorisation and coordination policies, which are mediated by the programmable coordination media: this makes it possible to find the right balance between the dual issues of security and coordination.

Finally, agents are allowed to know in advance which operations they are allowed to perform within TuCSoN nodes. This makes it possible to design intelligent agents which are able to *(i)* plan their course of actions so as to minimise the cost of exploration and access to resources, and *(ii)* reduce as much as possible the load of handling exceptions and access denials.

5   Related Works

As MAS become more and more a profitable solution in the Internet arena, new issues and challenges are raised, from both a conceptual and a technological viewpoint. In this paper, we presented an extension to the TuCSoN model for the coordination of Internet agents, which takes coordination as a basis for addressing both the topology and security issues in a uniform framework.

Despite the great deal of activity in both the coordination and security areas, their integration is still a neglected issue, as well as the definition of a comprehensive model meant to support system design. In particular, the mobile agent research field still lacks in-deep proposals addressing the issues of agent motion in a structured environment and agent interaction with resources. Most proposals in the area of intelligent agents address the issue of inter-agent interactions for knowledge exchange, without paying attention to architecture and security issues [10, 12].

The notion of programmable coordination medium [6], exploited in TuCSoN to deal with security and topology in a uniform way, has been already applied in the $\mathcal{ACLT}$ system [8] in the field of heterogeneous multi-agent systems, by MARS [1] in the context of mobile agents, and by Law-Governed Linda [19] to address security and efficiency issues in distributed environments. PageSpace [4] defines a general architecture for the coordination of Internet agents, where special-purpose agents are provided to influence the coordination activity of the applications agents. The ActorSpace model [13] is a comprehensive framework for building agent ensembles which addresses the coordination issue explicitly, but does not support agent exploration. In T Spaces [17], agents can add any new primitive to the tuple space, in order to implement any needed transaction on the stored data. However, none of the above coordination systems addresses in an integrated way the issues of authentication and authorisation in the access to the coordination media, which is instead one of the TuCSoN's key-features.

In the security area, well-known systems as Aglets and D'Agents [14] focused on the immediate usability of their tools, possibly supporting traditional cryptographic mechanisms and basic forms of access control lists (ACLs). In addition, a number of proposals are emerging, which address agent security with new interesting mechanisms, such as mobile cryptography [22]. However, the above systems lack a likewise attention to the definition of both appropriate models for the network topology and suitable coordination models.

To the best of our knowledge, the only proposals which address the issue of the hierarchical structure of many Internet application domains and explicitly model the migration of active entities across protected domains are Ambit [2] and Discovery [16]. However, both the above models fall short in supporting agent exploration and in providing for suitable coordination abstractions.

Acknowledgements

This work has been carried out under the financial support of the MURST (the Italian "Ministero dell'Università e della Ricerca Scientifica e Tecnologica") in the framework of the Project MOSAICO "Design Methodologies and Tools of High Performance Systems for Distributed Applications".

References

[1] G. Cabri, L. Leonardi, and F. Zambonelli. Reactive tuple spaces for mobile agent coordination. In *Proceedings of the 2nd Workshop on Mobile Agents*, volume 1477 of *LNCS*. Springer-Verlag, September 1998.

[2] L. Cardelli and A. D. Gordon. Mobile ambient, 1997. http://www.research. digital.com/SRC/personal/Luca_Cardelli/Ambit.

[3] P. Ciancarini. Coordination models and languages as software integrators. *ACM Computing Surveys*, 28(2), June 1996.

[4] P. Ciancarini, R. Tolksdorf, F. Vitali, D.Rossi, and A. Knoche. Coordinating multiagent applications on the WWW: A reference architecture. *IEEE Transactions on Software Engineering*, 24(5):362–375, 1998.

[5] *Coordination Languages and Models*, volume 1594 of *LNCS*. Springer-Verlag, 1999. 3rd Intl. Conf., COORDINATION'99, Amsterdam, The Nederlands, April 1999.

[6] E. Denti, A. Natali, and A. Omicini. Programmable coordination media. In *Coordination Languages and Models*, volume 1282 of *LNCS*, pages 274–288. Springer-Verlag, 1997.

[7] E. Denti, A. Natali, and A. Omicini. On the expressive power of a language for programming coordination media. In *Proceedings of SAC'98*, Atlanta, USA, 1998.

[8] E. Denti and A. Omicini. Designing multi-agent systems around an extensible communication abstraction. In *Proceedings of the 4th ModelAge Workshop on Formal Models of Agents*, LNAI. Springer-Verlag, 1999.

[9] S. Farrell. An Internet Attribute Certificate Profile for authorisation, August 1998. Internet Draft.

[10] T. Finin, R. Fritzson, D. McKay, and R. McEntire. KQML as an agent communication language. In *Proc. of the Third International Conference on Information and Knowledge Management*, Gaithersburg, Maryland, November 1994.

[11] D. Gelernter and N. Carriero. Coordination languages and their significance. *Communications of the ACM*, 35(2):97–107, February 1992.

[12] M.R. Genesereth and R.E. Filkes. Knowledge Interchange Format: Version 3.0 reference manual. Technical Report Logic-92-1, Computer Science Department, Stanford University, 1992.

[13] N. Jamali, P. Thati, and G.A. Agha. An actor-based architecture for customising and controlling agent ensembles. *IEEE Intelligent Systems – Special Issue on Intelligent Agents*, 1999. To appear.

[14] N.M. Karnik and A.R. Tripathi. Design issues in mobile-agent programming systems. *IEEE Concurrency*, 6(3):52–61, 1998.

[15] B. Lampson, M. Abadi, M. Burrows, and E. Wobber. Authentication in distributed systems: Theory and practice. *ACM Transactions on Computer Systems*, 10(4):265–310, November 1992.

[16] S. Lazar, I. Weerakoon, and D. Sidhu. A scalable location tracking and message delivery scheme for mobile agents. In *Proc. of the IEEE WETICE'98*, June 1998.

[17] T.J. Lehman, S. McLaughry, and P. Wyckoff. T Spaces: The next wave. http://www.almaden.ibm.com/TSpaces/.

[18] T. Malone and K. Crowstone. The interdisciplinary study of coordination. *ACM Computing Surveys*, 26(1):87–119, 1994.

[19] N. Minsky and J. Leichter. Law-governed Linda as a coordination model. In *Object-Based Models and Languages*, volume 924 of *LNCS*, pages 125–145. Springer-Verlag, 1994.

[20] A. Omicini and F. Zambonelli. Coordination for Internet application development. *Autonomous Agents and Multi-Agent Systems*, 1999. Special Issue on Coordination Mechanisms and Patterns for Web Agents.

[21] *Proceedings of the 1999 ACM Symposium on Applied Computing (SAC '99)*, The Menger, San Antonio, Texas, February 28 - March 2 1999. ACM. Track on Coordination Models, Languages and Applications.

[22] T. Sander and C.F. Tschudin. Towards mobile cryptography. In *IEEE Symposium on Security and Privacy*, May 1998.

[23] M. Woolridge and N. Jennings. Intelligent agents: Theory and practice. *Knowledge Engineering Review*, 10(2):115–152, 1995.

Protocol Engineering for Multi-agent Interaction

Amal El Fallah-Seghrouchni[1], Serge Haddad[2], and Hamza Mazouzi[2]

[1] LIPN - Université Paris Nord,
elfallah@lipn.univ-paris13.fr
[2] LAMSADE - Université paris Dauphine,
{haddad, mazouzi}@lamsade.dauphine.fr

Abstract. This paper focuses on the study of the pragmatics of multi-agent systems design, proposing an efficient approach for the interaction protocol engineering. This approach combines two complementary paradigms: 1) Distributed observation is used to capture the concurrent events inherent to the interactions between agents, through causal dependency, in order to explain the relationships within conversations or group utterances; 2) Colored Petri Nets are used as a suitable formalism to identify interaction-oriented designs while providing the means to model, analyze, and validate large scale applications.

1   Introduction

This paper focuses on the study of the pragmatics of multi-agent systems (MAS) design, proposing an efficient approach to build a robust and secure interaction between agents, as an essential component of the dynamics of MAS. Communication is often used by agents to enable cooperation, common tasks and goals achievement, and information exchanged, i.e. data, knowledge and plans. Message passing is a common paradigm for agents' communication. Such a paradigm is the necessary mean for cooperation which requires a shared background of the skills of the agents, specially when such skills are as complex as perception, learning, planning, and reasoning. Interaction modeling, as well as the development of standard languages for agents' communication (ACLs), remains a crucial problem in MAS design.

We propose an approach that tackles the problem of protocol engineering through the specification, the analysis, and the verification of such protocols when several agents are involved. This approach combines two complementary paradigms: Distributed observation is used to capture the relevant events underlying the interacting situations, while Colored Petri Nets (CPN) [11] provide an efficient formalism to specify, model, and study several kinds of communication protocols. We also claim that our approach is generic, in the sense that it is independent of any ACL.

1.1 Interaction languages

In order to support organizational interaction, communication, and cooperation in MAS, many frameworks [8] [9] have been proposed towards standardization for formalizing the flow of interaction between agents. These frameworks intend to develop a generic interaction languages by specifying messages and protocols for inter-agent communication and cooperation. Such languages focus especially on how to describe exhaustive speech acts [1] [18], both from the syntactical and semantical points of view that support a language of knowledge representation. Nevertheless, the ontological aspect and the resort to conventions may help to ensure a coherent collective behavior of the overall system, even if the conversational aspect is not easy to be guaranteed.

Research in interaction languages includes the Knowledge Sharing Effort (KSE) that outputs specification for the Knowledge Querying and Manipulation Language (KQML) [8], and the Knowledge Interchange Format (KIF). KQML proposes an extensible set of performatives, which define the permissible operations that agents may attempt on each other's knowledge and goal stores. Nevertheless, some observations about KQML has been pointed out, e.g., some performatives are ambiguous while others are not really performatives at all, and there are no performatives that commit an agent to do something. Another criticism to KQML is its deficiency regarding to a clear semantics independent of the structure of the agents [3].

More recently, the international collaboration of member organizations within FIPA (*Foundation for Intelligent Physical Agents*), proposed and specified some standards for the agent technology and especially, an agent communication language called ACL [9]. ACL recovers the syntactical idea of KQML which allows to build interactions enriched by a formalized semantics of performatives, and consequently, it enables the expression of a set of high level protocols and primitives to control the information exchange between agents.

However, few work related with the analysis and the validation of these protocols have been done. In [5] [6] a formal study of the FIPA Protocols is proposed and it shows that some of them may lead to some incorrect behaviour (e.g. deadlock situations between agents).

1.2 Interaction Models

The formal specification of interactions have been less successful. In fact, the modeling of interactions confines itself with the use of misfit formalisms, such as the graph of predefined states, to describe the progress of the agent according to the kind of received messages. Other models like automata or more specific graphs (e.g. the Dooly-graph [17]) have also been used to describe conversations between agents. These models of representation are practical to specify the structure of the conversations when they appear as isolated communications, but they exhibit poor capacity for computing complex protocols basically because: 1) any graph state includes all the local states of the agent leading to the combinatory explosion in the case of real and complex protocols; 2) most of the formalisms used take in charge only sequential processes. Moreover, when these formalisms take into account temporal aspects (in our case, specified through the causality concept), they assume the existence of a global clock what constitutes a strong constraint, i.e., agents must run on the same site. In addition, these models are very limited when it is useful to take into account the concurrency, which is the key stone of MAS since agents are often involved simultaneously in several interactions.

Our point of view is that it should be more judicious to resort to well-known and well-tested formalisms for concurrent systems, such as CPN [11] for at least three reasons: 1) they naturally take in charge concurrency; 2) they make easier the factorization process of treatments; and 3) they offer several methods for the analysis and the validation of the modeled protocols. Furthermore, even if at the present time the interaction protocols are quite simple, as the need of sophisticated protocols will grow, the complexity of those protocols will surely increase. The understanding and validating these complex protocols will be unavailable. CPN have been successfully and widely applied in analyzing protocols and thus are surely a good candidate for protocols' engineering. Hence some significant frameworks based on CPN formalism have been developed by different teams [5] [6] [4].

This paper is organized as follows: section 2 outlines both our framework hypotheses and our aims, namely the modeling and the analysis of interactions. Section 3 briefly introduces the paradigm of distributed observation through the causality concept and illustrates its usefulness to build the causal graph of interactions. Section 4 presents the CPN formalism through some modeling aspects. The pattern matching algorithm presented in Section 5 is our main focus in this paper. The algorithm leads to recognize the nature of interaction involved between agents. Section 6 concludes and lights up our future work.

2 Conceptual framework

Our approach is structured on five phases (see figure 1):

1. In [5] we have proposed an efficient study of interaction. Based on an *on-line* distributed observation of the MAS running, it allows to capture traces of the relevant events underlying the agents' interactions (see phase 1).
2. While exploiting the obtained traces, the second phase builds the causal graph of events [6] underlying the interactions that have been occurred during the distributed execution, i.e., agents may be situated and run on distinct sites (see phase 2). Let us remark that the reconstitution mechanism is ensured *off-line* and based on logical clocks proposed by J. Fidge [10] and F. Mattern [14] which take into account the local concurrency, i.e., on the same site, for multi-threading process for instance.
3. The third phase represents our main interest in this paper. It corresponds to the recognition of interactions based on a pattern matching algorithm. The algorithm is jointly based on the causal graph of events and the CPN models

as filters (CPN_patterns). Knowing that several computations may be associated with the same CPN model and consequently with the same protocol, it becomes necessary to identify the right instances of the right protocols. We overcome this difficulty thanks to the true-concurrency semantics by means of the unfolding Petri Net techniques. In fact, at the opposite of the interleaving concurrency semantics, the unfolding Petri nets method enables to associate a set of unfolding nets with a given protocol modeled as CPN.

4. and 5. Work in progress addresses the phases four and five that will not be detailed in this paper. Briefly, the fourth one aims to explain the behaviour of the MAS according to the adopted protocols while the fifth one corresponds to the learning process. Supported by the central agent, the learning process tries to deduce both qualitative and quantitative criteria to be communicated to the other agents. These criteria should be taken into account by the agents as guidelines to improve their behavior and especially their future interactions.

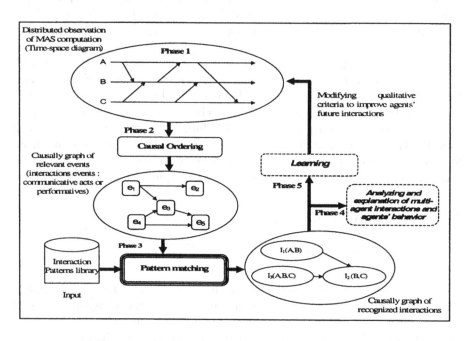

Fig. 1. A structured approach for interaction design in MAS

The hypotheses of our framework are:

- the MAS is composed of a set of cognitive agents distributed on different sites and may run concurrently.
- the agents communicate exclusively by asynchronous messages.
- each agent has a local strategy for problem solving, reasoning mechanisms, etc.

- all the protocols are modeled through CPN formalism and are available in the protocol library (CPN_Patterns) shared by agents.
- each agent communicates with each other w.r.t. the predefined protocols.
- the observation is distributed in the sense that each agent has a local module, which observes and traces the significant events corresponding to the emissions/receptions of the agent messages and some local events.
- the analysis and learning processes are ensured *off-line* by the central agent.

3 Distributed observation applied to interaction in MAS

Distributed problem solving involves complex interaction strategies of cooperation, in the sense that they are non-deterministic, hard to be interpreted and sometimes neither completely reproducible, nor predictable.

A possible solution is to observe the computation at run time in order to record the most significant events and their causality relation. Generally, at a given level of an application, only few events are relevant to the observation process. For example, in interaction protocol, only events according to the protocol running are significant. An observer of MAS may be any entity that attempts to watch the system while the computation is in progress or examine a post-mortem log or trace of events. In our framework, we consider a distributed execution as composed of a set of agents that communicate asynchronously by message passing over a communication network [13]. At the most abstract level, a computation of MAS can be defined as a set of events. Each agent generates an execution trace, which is a finite set of local atomic events in some specific order. There are two kinds of event: *interaction events*, i.e., sending and receiving messages, and *internal events* (e.g. updating internal state of the agent).

We are particularly interested about the concept of time in distributed systems which may be usefully used in many ways, especially for ordering events using logical clocks. Another aspect is that many applications require identifying *"cause and effect"* relationships in event occurrences (e.g. debugging programs). In any case, the model (called *happened-before*) [13] is necessary to give information about the *causally precedes* relation among the events. This relation can be defined as follows:

- *Locally precedes* relation between events on a single site which generally provides a total order,
- *Immediately precedes* relation between a couple of events e and f of exchange messages ; if e is the sending of the message and f is the reception of the same message.

Now, the *causally precedes* relation denoted by "$\rightarrow$" can be defined as the transitive closure of the union of the two relations above. Let us remark that one of the major difficulties in distributed agents is that the ordering relation between events is a *partial* order. Our model goes on to **partially order** the events on a single site which would allow events within an agent to be independent or concurrent (e.g. independent threads). This model [19] extends the happened-before model in order to: 1) address the problem of *false causality* when local events are independent; and 2) capture the semantics of multiple local threads of control. This relation can be represented with a **minimal oriented graph** denoted *causal dependency graph* (see [5] and [6] for the graph construction).

Finally, the mechanisms that capture causality are widely developed depending on the level of information required. In our approach, the vector clocks mechanism [10] [14] is adopted since it enables to exactly know the *causally precedes* relation between events.

4 Modeling interactions by means of CPN

The protocol engineering typically comprises various stages including specification, verification, performance analysis, implementation, and testing.A computational specification of complex interactions is the description of a combinatory of exchanging performatives between agents [12].We consider interaction protocols as the basic ones from which complex and high-level interactions can be built [2]. As argued in section 1.2, we adopt the CPN formalism to handle interactions. Next, we present the syntactical and semantical features of CPN [11] illustrated through a significant example, FIPA-Query-Protocol [9] (see figure 2). FIPA-Query-Protocol simply allows one agent to request another to perform some kind of inform action (*query-act*) and the receiver to answer with a normal *inform act* or, in some way, that it cannot answer (i.e. *refuse*, *failure* or *not-understood*). The presented example extends the FIPA-Query-Protocol since it involves one sender and any set of receiving agents (e.g. broadcast of a query).

4.1 Syntactical aspect of CPN

Petri Nets are state and action oriented models at the same time. In our framework, the modeling is concentrated on actions that represent the events to be observed. A Petri net is defined as usual: it consists of *places* (circles) and *transitions* (rectangles) which are connected by arcs.

- Places: each place contains tokens called *marking* which describe the state of the system. In ordinary Petri nets, tokens do not support information while in colored nets, the tokens are labeled by a type of data - possibly structured - called a color. Each token carries a data value which belongs to the type of the corresponding place. For instance the associated data type of the place *Init_Protocol* is the set AG which represents all the agents in our system and its initial marking is the involved agents' identifiers. Let us remark, that in the general case, a place may contain more than one token with the same data value, i.e. we have a multi-set of tokens. Hence a marking is a function which maps each place into multi-set of tokens of the associated type.
- Transitions: they model the change of states. In our model, each transition is associated with an action of an agent. The activation of a transition is called a firing, for instance as the result of the query communication act

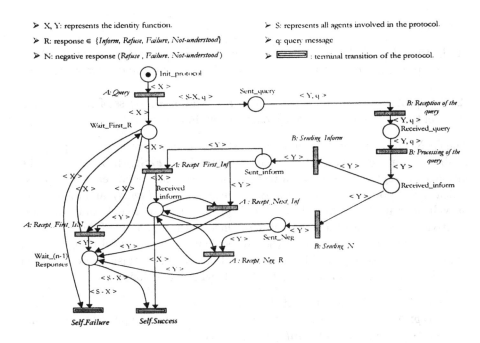

➢ X, Y: represents the identity function.
➢ R: response ∈ {*Inform, Refuse, Failure, Not-understood*}
➢ N: negative response (*Refuse , Failure. Not-understood*)

➢ S: represents all agents involved in the protocol.
➢ q: query message
➢ ▭▭▭ : terminal transition of the protocol.

Fig. 2. The CPN model of FIPA-Query Protocol

represented by the transition *Query*. When the condition of activation of a transition is fulfilled we say that the transition is fireable.

- Arcs: an *incoming arc* (from place to transition) indicates that the transition may consume tokens from the corresponding place while an *outgoing arc* (from transition to place) indicates that the transition may add tokens in the corresponding place. The exact number of tokens and their data values are determined by the arc expressions w.r.t. the semantics of the CPN (i.e. the firing rules of transitions).

4.2 Semantical aspect of CPN

The dynamic of the modeled system (i.e. the behaviour of the net) is given through the firing of transitions. The firing of a transition T_i is a two-steps operation: it consumes tokens from input places $(Pre(T_i))$ and produces tokens into output places $(Post(T_i))$. In colored Petri nets a set of variables is associated with each transition. The expressions that label the arcs around the transition are built with these variables. The firing of a transition involves an instantiation of the variables and an evaluation of the expressions which give the multi-set of tokens to be consumed or produced. For example, the arc labeled $< S\text{-}X, q >$, where q is a constant (query message), means that the firing of the transition *Query* needs to bind $< S\text{-}X >$ to a value from the set of all agents except the sender, i.e. $AG \setminus \{A_i\}$.

Remarks:

1. In the CPN model there is no connection between particular input tokens and particular output tokens, i.e. both their numbers and their values may differ.
2. The protocol execution is ensured by a thread or a process of each involved agent what allows then the concurrency within an agent.

The CPN-Protocol works as follows: The sender sends a *Query act* for a proposal to all the other agents and enters a waiting state (*Wait_First_R*). On receiving the message (*Reception_Query*), each receiver processes the query, sends a response which can be positive (*Sending_Inform*) or negative (*Sending_N*), and then enters in waiting state (*Sent_Inform* or *Sent_Neg*). The sender accepts only the first positive answer while others are rejected. Once all the responses of the agents are received, the agents come out of the protocol either in successful (*Self_Success*) or failure way (*Self_Failure*). Let us note that one can distinguish four cases when receiving the responses according to the following transitions:

- *Recept_First_Inf*: reception of the first inform,
- *Recept_Next_Inf*: reception of the next answers whose type is "Inform" and necessarily after the first *Inform* is received,
- *Recept_First_IsN*: the first response received is a negative response,
- *Recept_Neg_R*: reception of a negative responses that occurs after the first *Inform* is received.

The reader can easily verify that the protocol successes if the sender receives at least one positive answer, otherwise it fails.

5 Recognition Algorithm based on unfolding Petri Nets

Our algorithm is based on the partial-order semantics of Petri Nets and well-known as unfoldings of Petri Nets [16]. The main interest of this method is that, at the opposite of the interleaving concurrency semantics, it enables to associate a set of unfoldings with a given CPN, in our case, an interaction protocol. An unfolding, also called a "process net", formalizes a concurrent run of a protocol which can be interpreted in terms of causality between the associated events.

5.1 Partial-order semantics of Petri Nets

An unfolding is an acyclic Petri net where the places represent tokens of the markings and the transitions represent firings of the original net (see figure 4). To build an unfolding, the following steps have to be executed iteratively:

- start with the places corresponding to the initial marking,
- develop the transitions associated to the firings (w.r.t. to the semantics of CPN) of every initially enabling transition,
- link input places to the new transitions,

- produce output places,
- link the output places to the new transitions.

Let it be remarked that the unfolding may be infinite if the original net includes an infinite sequence. Several methods [15] [7] have been proposed in order to avoid the infinite state problem in the verification of systems and provide finite unfoldings. In our case, the infinite state is not faced since the unfolding we look for corresponds to a specific protocol computation and necessarily finite.

5.2 The recognition algorithm through an example

To begin, a partially ordered set of events is extracted from the global trace since our approach supports that an agent may be involved, simultaneously, in several interactions [6]. The algorithm inputs are the causal graph (CG) and the CPN_Patterns while the expected outputs are the process nets that match with the CG.

Hypothesis

The CPN_Patterns are one-safe (i.e. a place contains at most, one token per color). This makes the detection easier by avoiding the combinatory explosion of the number of states following multiple firings of a transition by the same color tokens. Let us note that since the CPN is one-safe and the events are associated with the transitions, given an event e to be recognized, there is exactly one state in the unfolding net reachable with a transition labeled by e.

Petri Net unfolding example

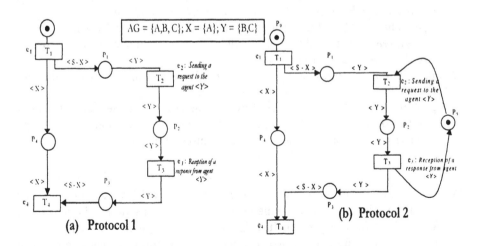

Fig. 3. Two CPN protocols to be recognized

Let us consider two protocols (cf. figure 3) which provide the same service (sending query messages to agents and reception of their answers). In the first protocol the execution is optimal, i.e., in parallel way; whereas in the second protocol the sending of messages and the reception of the associated answers are in sequence. One can easily verify in $Protocol_2$ that, except for the first firing of T_2 initially enabled from the initial marking, each following firing of T_2 requires at least a token in the input places P_1 and in P_5. As for P_1, (n-1) tokens have been produced by T_1, while a token in P_5 imposes the firing of T_3 which corresponds to a (n-1) sequences of T_2 followed by T_3 .

Let us now observe a computation of one of the two protocols given through a CG in (figure 4.b). The algorithm presented below develops all the possible process nets (see figure 4.a) in order to recognize the right CPN and the right process. The cycle of our algorithm (Step 1 to 5) is executed iteratively until all the events of CG are not examined.

Step 0: the algorithm begins at the places corresponding to the initial marking of each CPN (P_0 in $Protocol_1$ and (P_0, P_5) in $Protocol_2$). The set of events without predecessors is extracted from the GC (i.e. initially the only event ($e_1(A)$).

Step 1-2: For each of the expected events (here $e_1(A)$), the algorithm tries to recognize while firing the transitions labeled by these events concurrently in the two CPNs. In our example, only the transition T_1 labeled by $e_1(A)$ is fired both in $Protocol_1$ and $Protocol_2$. Consequently, the event is recognized by the two protocols and the output places are created and linked accordingly.

Step 3-4: Step 3 checks that the causal dependency of the recognized events through the process net is the same one as the CG. In the contrary case, the corresponding process net is rejected. When the transition labeled by an event is not fireable (*Step 4*) the associated process net is rejected. This is the case if the $Protocol_2$ for the transitions $T_2(A)$ and $T_2(B)$.

Step 5: The set of events without predecessors is updated by removing the events already examined and adding new ones, i.e. their successors (of course, only those without predecessors).

Step 6: The algorithm fails because all the developed process nets are eliminated.

Step 7: if the CG has been covered by the algorithm, it is necessary to check that the obtained process net is maximal, i.e. no transition can be fired. Otherwise, the protocol has not been executed completely.

Remarks:

1. In the general case, the same event may be associated with more than one transition labeled with the same event (cf. transitions *Recept_First_Inf* and *Recept_Next_Inf* in figure 2). In this case, the ambiguity is solved by introducing a choice function which returns the transition to be considered for a given event during the pattern matching process. Obviously, if the choice is wrong, we have to backtrack and consider an other alternative.

2. From the modelling point of view we have assumed that the CPN-Patterns are one-safe and without cycle. Let us remark that these limitations are introduced to gain simplicity but our algorithm may be applied to any kind

of CPN. In the most general case (possible ambiguity and any CPN) the algorithm complexity is P-Space, otherwise it is P-Time.

The algorithm:

Inputs:

The causal graph $CG = (E, U)$: *Where E is the set of events and U denotes the Causal dependency relation*

CPN_Patterns $= \{\sum_i / \sum_i = (CPN_i, M0_i)\}$: *The set of CPN-Patterns available in our library of protocols*

Output:

The set of expected unfoldings (i.e. process nets)

Begin

    Unfold_Nets:=CPN_Patterns

    $Ewp = \{e \in E/e$ is without predecessor$\}$

    $MC_i = M0_i$: *the current marking of $\sum_i$ initialized with the initial marking*

1:    **while** $Ewp \neq \emptyset$ **do**

        for_each e_j such that $e_j \in Ewp$ **do**

2:        **for_each** $\sum_i \in$ Unfold_Nets **do**

            if $\forall t_{k,i} in \sum_i /e_j$ is labeled by $t_{k,i}$ and is fireable from MC_i **then**

                $MC_i := MC_i \oplus Post(t_{k,i}) \ominus Pre(t_{k,i})$: *update the marking after firing $t_{k,i}$*

3:                **if** not (Causal-Dependency-Satisfied (CG,Ewp)) **then**

                    Unfold_Nets:= Unfold_Nets $\setminus \{\sum_i\}$: *eliminate $\sum_i$ unfolding: causal dependency violation*

                end_if

            else

4:            **if** $(\exists t_{k,i}/e_j$ is labeled by $t_{k,i}$ and $t_{k,i}$ is not fireable with $MC_i)$ **then**

                Unfold_Nets:= Unfold_Nets $\setminus \{\sum_i\}$: *abort unfolding : transition $t_{k,i}$ cannot be fired*

            end_if

        end_if

        end_for_each

        end_for_each

5:        $Ewp = Ewp \setminus \{e_j\} \cup \{e' \in E$ such that: $e' = succ(e_j)$ and e' is without predecessor$\}$

    end_while

6:    **if** Unfold_Nets$=\emptyset$ **then** return FAILURE : *No unfolding net found*

    else

7:        **for_each** $\sum_i \in$ Unfold_Nets **do**

        if there is no more transition $t_{k,i}$ fireable with the marking MC_i **then**

        return SUCCESS: $\sum_i$ *matches with CG*

        else

        Unfold_Nets:= Unfold_Nets $\setminus \{\sum_i\}$: *The unfolding of $\sum_i$ is not maximal*

        end_if

    end_if

End

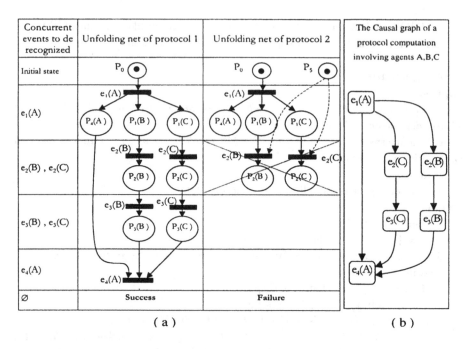

(a)   (b)

Fig. 4. The unfolding process of the two protocols according to the CG

6   Conclusion and future work

This paper proposes an original approach for protocol engineering in the case of complex interactions. The main advantages of our approach may be summarized as follows:

- It is generic, i.e. independent of any communication protocols and languages;
- It enables a formal study of complex interactions (i.e. modeling, analysis and verification) through a suitable formalism namely the Colored Petri Nets;
- Our algorithm is based on the partial-order semantics of Petri Nets unfolding (i.e. true concurrency) and enables, at the opposite of the interleaving concurrency semantics, the partial order representation of concurrent behaviours;
- Based on distributed observation, our approach develops the causal graph of events (the most relevant ones) w.r.t. the local concurrency and hence it addresses the problem of *false causality*;
- Finally, it allows not only the detection of the success/failure situations but also the explanation of such situations.

Our future work, intends to use the results of the analyzed situations analysis, and consequently the evaluation that it provides regarding to a set of interactions, in the following way: a learner agent recovers these results and generates a qualitative criteria to be communicated to other agents in order to enrich their social knowledge and improving their future interactions.

References

1. J.L. Austin:How To Do Things With Words. Oxford University Press. (1962).
2. H. Bachatène, M. Coriat and A. El Fallah Seghrouchni: Using Software Engineering Principles to Design Intelligent Cooperative Systems. In: Proc. of SEKE'93 (KSI Press. San Fransisco, USA. (1993).
3. P.R. Cohen and H.J. Levesque: Communicative actions for artificial agent. In Proc. of ICMAS'95, San Francisco, CA (1995).
4. R. S. Cost, Y. Chen,T.Finin, Y. Labrou and Y. Peng. Modeling Agent Conversations with colored Petri Nets. To appear in Working Notes of the Workshop on Specifying and Implementing Conversation Policies, Autonomous Agents '99. Seattle, Whashington, May 1999.
5. A. El Fallah Seghrouchni, S. Haddad and H. Mazouzi: Etude des interactions basée sur l'observation répartie dans un systéme multi-agents. In Proc. of JFIADSMA'98, Eds Hermès. Nancy.(1998).
6. A. El Fallah Seghrouchni, S. Haddad and H. Mazouzi: A Formal Study of Interactions in Multi-Agent Systems. In Proc. of CATA'99. pp 240-246. April, Cancun, Mexico.
7. J. Esparza, S. Romer, and W. Volger: An improvement of McMillan's unfolding algorithm. In Proc. of the second international workshop TACAS'96, volume 1055 of LNCS, pp. 87-106, Passau, Germany, 1996. Springer Verlag.
8. T. Finin, R. Fritzon, D. McKay et R. McEntire. KQML as an agent Communication Language. In 3rd International Conference on Information and Knowledge Management (CIKM'94), ACM Press, 1994.
9. Foundation for Intelligent Physical Agents: FIPA 97 Specification. Part 2, Agent Communication Language, (1997).
10. J. Fidge: Timestamps in message passing systems that preserve the partial ordering. In Proc. 11th Australian Computer Science Conference,(1988), 55-66.
11. K. Jensen and G. Rozenberg: High Level Petri Nets, Theory and Applications. Springer-Verlag (1991).
12. J.L. Koning, G. Franois and Y. Demazeau : Formalization and pre-validation for interaction protocols in multi agent systems, ECAI'98, Brighton, (1998).
13. L. Lamport: Time, Clocks, and the ordering of events, in distributed system. Communication of the ACM. 21(7), pp. 558-565.(1978).
14. F. Mattern: Virtual time and global states of distibuted systems. In. Proc. of the Workshop on Parallel and Distributed Algorithms, Bonas, North Holland (1988).
15. K.L. McMillan: On-the-fly verification with stubborn sets. In Proc. of Computer Aided Verification, vol. 663 of LNCS, 164-175, Montreal, June 1992. Springer Verlag.
16. M. Niellsen. G. Plotkin and G. Winskel: Petri Nets, Event Structures and Domains. Theoretical Computer Science (13)1, pp. 85-108 (1980).
17. V. Parunak: Visualizing Agent Conversations: Using Enhanced Dooley Graphs for Agent Design and Analysis. In. Proc. of ICMAS'96.(1996).
18. J.R. Searle: Speech Acts. Cambridge University Press (1969).
19. A. Tarafdar and V. K. Garg: Adressing False Causality while Detecting Predicates in Distributed Programs. Proceedings of the IEEE 18th ICDCS, pages 94 - 101, Amsterdam, Netherlands, May 1998.

Designing Agent Communication Languages for Multi-agent Systems

Jeremy Pitt and Abe Mamdani

Intelligent & Interactive Systems, Dept. of Electrical & Electronic Engineering
Imperial College of Science, Technology & Medicine, London, SW7 2BZ
Email: {j.pitt,e.mamdani}@ic.ac.uk   URL: http://www-ics.ee.ic.ac.uk/

Abstract. To provide inter-operability between heterogeneous agents in open systems, a commonly understood agent communication language (ACL) is used. To ensure that it is commonly understood, a formal semantics for the ACL is required. In this paper, we explore ideas from the semantics of natual language dialogues for defining the meaning of ACL messages. Using a general semantic framework for characterising the semantics of a class of ACLs in terms of protocols, we introduce a method for designing an ACL for a particular application. We illustrate this idea with respect to a small ACL called sACL. The advantages of this approach are that the specification is considerably less complex and more general, the potential for interoperability is improved, and verification of compliance to the semantics is easier.

1   Introduction

Traditionally, distributed systems designed with object-oriented methodologies were generally concerned with the physical distribution of data and resources. In contrast, systems engineering with agents as the primary design abstraction are generally concerned with the logical distribution of knowledge, responsibility and control. An agent is then a software process that encapsulates some domain information (knowledge) and responsibility for some complex functionality ('know how'). Multiple agents co-operate to solve problems: when one agent determines that a given problem is beyond its capabilities or jurisdiction, it finds another one to help it. However, when an agent receives a request to assist with some task, it measures the desirability of doing so against its own goals. The agent itself makes a decision on whether to accept, decline or enter negotiation.

There are several issues here, one of which is the communication which underpins the multi-agent problem solving. The requirement for communication has determined that some kind of message passing between agents be implemented. To provide inter-operability between heterogeneous agents in open systems, a commonly understood agent communication language (ACL) is used, and to ensure that it is commonly understood, a formal semantics for the ACL is required.

Example ACLs include KQML [3], ARCOL [11], and FIPA's ACL [4]. The semantics of these languages has typically been characterised in terms of speech act theory and framed in terms of the intentional stance (i.e. mentalistic notions such as beliefs, desires and intentions) [2, 7, 11, 4].

For MAS engineering, the ACL proposed by the standardisation body FIPA (Foundation for Intelligent Physical Agents) has been a significant development. FIPA has endeavoured to standardise both the syntax and the semantics of this language. However, there are a number of limitations associated with the specification of the FIPA ACL semantics, e.g. for generality [12] and compliance [14]. We believe that these problems stem from trying to standardise the semantics of an ACL based on the intentional stance. In this paper, we consider how to design and specify interactions in a multi-agent system based on 'standard' performatives and protocols. The intuitions behind the intentional semantics can then be interpreted informatively and accommodated as required (cf. [13]).

We conclude that a 'standard' ACL semantics for all agents, applications and domains is unrealistic, but that we can provide a generic ACL and customise it for particular agent societies. We can view a multi-agent system as a social organization, and analyse the communicative acts from the implicit authority, trust, sincerity and belief revision required for dynamic social systems [1, 12]. Further mechanisms are required for agents to publicise their behaviour and to learn the protocols required to interact in new social situations.

2   A Layered Semantics

An intentional formalisation of an ACL semantics often involves the axiomatisation of the felicity conditions of Searle and/or the conversational maxims of Grice. For example, Grice's analysis of conversational implicatures was underpinned by the sincerity condition to support the co-operativity principle. For agents to converse co-operatively (e.g. for negotiation, co-ordination, etc.), the sincerity condition is a reasonable requirement, but is often hard-wired into the semantics as a feasibility precondition on performing a simple speech act, e.g. KQML tell and FIPA inform. Thus an agent believes what it says and only says what it believes, but this may not be appropriate in all situations [Singh, 1998].

To address this problem, we are inclined to take a more protocol-oriented view of the ACL semantics, so that the communication between two (or more) agents can be seen as a conversation. The meaning of agent dialogues using ACL can also be analysed by applying ideas from the formal semantics of natural languages. Now it is well known that the 'meaning' of a sequence of statements (assuming each statement is a formula in some logical language, or translation into such a formula) as exchanged between two agents cannot usually be represented as the simple conjunction of each of the individual formulas. The limitations of this approach may be overcome by using the theory and techniques of discourse representation, and considering 'meaning' at different levels of abstraction. Guenthner [6] identified three levels of 'meaning' of an expression:

- the linguistic meaning of an statement (simple or complex), which is what determines its contribution to an information state, or better, the conditions of its contribution to an information state;
- the representational meaning of a statement, which is the particular change the statement induces on an information state;
- the model-theoretic meaning of a statement, which is the set of satisfiability conditions induced by the change given a particular class of models for the information states.

One of our defining characteristics for an 'intelligent' agent is a large number of internal states (combining belief and goal states, for example). Each state of an agent, including any preceding dialogue, can be thought of as an information state. The content of a speech act can be thought of as *changing* one information state into another. Therefore if we had the totality of possible states, i.e. the set of all information states U_s for an agent s given by $U_s = \{s_1, s_2, \ldots, s_n, \ldots\}$, we could think of a proposition p (with p being the content of an inform performative, say) as defining a diadic relation R_p between members of U_s.

In principle, given any two information states of an agent, we could determine whether or not they stood in some relation R_p. In practice, however, we are only given an initial state of an agent s, s_i say, and a proposition p 'corresponding to' the relation R_p, and nothing about the resulting state s_j. We can however use the proposition to infer the conditions on and information content of p, i.e. its *linguistic meaning*. Thus the linguistic meaning of the content p of an inform performative is defined as the set of pre-conditions in s_i and post-conditions in s_j that the information states must satisfy, plus the information content of p itself. In the following we will refer to this as the *content meaning*, as this meaning is derived from the :content slot of the agent's speech acts in the ACL.

The change in context induced by a proposition p need not be restricted to merely checking the pre-conditions and adding the post-conditions and information content of p. The new information may be used to derive further inferences, for example, and we may get different results for different values (states) of s_i. Thus the particular change an expression effects on an information state is dependent on that state. For a 'logical' agent, the resulting state s_j can be computed from that agent's reasoning principle (or principles), parameterised by the initial information state s_i and the content meaning of the speech act. The representational meaning of a proposition, i.e. what it really means for the agent to 'understand' the proposition, is then defined as the difference between information states induced by the content meaning and the reasoning principles.

The level of model-theoretic meaning identified above by Guenthner [6] is effectively the semantics of the knowledge representation language used to specify the content and representational meanings, and need not concern us further here.

In the general case of two agents communicating, We would argue that there are three layers of semantics:

i the content level semantics, which is concerned with interpreting and understanding the content of a message, and is internal to an agent;

ii the action level semantics, which is concerned with replying in appropriate ways to received messages, and is external to the agents;

iii the intentional semantics, which is concerned with making a communication in the first place, and with replying, and again is internal to the agent.

We would argue that the current FIPA ACL semantics for example, is level 3. This is internal to an agent, and so its usefulness in standardisation has been questioned [14, 12]. The only part of the communication that is amenable to standardisation is the observable tip of the iceberg: namely the communication itself. Note that this properly includes ontologies, so that there may be a standard interpretation, but the actual interpretation of the content of the message is once again internal to the agent.

3 The ACL Development Method

In related work [9], we define a general semantic framework for defining a protocol-based semantics for a class of ACLs, wherein the meaning of a speech act was given as an intention to reply. This was done by defining an ACL to be a 3-tuple $ACL = <$ Perf, Prot, $reply >$ defining performatives, protocols, and a $reply$ function, which for each state of a protocol determines which performatives are acceptable replies. This gave the action level semantics.

Each agent then had its *own* definition of two functions, one for changing state after receiving new information, and one for formulating and selecting a response to a speech act, according to the history of the conversation, the information state of the recipient, and the state of the protocol. This could be given as an intentional semantics.

The definition of a particular ACL by a 3-tuple effectively defines a set of finite state diagrams with arcs labeled by performatives and states labeled by which agent's turn it is to 'speak' in the conversation. Some attention needs to be paid to protocols where there are more than two participants, the sequence of speech acts is not simple turn-taking, there are timing constraints which affect which actions that may be taken, and so on. However, in general our approach allows us to define a class of ACLs, rooted on a common core. We envisage starting from a set of core performatives and possibly some protocols (i.e. performatives whose intended meaning is intuitively clear and protocols for some common functions). This would be the 'standard' ACL, the root of this class of ACLs, which could then be extended within the same semantic framework for particular applications. We use as our core core-sACL (see the next section).

There are three directions in which core-sACL could be extended, as illustrated in Figure 1:

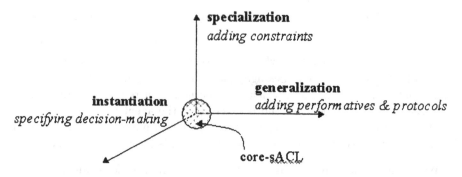

Fig. 1. Framework for Extending core-sACL

- *generalization.* New performatives and new protocols can be defined to create a new ACL where there were general interactions not covered by the standard. For example, auction protocols are a common requirement in some multi-agent systems, and new protocols could be added for the particular type of auction demanded by an application (Dutch, English, etc.);
- *specialization.* Additional constraints can be added to transitions, and/or richer description of states can be specified. For example, in the development of a FIPA'97-compliant multi-agent system for real-time load control [10], we required some interactions to be 'timed out'. Also, a state could be associated with a set of conversation variables that determine the conversation state, and there could be a complex interaction of state changes according to certain transitions given a particular conversation state;
- *instantiation.* The specific decision-making functionality for deciding which reply from a set of allowed replies can also be specified. For example, the same protocol may be used in quite different application domains. The decision-making that characterises whether to reply with performative X or performative Y from the same state may then be dependent on very different functions. In principle, application designers can take an ACL "off the shelf", if it contains a protocol that serves the task required, and specify the application-specific functions which the system developers can then implement.

In the following sections, we fully define core-sACL and demonstrate how this can be generalized, specialised and instantiated.

4 sACL: A small Agent Communication Language

Using this framework in conjunction with the design method just introduced, we can develop a semantic definition for sACL, a small Agent Communication Language. We begin with core-sACL, which comprises just three basic speech acts, declarative (statement), interrogative (question), and directive (command),

and no protocols. We will use the undefined symbol $\perp$ to indicate that there is no conversation involved in one off communications, and so of course the *reply* function returns no state.

Let core-sACL be the 3-tuple <Perf, Prot, *reply*> where:

$$\text{Perf} = \{\text{inform}, \text{query}, \text{command}\} \qquad \text{Prot} = \{\textbf{no\_protocol}\}$$
$$reply(\text{inform}, \textbf{no\_protocol}, \perp) = \{\text{null}\}$$
$$reply(\text{query}, \textbf{no\_protocol}, \perp) = \{\text{inform}\}$$
$$reply(\text{command}, \textbf{no\_protocol}, \perp) = \{\text{inform}, \text{null}\}$$

This defines the action level semantics of core-sACL, i.e. a semantics at level (ii) as identified earlier. We next define an intentional semantics (a semantics at level (iii)). We do this using a BDI (Beliefs-Desires-Intentions) logic, where there are modal operators $\mathcal{B}$, $\mathcal{D}$ and $\mathcal{I}$ for respectively the beliefs, desires (goals) and intends modalities. The notation in the following includes: $\mathcal{K}_s$ denotes 'knowledge' and is defined by $\mathcal{K}_s p \leftrightarrow \mathcal{B}_s p \vee \mathcal{B}_s \neg p$; DONE is an operator on actions, which is true after action A has taken place; and $[a, A]$ is an agent-action modality, so that the formula $[a, A]p$ is read "after agent a does action A, then p holds". For any agent i, $\mathcal{I}_i < i, A >$ is logically equivalent to $\mathcal{I}_i < A >$ (i.e. the agent intends to do action A itself). For clarity of presentation, we have omitted the language, ontology and conversation identifier parameters. The protocol parameter is also omitted but it is **no_protocol** in all cases.

$$\models \mathcal{B}_s p \wedge \mathcal{D}_s \mathcal{B}_r p \rightarrow \mathcal{I}_s < \text{inform}(r, p) >$$
$$\models \mathcal{D}_s \mathcal{K}_s p \wedge \mathcal{B}_s \mathcal{K}_r p \rightarrow \mathcal{I}_s < \text{query}(r, p) >$$
$$\models \mathcal{D}_s \text{DONE}(A) \wedge \mathcal{B}_s \, capable(r, A) \rightarrow \mathcal{I}_s < \text{command}(r, A) >$$
$$\models [s, \text{inform}(r, p)]\mathcal{B}_r p$$
$$\models [s, \text{query}(r, p)](\mathcal{B}_r p \rightarrow \mathcal{I}_r < \text{inform}(s, \textbf{true}) >) \vee$$
$$(\mathcal{B}_r \neg p \rightarrow \mathcal{I}_r < \text{inform}(s, \textbf{false}) >)$$
$$\models [s, \text{command}(r, A)]\mathcal{I}_r < A > \wedge$$
$$[r, A](\text{DONE}(A) \rightarrow \mathcal{I}_r < \text{inform}(s, \text{DONE}(A)) >)$$

However, communication rarely takes place in isolation. The first three axioms above show a possible axiomatic combination of beliefs and desires that trigger the intention to perform each of the three specified speech acts, for a given sending agent s and an intended receiving agent r. The last three axioms are then a logical specification of how the receiving agent complies with the specification of the ACL as a 3-tuple. These specifications also determine which performative to use in a reply in order to comply with the semantic definition, the extra information that is required to parameterise the performative to turn it into a speech act, and how the information state of the receiving agent changes after the speech act.

Note, however, that this is a 'non-binding' specification only, and other agents may respond differently provided they comply with the action level semantic definition. This is why we describe the 3-tuple as specifying *the* action level semantics, as all agents 'talking' core-sACL should comply with this specification. The specification of the axioms below *an* intentional semantics, as different agents may act and re-act in different ways (i.e. it will depend on how each one has its *add* and *select* functions implemented).

Communication is more likely to occur in the context of a conversation and/or a social situation. We can further analyse the logical formulation above with respect to issues of sincerity, trust, authority and belief revision, i.e. interactions in a dynamic social context (cf. [1, 12]). We consider the effect of conversations on core-sACL in the next section.

The logical formulation of the intention to inform includes the 'precondition' that the agent believes what it is saying. This is the behaviour of a sincere agent that may be trying to co-operate. Alternatively, or additionally, we could define the behaviour of a 'rapacious' agent by the axiom:

$$\models \mathcal{D}_s \psi \wedge \mathcal{B}_s(\text{DONE}(A) \rightarrow \psi) \rightarrow \mathcal{I}_s \text{DONE}(A)$$

This axiom states that if s desires (wants) ψ and believes that doing A will achieve ψ then s will intend to do A. If $\psi = \mathcal{B}_r \phi$, the same communication occurs (A is $< s, \text{inform}(r, \phi) >$), without s having an explicitly held belief in ϕ. However, it is important to note that with the first axiom the agent is being sincere with respect to its beliefs, and with the second axiom it is being sincere with respect to its desires.

Given this possibility, whether or not the receiving agent does or does believe that the content of an inform is true, is a function of the trust or reliability that the receiving agent has in the sender. Therefore, in a multi-agent system, we may need some representation of the trust relationships between two agents. One agent may come to trust another if there is an agreed commitment to abide by the sincerity axiom for communication via informs.

Then we could put an extra condition on the action modality for treating the content of inform speech acts, e.g. by making belief in the content contingent on trust in the sender:

$$\models [s, \text{inform}(r, p)](trust(r, s) \rightarrow \mathcal{B}_r p)$$

This is saying simply that: after s informs r that p holds, if r trusts s then r will believe p. If the trust relationship is mutually known to both sending and receiving agents, then this formula can equally apply to the reasoning of both sending and receiving agents about the consequences of a speech act. The sending agent can infer that the receiving agent will believe the content, and the receiving agent can safely take the information 'on trust' as it were.

However, there is an asymmetry for the logical consequence of an inform for a sending agent and a receiving agent in situations where the trust relationship has not been established. The receiving agent may believe the content p or not, as it wishes. The sending agent cannot assume that $\mathcal{B}_r p$ will necessarily result from the speech act, but the sending agent can assume that it may be the result. The sending will have to revise this belief, though if it turns out that the receiver did not trust the sender and/or did not believe the content. There are various methods for doing this (e.g. [5]).

One of the features of agents, as mentioned in the Introduction, is that they are autonomous. This implied they made their own decisions on whether to co-operate, and of course, whether they took actions that they were asked or told to do. Therefore, in a multi-agent system, in order to co-operate effectively, there may be some requirement to negotiate authority relationships for the suspension of autonomy. So one agent s might establish a permission to command r to do an action A, otherwise it would have to request that r to do A (which might be refused). For this, of course, we would need to generalise core-sACL with new performatives, and modify the *reply* function as appropriate. These two alternatives could be represented by:

$$\models \mathcal{D}_s \text{DONE}(A) \wedge \mathcal{B}_s \, capable(r,A) \wedge \mathcal{B}_s \, authority(s,r) \rightarrow \mathcal{I}_s < \text{command}(r,A) >$$

and:

$$\models \mathcal{D}_s \text{DONE}(A) \wedge \mathcal{B}_s \, capable(r,A) \wedge \neg \mathcal{B}_s \, authority(s,r) \rightarrow \mathcal{I}_s < \text{request}(r,A) >$$

For receiving agent r, the action modality a command and a request might be modified to:

$$\models [s, \text{command}(r,A)](authority(s,r) \rightarrow$$
$$(\mathcal{I}_r < A > \wedge [r,A](\text{DONE}(A) \rightarrow \mathcal{I}_r < \text{inform}(s,\text{DONE}(A)) >)))$$
$$\vee (\neg authority(s,r) \rightarrow \mathcal{I}_r < \text{refuse}(s,A) >)$$

$$\models [s, \text{request}(r,A)] \, (\mathcal{D}_r \text{DONE}(A) \rightarrow$$
$$(\mathcal{I}_r < A > \wedge [r,A](\text{DONE}(A) \rightarrow \mathcal{I}_r < \text{inform}(s,\text{DONE}(A)) >)))$$
$$\vee (\neg(\mathcal{D}_r \text{DONE}(A) \rightarrow \mathcal{I}_r < \text{refuse}(s,A) >))$$

In the former case r will only do the action A if the appropriate authority exists, in the latter case r will only do A if it fits in with r's own desires.

The summary of all this discussion is that the beliefs, desires and intentions of the sending receiving agents are external to the semantics of sACL, because the required combinations differ according to the agents, applications and domains in which the multi-agent system is set. There are also 'social' factors which have to be considered. We conclude that it is impossible to produce a single ACL whose semantics is defined in terms of the intentional stance. However, we can define a semantics for an Agent Communication Language where the normative part is based on a commitment to reply and an informative specification is provided for a particular application. In the next section, we consider the effect of adding protocols to sACL.

5   Protocol Communications

In this section, we devleop the ACL sACL by generalising core-sACL to include some simple ptotocols, which also entails introducing a number of new performatives. Let sACL be the 3-tuple $<$ Perf, Prot, *reply* $>$ given by specifying:

Perf = {inform, query, command, acknowledge, end, request, agree, cancel, fail, null}

Prot = {*yesno_query*, *confirmation*, *commitment*, *continuous_update*,
no_protocol}

The finite state diagrams for the four protocols are illustrated in Figure 2. The corresponding extension to the *reply* function can be constructed from the finite state diagrams.

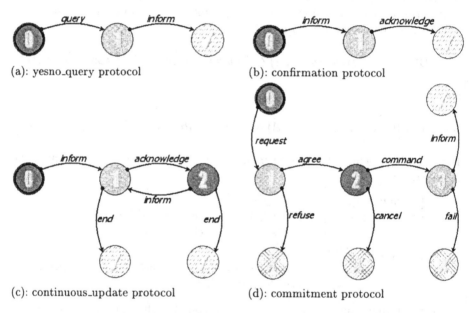

(a): yesno_query protocol

(b): confirmation protocol

(c): continuous_update protocol

(d): commitment protocol

Fig. 2. Simple protocols for sACL

The notation used in Figure 2 is as follows. States are numbered, and arcs are labelled with the speech act that causes the transition between states. The state with the heavy border (state 0) is the start state. States labelled with a tick or cross are end states, with the conversation terminating successfully or not respectively. The different shading on each state indicates which agent's turn it is to continue the dialogue, so here we are specifying turn-taking conversations between only two agents. The notation needs to be extended to accommodate conversations involving multiple participants and/or sequences from one agent; or for making 'terminate' and 'interrupt' performatives available from any state. These would respectively end or change the state of the conversation.

These protocols can be used by one agent to communicate with another in order to:

- query another agent about the value of some proposition (note this is protocol instance of the expected behaviour for one shot query speech acts);
- inform an agent of some proposition and receive an acknowledgement (of belief and/or receipt);
- continuously update the other agent about the value of some proposition;
- ask an agent if it will undertake some action, and, if it is agreeable, to tell (command) it to do that action. The final communication will be the result of doing the action (if it succeeds or fails).

It is now straightforward to construct the actual *reply* function from the finite state diagrams. Furthermore, each protocol can be supplemented by an additional specification (which may be intentional) of a version of the *add* and *select* functions which have been implemented by an agent in order to comply with this action level semantics. However, agents are not constrained to implement this specification. Each agent may have its own way of doing things and can do that, provided that its behaviour (in terms of responses to received messages) complies with the action level semantics.

We now reconsider the communicating agents illustrated in Section 2. Suppose one is telling the other when it has changed something in the environment in which they are embedded, which is of mutual interest. To ensure that their perceptions of the environment are aligned, they will use the agreed protocol *continuous-update*. This is the protocol illustrated as the finite state diagram shown in Figure 2(c). The idea is for one agent to inform the other agent of changes in the environment, and for this other agent to acknowledge receipt of the message, via the **acknowledge** performative. The content of the speech act will indicate whether or not the receiving agent accepts (believes) the change.

We assume that previously the receiving agent has indicated to the other agent an interest in some value p in the shared environment. For example, given the goal $\mathcal{D}_a\mathcal{K}_a p$ agent a would seek to find an agent that knew about p (agent s say, so $\mathcal{B}_a\mathcal{K}_s p$), but because of the desire to be repeatedly informed of the change it will intend to use the *continuous-update* protocol rather than the *yesno-query* protocol. This might be initiated by a one-shot communication via an *inform*, which also indicated when agent s should inform a of any change (i.e. by period, or on change).

Ignoring for now issues like language, time, ontology and protocol, an agent designer could specify (and implement) an agent a's behaviour for add_a (in this application) to be as shown below. It treats each of the three cases: when the content of the *inform* is already known, new, or contradictory. Note that the formula ϕ^c denotes the complement of formula ϕ, and that function *belief_revise$_a$* is a gloss on a's belief revision for contradictory statements (cf. [5]). We are not saying how the agent ensures its database is consistent (but there are algorithms for doing this, e.g. forward chaining).

$add_a(\text{inform}, datasync, \phi, \Delta_a) = \Delta'_a$, where

$\phi \in \Delta_a \rightarrow \Delta'_a = \Delta_a$

$\phi \notin \Delta_a \rightarrow \Delta'_a = \Delta_a \cup \{\phi, \mathcal{D}_a\mathcal{B}_s\mathcal{B}_a\phi\}$, if $\Delta_a \cup \{\phi\}$ is consistent

$\quad\quad\quad \rightarrow \Delta'_a = \Delta_a \cup \{\phi^c, \mathcal{D}_a\mathcal{B}_s\phi^c\}$, if $\Delta_a \cup \{\phi\}$ is inconsistent

$\phi^c \in \Delta_a \rightarrow \Delta'_a = \Delta_a - \{\phi^c\} \cup \{\phi, \mathcal{D}_a\mathcal{B}_s\mathcal{B}_a\phi\}$, if $belief\_revise_a(\Delta_a, \phi, \phi^c) = \phi$

$\quad\quad\quad \rightarrow \Delta'_a = \Delta_a \cup \{\mathcal{D}_a\mathcal{B}_s\phi^c\}$, otherwise

This is only an exemplary specification in a semi-formal notation. Different agents may have alternative ways of reacting to messages in this protocol, and this would be realised through different implementations of the *add* and *select* functions (and result in/from different specifications).

This intentional specification of an agent a's reactions to information received in the *datasync* protocol can be paraphrased informally as follows (where all replies are *intentions*, to be consistent with the ACL semantics):

If you tell me something I already know, my information state Δ is unchanged;
If you tell me something I don't know, then
if it is consistent with Δ, then I'll add it to Δ and acknowledge it
else if it is inconsistent with Δ, then I'll inform you that I disagree;
If you tell me something that I disagree with, then
if I prefer your version, then I'll revise Δ and acknowledge it
else if I prefer my version, then I'll keep Δ as it is and inform you otherwise

The implementation of the *select* for the agent will now use the new desires that result from 'understanding' the speech act in conjunction with the valid replies as given by the semantics of the protocol to generate (the intention) to reply accordingly.

This is of course just one formulation: the treatment of new and contradictory information may not be treated in the same way, for example. It is also easy to refine such a specification to incorporate elements of trust. Furthermore, since the sincerity condition is predicated on the notion of co-operation; and all speech acts involve the receiver recognizing an intention on the part of the sender, agents are free (but not forced) to make further inferences about the other agent's beliefs and intentions. Different inferences may be more appropriate for particular types of agents in different kinds of application.

6 Conclusions and Further Work

The specification of standards are extremely important engineering tool for achieving interoperability in heterogeneously designed and implemented multi-agent systems. The FIPA standardization body has produced a specification of a syntax and semantics for a 'standard' ACL to address the essential requirement for communication between agents. This is loosely based on speech act theory, and defined in terms of a set of performatives or communicative acts. A communicative act occurs whenever one agent sends a message to another.

In the FIPA specification, each performative is given a meaning informally via English descriptions, and a formal semantics in a first order modal logic of mental attitudes and actions, which define feasibility preconditions and rational effects of communicative acts, and various agent properties. The logical definitions generally characterise the belief state of the sending agent before performing the communicative act, and the intended belief state of the receiving agent after the act has been performed. Underlying these definitions are a number of properties which an agent can use either to plan a communicative act (i.e. send a message), or to make inferences from 'hearing' a communicative act (i.e. receiving a message). These properties are formalised as axioms of the logic.

At present, though, it is not clear whether the specification of the formal semantics is intended to be normative or informative, so that the semantics and axioms are providing guidance for the developers or are requirements that the agents themselves are responsible for satisfying. This paper has instead been concerned with applying a general semantic framework which could give a formal normative meaning to ACL performatives and a formal informative meaning to speech acts used in different circumstances (e.g. social contexts and/or application domains).

This approach allows us to define a class of ACLs. We envisage starting from a set of core performatives and protocols (i.e. performatives whose intended meaning is intuitively clear and protocols from some common functions). This would be the 'standard' ACL, the root of the class of ACLs, which could then be extended within the same semantic framework for particular applications. New performatives and protocols could then be defined to create a new ACL where there were general interactions not covered by the standard. The protocols could then be reified and specialized for particular tasks, i.e. any time constraints or decision-making needed to determine actions in a conversation for a particular application domain (cf. [8]).

The definition of a particular ACL by a 3-tuple $< \mathsf{Perf}, \mathsf{Prot}, reply >$ effectively defines a set of finite state diagrams with arcs labeled by performatives and states labeled by which agent's turn it is to 'speak' in the conversation. All agents should then react to a speech act according to the protocol, and we try to constrain and predict the possible reactions with protocols. These, we argue, are the normative standard items: what an agent can do, not how it does it. add_a and $select_a$ are specifying what agent a should do, not how it should do it. Examples of how to do it can be specified, as illustrated in Sections 4 and 5, but these are informative specifications. Mental attitudes can be used for determining how to reply (although still cannot be used for generating content). However, even if an ACL with a standard external semantics can be agreed, it is unlikely to be testable as the agents are complex entities. 'Anti-social' behaviour may not be immediately obvious and the history of communications needs logging, and a means of auditing, policing and accountability is required.

Acknowledgements

This research has been undertaken in the context of the UK EPSRC/Nortel Networks joint funded project CASBAh (GR/L34440) and the EU funded ACTS project MARINER (AC333). We are grateful for the constructive comments of the anonymous reviewers.

References

1. C. Castelfranchi. Commitments: From individual intentions to groups and organizations. In V. Lesser, editor, *Proceedings ICMAS-95*. AAAI-MIT Press, 1995.
2. P. Cohen and H. Levesque. Communicative actions for artificial agents. In V. Lesser, editor, *Proceedings ICMAS95*. AAAI Press, 1995.
3. T. Finin, Y. Labrou, and J. Mayfield. KQML as an agent communication language. In J. Bradshaw, editor, *Software Agents*. MIT Press, 1995.
4. FIPA. Fipa'97 specification part 2: Agent communication language. FIPA (Foundation for Intelligent Physical Agents), http://drogo.cselt.stet.it/fipa/, 1997.
5. J. Galliers. Autonomous belief revision and communication. In P. Gardenfors, editor, *Belief Revision*. Cambridge University Press, 1992.
6. F. Guenthner. From sentences to discourse: Some aspects of the computational treatment of language. In A. Blaser, editor, *Natural Language at the Computer*, volume 320 of *LNCS*, pages 147–165. Springer-Verlag, 1988.
7. Y. Labrou and T. Finin. Semantics for an agent communication language. In M. Singh, A. Rao, and M. Wooldridge, editors, *Intelligent Agents IV*, volume 1365 of *LNAI*. Springer-Verlag, 1998.
8. J. Pitt, M. Anderton, and J. Cunningham. Normalized interactions between autonomous agents: A case study in inter-organizational project management. *Computer-Supported Cooperative Work*, 5:201–222, 1996.
9. J. Pitt and A. Mamdani. A protocol-based semantics for an agent communication language. In *Proceedings IJCAI'99*. Stockholm, Sweden, to appear.
10. J. Pitt and K. Prouskas. Initial specification of multi-agent system for realisation of load control and overload protection strategy. MARINER Project (EU ACTS AC333) Deliverable D3, http://www.teltec.dcu.ie/mariner, 1998.
11. D. Sadek. Dialogue acts are rational plans. In *Proceedings ESCA/ETRW Workshop on The Structure of Multimodal Dialogue*, pages 1–29. Maratea, Italy, 1991.
12. M. Singh. Agent communication languages: Rethinking the principles. *IEEE Computer*, pages 40–47, 1998.
13. I. Smith, P. Cohen, J. Bradshaw, M. Greaves, and H. Holmback. Designing conversation policies using joint intention theory. In Y. Demazeau, editor, *Proceedings ICSMAS98*. IEEE Press, 1998.
14. M. Wooldridge. Verifiable semantics for agent communication languages. In Y. Demazeau, editor, *Proceedings ICMAS98*. IEEE Press, 1998.

A Temporal Agent Communication Language for Dynamic Multi-agent Systems

T. Carron, H. Proton, and O. Boissier

Multi Agent Systems Group
Department of Industrial Cooperative Systems,
Ecole Nationale Supérieure des Mines,
158 Cours Fauriel,
F-42023 Saint-Etienne Cedex, France,
{Thibault.Carron,Hubert.Proton,Olivier.Boissier}@emse.fr

Abstract. A temporal dimension must be present in interactions between agents that must cooperate in continuously changing environments. In this paper, we present the definition of a temporal agent communication language. This language uses a sophisticated communication model based on the speech act theory. It is the component of a more important research dealing with the study of temporal reasoning in multi-agent systems. This work takes place, also, in the building of an interaction toolbox with temporal abilities in the context of a Multi-Agent System Platform in construction in our laboratory.

1 Introduction

As it is naturally present in natural language interactions, the temporal dimension has also to be present in interactions between agents that must cooperate in a continuously changing environment. This presence has many aspects such as datation, duration, expression of past and future, exchange of historic chronicles. It can also be more complex, like exchange of temporal constraints dealing with the action to execute or with the resources to use, but also temporal constraints bearing on the exchanges themselves. As a matter of fact, agents living in a dynamic world need not only to reason internally about temporal relations but also to communicate *in* a temporal dimension and *about* time.

The work which is presented here, is concerned with these dimensions, and more particularly, with the definition of a temporal communication language. This language uses a sophisticated communication model based on the speech act theory [16] [20]. It is the component of a more important research [2] dealing with the study of temporal reasoning in multi-agent systems. This work takes place, also, in the building of an interaction toolbox with temporal abilities, in the context of a Multi-Agent System Platform under construction [4].

In a first section, we will describe the problem that we want to solve. Then, we define the model of actions and times that we use to specify on one side, the speech acts of the language and on the second side, the language itself. We end with an example issued of an application of supervision of a bus fleet by temporal agents that communicate through the language that we defined.

2 Motivations

In Multi-Agent Systems (MAS), some researches have studied how to specify MAS having temporal properties [21] [18] [10]. Some have been mostly interested in the individual temporal reasoning capabilities [19], [6], whereas others studied the temporal properties of the social part of an agent : use of temporal dependence networks [2], study of the temporal dimension in discourse [13].

If we give a look at natural language interactions between humans, we can observe that time is an important property. It is conveyed by several features such as verb tenses, temporal conjunctions, ... Our aim is not to build a general representation of time in discourse. We are mainly interested in the expression of time in an agent communication language in the framework of a temporal interaction toolbox of our MAS platform. In this context, we consider that time has to be managed at three different layers in a multi-agent system :

1. at the *communication* layer dealing with the routing of the message. It deals among others with the identities of the sender and of the receiver, the mode of emission ... Depending on the middleware on which the agents are executed, time has to do with the sending or receiving dates, with synchronization issues, ...

2. at the *multi-agent system* layer that constrains the cooperation process between the agents. This layer is characteristic of the use of a multi-agent system [5] [3]. In the context of the speech act theory, this layer has to do, for example, with the illocutionary force that expresses the intention of the sender of the message. It handles also the whole of information necessary for the management of a conversation between the agents, as well as information necessary for the interpretation of the message.
We will give, below, examples of temporal aspects at this layer.

3. At the *application* layer that deals with the informations that are relevant to the particular application which is implemented by the multi-agent system. At this level, time is relevant to the content of the message itself: agents must be able to specify temporal constraints in the message that are to be taken by the individual reasoning capabilities of the receiver. Insofar, this one can use her individual temporal reasoning capabilities to reason on the temporal constraints in order to take it into account in her planning process for example.

In this article, we are mainly interested in the study of the temporal dimensions at the second layer which is the one concerned by our interaction toolbox. We will give some examples to better illustrate these temporal dimensions. These examples will be used in the following sections to illustrate the use of our temporal communication language.

Let's consider agent A that wants to communicate with agent B in two different situations:

1. A wants B to tell her what time it is.
2. A wants B to tell her what she will do next week.

We know that in (1), A doesn't know the current time and wants to know it. But we also know that A waits for an answer in a short time, whereas in (2), Agent A is less impatient. Both examples express a different temporal constraint on the sequencing of messages. In natural language, all this is implicit. In an artificial language, these have to be made explicit: the illocutionary force takes a different strength according to the temporal constraint that qualifies it.

In the same vein, we also want to express temporal constraints on the execution of an action compared to the communicative action. An example of such a constraint could be to ask for the execution of an action just 10 min. after, or as soon as, has been received the message asking to execute it.

We will now introduce the languages that we will use to specify the temporal communication language able to express such dimensions.

3 Action and Time

In the following, we will use the letters x, y, z to denote the agents of the system. Our approach separates the temporal and non-temporal constructs in the language. Thus we will start by presenting a language for describing actions and continue with a language for describing the world and the mental states of the agents. Then, we end with the description of a temporal expression language.

3.1 Actions

The action language, L_α, expresses the two types of actions that an agent can perform: one that an agent can execute $\underline{a}$ and one that is a communicative action $\underline{sa}$ (speech act). The action language is defined by the following BNF formula:

$$\alpha ::= \underline{a} \mid \underline{sa} \mid \alpha_1; \alpha_2 \mid \alpha_1 \& \alpha_2 \mid \alpha_1 \vee \alpha_2 \mid \neg\alpha \mid \text{any} \mid \alpha(\phi)$$

$\underline{a} \in L_{act}$ and $\underline{sa} \in L_{speech}$. L_{act} is the set of all the atomic actions that the agents can exchange and execute locally. L_{speech} is the set of all the communicative actions (performatives) that can be used by the agents to communicate (their semantic will be defined in Sect. 4).

$$L_{speech} = \{\text{inform, command, propose, refuse, accept, } \ldots\}$$

The meaning of $\alpha_1; \alpha_2$ is the sequential execution of actions α_1 and α_2. The meaning of $\alpha_1 \& \alpha_2$ is the parallel execution of both actions. $\alpha_1 \vee \alpha_2$ means the choice between actions α_1 and α_2. The expression $\neg\alpha$ stands for the non-execution of the action α. The any action is a universal action. Finally the action $\alpha(\phi)$ stands for the action α that leads to the world state described by ϕ.

3.2 Formula

In order to describe the world and the mental states of the agents we define the language L_ϕ. This language is based on "Belief-Desire-Intention" [9]. A formula of L_ϕ is defined with the following BNF :

$$\phi ::= \underline{\phi} \mid B(x, exp, \phi) \mid I(x, exp, \alpha) \mid S\_C(x, y, exp, \alpha)$$

where $exp \in L_T$ (see below).
$\underline{\phi}$ is a first order formula, $\alpha \in L_\alpha$.

- The meaning of $B(x, exp, \phi)$ is that agent x believes ϕ at any time t such that exp is verified at t. The semantic is defined by the classic axioms of belief [19].
- $I(x, exp, \alpha)$ means that agent x intends to do α such that the temporal expression exp will be satisfied.
- $S\_C(x, y, exp, \alpha)$ means that agent x is committed near agent y to execute action α such that exp is verified.

We define the modality Can to express the ability of an agent to execute an action as follow: $Can(x, exp, \alpha)$.

3.3 Time

In order to be more expressive, the denotations of temporal elements are interpreted at intervals [1], not at points [11]. We want to express explicit temporal constraints on actions or on formulas.

The language L_T allows the definition of temporal expressions consisting in the composition of temporal expressions with conjunction $\wedge$ or choice $\vee$, or simply in a temporal expression exp :

$$exp ::= \underline{exp} \mid exp_1 \wedge exp_2 \mid exp_1 \vee exp_2$$

A simple temporal expression $\underline{exp}$ consists in basic temporal expressions $(i, [\alpha], [\phi])$ or in the relative positioning of two simple temporal expressions. It is done through the use of temporal connectives **periodic** or $\mathcal{R}$, which are based on Allen's interval calculus :

$$\underline{exp} ::= i \mid [\alpha] \mid [\phi] \mid \underline{exp}_1 \, \mathcal{R} \, \underline{exp}_2 \mid \underline{exp}_1 \, \textbf{periodic} \, \underline{exp}_2 \, exp_3$$

The basic temporal expressions are :

- a temporal interval i that can be a duration d or an interval with a starting point t_s and an ending point t_e :

$$i ::= [d] \mid [t_s, t_e]$$

The expression $[d]$ is equivalent to the following interval $[t_?, t_? + d]$ where $t_?$ is an undetermined instant. We will use t_{now} for the current time and i_+ for denoting the interval $[t_{now}, +\infty[$.

- the interval $[\alpha]$. Its limits are respectively the starting point and the ending point of the execution of α ($\alpha \in L_\alpha$). Let's remember that α can be either $\underline{a}$, either $\underline{sa}$.
- the interval $[\phi]$. Its limits are respectively the starting point and the ending point of ϕ being true.

The temporal connectives are defined as follows:

$$\mathcal{R} ::= < \mid > \mid = \mid m \mid mi \mid o \mid oi \mid d \mid di \mid s \mid si \mid f \mid fi \mid \mathsf{beg} \mid \mathsf{end} \mid \mathsf{in}$$

The meaning of $<, >, =$, m, mi, o, oi, d, di, s, si, f, fi is the same as the one defined by Allen, (before, after, equal, meet, meet-inverse, overlap, overlap-inverse, during, during-inverse, start, start-inverse, finish, finish-inverse). A precise axiomatic of all these operators as well as their transitivity are given in [1].

For convenience, additional operators have been defined. The operator **beg** (resp. **end**) expresses that the starting (resp. ending) point of the first interval must be in the second interval.

Whereas all these operators are diadic, the operator **periodic** is triadic. It requires to have an action $[\alpha]$ or a formula $[\phi]$ interval as first terms. It is used to specify a periodic execution of the action with a frequency expressed in the second term and during an interval specified in the third term.

3.4 Example

These temporal notations are complex and multiple. This shows the difficulty of the problem. To illustrate the use of all these definitions, we will give some examples:

- "[FillIn] in $[10, 20]$" means that the action FillIn must be executed within the temporal interval $[10, 20]$,
- "[tank filled up to 75%] $= [10, 20]$" means that the state tank filled up to 75% must be maintained during an interval equal to $[10, 20]$,

We will show now, how to write more complex expressions. Let's imagine, that the action FillIn to achieve tank filled up to 75%, must be executed within $[10, 20]$, and as soon as this action ends, the state tank filled up to 75% must be maintained during 20. We will write:

([FillIn(tank filled up to 75%)] in $[10,20]$) $\land$ ([tank filled up to 75%] $= [20]$)$\land$
　　([FillIn(tank filled up to 75%)] m [tank filled up to 75%])

4　Semantic of Temporal Speech Acts

Placing our work in the same vein of [8], [15], in this section, we will express the semantic of the different communicative actions that are defined in L_{speech}. This semantic has no other goal to enable us to express the temporal dimensions in the illocutionary force. It doesn't pretend to define yet a new semantic of speech acts.

A speech act is a communicative action which is parameterized by a temporal expression $(exp \in L_T)$ and an action $(\alpha \in L_\alpha)$ or a first order formula $(\phi \in L_\phi)$:

$\underline{sa} \in L_{speech} : \underline{sa}(sender, receiver, exp, \phi) \quad \vee \quad \underline{sa}(sender, receiver, exp, \alpha)$

sender and *receiver* are the identity of the agents that respectively send and receive the communicative action. The *receiver* can also be a group in case of broadcasting.

A communicative action $\underline{sa}$ has to be matched against the mental state of the agent in order to know if it is possible. It has also to define explicitly the modifications to do on this mental state when the speech act is successful. This is why we define a communicative action as a triple ⟨ Prec, Post, Pe ⟩ where Prec, Post and Pe are respectively, the pre-conditions, the post-conditions and the perlocutionary effect. Each of them is expressed using the above definitions.

- Prec : it is the set of necessary conditions for the triggering of the action. These are the conditions on the propositional content, the preparatory conditions and the sincerity conditions described in [20].
- Post : it is the set of postconditions. It is composed of an add list (+) and a retract list (-), that are to be done on the mental state of the sender.
- Pe : the perlocutionary effect is a description of the mental state that is wanted to be in the receiver.

4.1 Temporal Speech Acts

In the following, in order to simplify the presentation, we will use i, j, k to express temporal expression as defined above. A prime is added to an expression i, to express that i' is computed using i, t_{now} and the duration of the sending of the message. Let's present some examples of speech acts.

Assertive Acts.

- The communicative act inform is an assertive action that is used by agent x to inform agent y of the truth of ϕ.

inform(x, y, i, ϕ)
Prec : $B(x, i, \phi) \wedge B(x, j, \neg B(y, k, \phi)) \wedge t_{now} \in i \cap j \cap k$
Post : (+) $B(x, i', B(y, i'', \phi))$ (-) $B(x, j, \neg B(y, k, \phi))$
Pe : $B(y, i'', \phi)$

Directive Acts.

- The communicative action command is a directive act that commits the receiver to execute the action expressed in the parameters.

command(x, y, i, α)
Prec : $I(x, i, \alpha) \wedge B(x, j, Can(y, k, \alpha)) \wedge (k$ in $i) \wedge t_{now} \in i \cap j \cap k$
Post : $(+)$ $B(x, i', S\_C(y, x, i'', \alpha))$ $(-)$ $I(x, i, \alpha)$
Pe : $S\_C(y, x, i'', \alpha)$

– The propose act is a directive act making it possible for the transmitter to require of the receiver to achieve the action α in the future with the possibility of refusing.

propose(x, y, i, α)
Prec : $I(x, i, \alpha) \wedge B(x, j, Can(y, k, \alpha)) \wedge (k$ in $i) \wedge t_{now} \in i \cap j \cap k$
Post : $(+)$ $B(x, i', S\_C(y, x, i'', \alpha))$ $(-)$ $I(x, i, \alpha)$
Pe : $S\_C(y, x, i'', \alpha)$

Commissive Acts.

– The act accept is a commissive act making it possible for the transmitter to commit herself near the receiver to achieve an action in the future.

accept(x, y, i, α)
Prec : $B(x, k, I(y, j, S\_C(x, y, i, \alpha))) \wedge B(x, l, S\_C(x, y, i, \alpha)) \wedge t_{now} \in k \cap l$
Post : $(-)$ $B(x, k, I(y, j, S\_C(x, y, i, \alpha)))$
Pe : $B(y, l', S\_C(x, y, i, \alpha)))$

– The act refuse is a commissive act making it possible for the transmitter to refuse to commit herself near the receiver to achieve an action in the future.

refuse(x, y, i, α) :
Prec : $B(x, k, I(y, j, S\_C(x, y, i, \alpha))) \wedge B(x, l, \neg S\_C(x, y, i, \alpha)) \wedge t_{now} \in k \cap l$
Post : $(-)$ $B(x, k, I(y, j, S\_C(x, y, i, \alpha)))$
Pe : $B(y, l', \neg S\_C(x, y, i, \alpha))$

4.2 Examples

Going back to the examples given in Sect. 2, we will show, how we can express them with the above definitions.

Let's suppose that agent A uses a command to ask B for the current time or what she will do next week.

1. The first case is written as :

command$(A, B,$ [inform] in $[t_{now}, 0{:}0{:}10]$, inform(current_time))

A asks B to inform her at least in 10 seconds about the current time : the communicative action inform must take place within the interval $[t_{now}, 0{:}0{:}10]$.

2. The second case is written as :

command$(A, B,$ [inform] in $[t_{now}, 48{:}0{:}0]$, inform(about next_week))

A asks *B* to inform her at least in two days about what she will do next week : the communicative action inform must take place within the interval $[t_{now},48{:}0{:}0]$.

We will, now, give an example, where the temporal constraint doesn't bear on the action or formula given in the fourth parameter of the speech act, but on the speech act itself. Let's imagine, that *A* wants to require of the receiver *B* to achieve the action FillIn in the future, with the possibility of refusing (use of a **propose**). She wants, also, to tell her that she will send the same message periodically every 5 min. for one day. Moreover, she wants the action to start as soon as the message is received.

propose(A, B, ([propose] periodic [0:5:0] [24:0:0]) $\land$ [FillIn] mi [propose], FillIn)

At the reception of such an act, the receiver *B* will know that *A* will send her periodically the same act. So the receiver can use this information to anticipate this demand and be ready for executing the action given the constraints specified in the message.

5 The temporal Agent Communication Language

The semantics of the various acts of language, being defined, we define the syntax of our temporal communication language and illustrate it with an example in the context of the supervision of a bus fleet.

5.1 Syntax

The syntax of the language is inspired by the one described in ASIC [3]. It is composed of three fields, that make explicit the three kinds of information according to the layers, which were presented in Sect. 2 : :comm for the communication layer, :mas for the multi-agent system layer, and :content for the application layer. We will describe in detail only the :mas one.

⟨message⟩::=(:comm (⟨communication⟩)
               :mas (⟨mas⟩)
               :content (⟨application⟩)))

The field ⟨communication⟩ comprises the whole of information related to the routing of the message. It contains among others the identities of the sender and of the receiver, the date of emission.

The field ⟨mas⟩ comprises the whole of information necessary for the management of a conversation between the agents, as well as information necessary for the interpretation of the message. This field is still under definition. Currently it consists of the following sub-fields :

⟨mas⟩::= :act ⟨act⟩
       :time ⟨time⟩

:nature ⟨descriptor⟩
:protocol ⟨protocol⟩
:conversation ⟨conversation⟩

– ⟨act⟩ defines the set of speech acts that will be used. The semantic of these acts is the one that was defined in Sect. 4.

⟨act⟩ ::= inform | command | propose | accept | refuse

– ⟨descriptor⟩ allows to interpret correctly the content of the field :content as a resource, a plan, an action or a goal.

⟨descriptor⟩ ::= resource | plan | action | goal

– the field ⟨time⟩ is directly defined according to the temporal language L_T :

⟨time⟩ ::= (⟨expr⟩)
⟨expr⟩ ::= ⟨texp⟩ | ⟨expr⟩ AND ⟨expr⟩ | ⟨expr⟩ OR ⟨expr⟩
⟨texp⟩ ::= A | P | Ss | Sr | ⟨inte⟩ | ⟨texp⟩ ⟨rel⟩ ⟨texp⟩ |
           ⟨texp⟩ periodic ⟨texp⟩ ⟨texp⟩
⟨inte⟩ ::= [*duration*] | [⟨t⟩, ⟨t⟩]
⟨t⟩ ::= now | ? | infty | *real*

where :
- ⟨*rel*⟩ is defined according to the temporal connectives $\mathcal{R}$ (cf. Sect. 3.3).
- *duration* is a value expressed in a time format,
- now is t_{now}, ? is $t_?$, infty is $+\infty$,
- A, P, respectively, denotes the action and the formula contained in the field :content. They are used to build the basic temporal expressions such as [α] and [ϕ].
- Ss denotes the speech act which is expressed in :act (for the sending). Sr denotes the speech act that is specified in the next step of the protocol (it is equivalent to the *reply-by* of [8]). Both are used to build basic temporal expressions such as [*sa*].
– The fields ⟨protocol⟩ and ⟨conversation⟩ are used for the management of, respectively, the protocol and the conversation. For simplicity, we don't describe them here, being out of context.

The field ⟨application⟩ comprises the whole of information suitable for the application. We will not detail it here, being irrelevant. Insofar as we said in introduction, temporal dimension is clarified within the field ⟨mas⟩. We can however notice that nothing prevents this field ⟨application⟩ from also containing a temporal component.

6 Examples of Temporal Messages

In order to illustrate the use of the temporal communication language that we have just presented, we will use an example of supervision of a fleet of bus

[2]. Each bus runs along a line and serves different bus-stops which are on it. The multi-agent system that was built for this application acts to control the activity of the fleet of bus. Each agent uses a temporal reasoning mechanism to reason on the functioning of the buses and of the lines. To this aim, she takes into account on the one hand, the possible functioning that she must supervise, and, on the other hand, a continuous flow of events coming from the supervised system. The different functionings are described with temporal scenarios[7] that are matched against the events coming at different times from the supervised system (the buses and the lines). This continuous flow of events constitutes an important source of evolution to which the agents must adapt. It constitutes also the global referential of time. Dependence networks [17] that exhibit a temporal dimension[2] are used to enable the cooperation in the system.

In the context of this article, we just point the course of the exchange of messages between the agents using our temporal communication language. Particularly, we will follow a protocol allowing to anticipate a delay due, for example, to a congestion on a segment of the route. We lay out for that, a human-interface agent A_3 which will make it possible to impose a new way with times for each part of the new course, and three software agents: A_1 supervises the bus 1, A_2 monitors the traffic and A_4 is the general agent of supervision. We choose randomly 12:00:00 as starting date. In that way, we are able to observe three cases.

6.1 Normal Course

This first case deals with a normal course with no congestion. During the totality of the course, agent A_1 requires periodically (every 5 minutes) to be informed about the state of the traffic by agent A_2 and this within 1 minute compared to the sending of the message. This is expressed by writing a temporal expression bearing on the communicative action used to answer, which is specified by the protocol (use of Sr):

```
(message :com (:sender A_1 :receiver A_2 ...)
        :mas (:act command
              :time ((Sr periodic [0:05:00] [12:00:00,13:00:00])
                    AND (Sr s [12:00:00,12:01:00]) AND (P = [now,?])) ... )
        :content (Get(traffic_State))    )
```

where s stands for Allen's operator: start.

When agent A_2 receives the message, she will know, that she will have to send periodically the state of traffic to agent A_1. She has to do that for the first time within the interval [12:00:00,12:01:00]. In this scenario, there is no congestion thus agent A_1 will obtain the following answer from A_2:

```
(message :com (:sender A_2 :receiver A_1 ...)
        :mas (:act inform
              :time (P = [12:00:30,infty]) ... )
        :content ("Traffic_State=OK")    )
```

6.2 Congestion with a Possible Correction

In this example there is a congestion on a part of the course. The course must be modified in order to avoid a delay.

As we saw for the first case, during the totality of the course, agent A_1 required to be informed periodically about the state of the traffic by agent A_2. We suppose, here, that there is a congestion of 5 minutes on the part [D,E] of the course. Therefore agent A_1 will receive the following answer from agent A_2:

```
(message :comm (:sender A₂ :receiver A₁ ...)
        :mas (:act inform
               :time (P = [12:00:30,infty]) ...)
        :content ( "Traffic_State=Delay[D,E][00:05:00]" )   )
```

Agent A_1 decides to require from agent A_3 an other route avoiding the congestion. This new way has to be at least as fast as the one which is congested. Agent A_1 also transmits a temporal constraint for the course of replacement (a reply must be sent within [12:02:00,12:05:00]):

```
(message :com (:sender A₁ :receiver A₃ ...)
        :mas (:act command
               :time (Sr in [12:02:00,12:05:00]) ... )
        :content ( Get(New_Way([D,E],[00:15:00]))) )
```

Agent A_3 answers the new course with the new times to agent A_1 and to the general supervisor, A_4:

```
(message :com (:sender A₃ :receiver A₁ ...)
        :mas (:act inform
               :time (P = [12:04:00,infty]) ... )
        :content ("New Way Bus1 = { [D,H][00:04:00],
                                    [H,S][00:07:00],
                                    [S,E][00:01:30] }" )   )
```

6.3 Congestion without any Possible Correction

Let's imagine, now, that the answer of A_3 to A_1 did not arrive in time. We are still in case of the existence of a congestion of 5 minutes on the part [D,E] of the course (agent A_1 has been made aware of that by agent A_2 (see Sect. 6.2)). As we saw in Sect. 6.1, agent A_1 required to be informed periodically during the totality of the course, about the state of the traffic by agent A_2. Agent A_1 required agent A_3 (see Sect. 6.2) a new route avoiding the congestion. The answer did not arrive within the deadlines (3 minutes), therefore at the end of a certain time, agent A_1 informs A_4 that the bus 1 is late:

```
(message :comm (:sender A₁ :receiver A₄ ...)
        :mas (:act inform
               :time (P = [12:07:30, infty]) ...)
        :content ( "Delay=[00:07:00]" )   )
```

These examples show clearly that time is made explicit at the mas layer while there can exist, also, an expression of time at the application layer.

7 Results and Conclusion

In this paper, we have presented a temporal agent communication language for MAS that runs in continuously changing environment. We illustrated the use of this language with an example of the supervision of fleet of buses.

This language is build from already existing ideas [1],[12],[14]. However, it makes explicit the temporal aspects relevant to the multi-agent system layer. Due to that, we can envision the integration on this layer, of individual reasoning systems that don't possess any temporal reasoning capabilities. Time will be handled only at the mas layer. This aspect is illustrated particularly in the first example (cf. Sect. 6.1). The periodic sending of the state of the traffic is managed directly by the mas layer by taking into account the temporal constraints.

Moreover, the temporal language is more general than its current application to the interaction dimension in MAS. We envision to broaden its use to the different aspects of temporal reasoning in a MAS : organizational dimension, temporal social reasoning for example. We are currently interested in two practical applications which both reveal some strong temporal dependences: crisis management and alliance management of printing workshops groups distributed all over the world.

Acknowledgments

Thibault Carron is supported by a Région Rhône-Alpes Fellowship. We would like to thank C. Sayettat and M.Allouche for fruitful discussions on the temporal aspects of this work as well as the anonymous referees for their valuable suggestions.

References

1. Allen, J.F.: Maintaining knowledge about Temporal Intervals. Communications of the ACM, **26** (11) (1983) 832–843
2. Allouche, M.: A temporal agent society for the supervision of industrial systems. Phd thesis, ENSMSE/Université de Saint-Etienne (1998) (in french)
3. Boissier, O., Demazeau, Y.: A multi-agent architecture for open and decentralized vision systems. (in french), Technique et Science Informatiques, (October 1997) 1039–1062
4. Boissier, O., Beaune, P., Proton, H., Hannoun, M., Carron, T., Vercouter, L., Sayettat, C.: The Multi-Agent System Testbed. Internal Report SIC/ENSM.SE (in french) (1998)
5. Demazeau, Y.: From interactions to collective behaviour in agent-based systems. European conference on cognitive science, Saint-Malo (Avril 1995)

6. Dojat, M., Sayettat, C.: A Realistic Model for Temporal Reasoning in Real-time Patient Monitoring. Applied Artificial Intelligence, **10 (2)** (1996), 121–143

7. Fontaine, D.: Temporal scenario recognition. Technical report 93/106, Université de Technologie de Compiègne , (in french), (June 1993)

8. Fipa: Specification, Agent Communication Language. (28th November 1997)

9. Georgeff, M.P., Lansky, A.L.: Reactive Reasoning and Planning. Proceeeding of the AAAI Conference (1987) 677–682

10. Haddadi, A.: Communication and cooperation in agent systems. LNCS Volume 1056, Springer-Verlag (1996)

11. Mac Dermott, D.: A Temporal Logic for Reasoning About Processes and Plans. Cognitive Science **6** (1982) 101–155

12. Millner, R.: A Calculus of Communication Systems. LNCS Volume 92, Springer-Verlag (1980)

13. Moulin, B.: Temporal Contexts for Discourse Representation : An Extension of the Conceptual Graph Approach. Journal of Applied Intelligence, **7 (3)** (1997) 227–255.

14. Pnueli, A.: The temporal logic of programs. In Proc. 18th IEEE Symp. Foundations of Computer Science, Providence (November 1977) 46–57

15. Sadek, D.: Dialogue acts are rational plans. Proceedings of the ESCA/ETRW Workshop on the Structure of Multimodal Dialogue, Maratea, Italy, (1991) 1–29

16. Searle, J.R.: Speech Acts. Cambridge University Press (1969)

17. Sichman, J.S.: Du raisonnement social chez les agents. Une approche fondée sur la théorie de la Dépendance. Phd Thesis (in french), Institut National Polytechnique de Grenoble (1995)

18. Singh, M.P.: Multiagent Systems: A Theoretical Framework for Intentions, Know-How, and Communications. LNAI Volume 799, Springer-Verlag (1994)

19. Shoham, Y.: Temporal logic in AI : semantical and ontological considerations. Artificial Intelligence, **33** (1987) 89–104

20. Vanderveken, D.: Les actes de discours. P. Mardaga Ed. (1988)

21. Wooldridge, M.: The logical Modelling of Computational Multi-Agent Systems. Phd Thesis, UMIST, Manchester UK, (October 1992)

Multi-paradigm Languages Supporting Multi-agent Development

Analía Amandi, Alejandro Zunino, Ramiro Iturregui

ISISTAN Research Institute, Facultad de Ciencias Exactas,
Universidad Nacional del Centro de la Pcia. de Buenos Aires
Campus Paraje Arroyo Seco - (7000) Tandil - Bs. As., Argentina
email: {amandi,azunino,riturr}@exa.unicen.edu.ar

Abstract. Object-oriented languages generally support agent developments despite logic languages are more appropriate for managing mental attitudes. The alternative of a multi-paradigm language is a way for supporting agent constructions we explore. A multi-paradigm language that supports the encapsulation of actions, the hiding of private knowledge and the flexible manipulation of knowledge could be a good candidate for programming agents. Therefore, we present an approach for integrating object and logic paradigms based on logic modules combined with object-oriented abstractions. This approach aims at the construction of flexible agents in terms of easy extensions of the components of the logic interpreter. JavaLog, a particular implementation based on Java and Prolog, is also introduced.

1 Introduction

Object-oriented programming is currently supporting the building of intelligent agents despite it does not allow complex mental attitudes to be represented. Logic programming is an obvious support for representing and inferring relationships among mental attitudes such as intentions, goals and beliefs, but it presents several limitations in the definition of action capabilities.

Certainly, multi-paradigm languages [5,7,8,9,12] that integrate logic and object-oriented paradigms can guide the definition of a language for supporting multi-agent development. The old multi-paradigm languages have pointed to the management of both modularization and inference of knowledge; modularization provided by object-oriented languages and inference of knowledge provided by logic languages.

Those proposals show us their potential for programming agents in terms of actions as well as the manipulation of mental attitudes. However, our analysis on these languages has given evidence of some limitations for programming agents, related mainly to inheritance. Therefore, we have defined a particular approach for integrating both paradigms. It is based on logic modules that encapsulate clauses enabling a common manipulation of element in the resulting integration.

This article presents our approach for integrating object-oriented and logic paradigms for agent programming that follows the guides for developing agents of the

Brainstorm architecture [1,2]. Moreover, a particular materialization of this approach using two known programming languages, Java and Prolog, is also presented. It is named JavaLog and it is used in our agent examples.

In the remainder of the article, we will first present the analysis on the usefulness of old multi-paradigm languages for agent programming. Second, we expose our approach based on logic modules for agent programming, and then summarize relevant characteristics of the Javalog language. Then, we describe how to use this integration in agent developments and present data on the cost of integrating these paradigms.

2   The usefulness of old multi-paradigm languages

The old proposals on multi-paradigm languages work on logic and object-oriented components present several ways of putting those different components together. These can be classified into two main focus: (i) the incorporation of modularization to logic languages and (ii) object-oriented languages manipulating logic clauses.

There are several proposals for modularizing logic languages (i.e. CPU [8], SPOOL [5], LOO [9] and SCOOP [12]). These languages show different alternatives to incorporate modularity from object-orientation view into logic languages.

These languages define classes as a set of clauses, where generally each clause represents a method. Inheritance is managed under three different interpretations. Some languages considers that clauses in a subclass with the same head and arity that those clauses in the superclass mean an addition on the definition of such a method. Therefore, the languages that apply this view of inheritance do not accept the redefinition of methods.

Other languages apply a second inheritance view. It is drawn in the picture formed by a method which contains a clause with the same head and arity that a clause in the same method in the superclass and the result is the redefinition of those inherit clauses. This combination of clauses is one that rewrites clauses with the same name, allowing thus the redefinition of some clauses.

Finally, a third inheritance view is applied in other languages. It represents a complete redefinition of a method. Here the definition of a method with the same name in the superclass indicates the redefinition of the inherited method. Using only this inheritance perspective, the combination of clauses into methods is avoided.

In the first alternative, a subclass can complete the definition of a subject adding new clauses with the same head, but it can not redefine clauses. In the second the subclass redefines clauses with the same name, but it can not add clauses with the same name. Finally, the third allows the redefinition of all the methods in the superclass. Certainly, these combinations of logical clauses are useful but they are not all together available in the old multi-paradigm languages.

On the other hand, proposals of object-oriented languages manipulating logic clauses show another alternative on the usages of clauses. Here, a sequence of clauses is viewed as knowledge recorded in instance variables, contracting the behavior view. These languages (i.e. ORIENT/84 [7]) enable the creation of knowledge bases in objects and their management through a set of given tools.

From these experiences we have learned the importance of both usages of clauses, in inner knowledge specification and behavior codification. Specifically, it is due to the need of agent-oriented languages for managing clauses as internal mental attitudes and as part of decision actions.

We can conclude that the old languages proposed for combining logic and objects show different applications of a set of clauses in variables and methods, but there is not any language that supports all management of clauses. Our proposal aims at solving these limitations.

3 Integration of Logic and Object Paradigms for Agent-Oriented Programming

The object-oriented and logic paradigms work on different worlds. To integrate these worlds presents several troubles. The troubles are a direct consequence of the different nature of the elements involved and the way in which they are manipulated in each paradigm.

The object-oriented paradigm only works on entities named objects, which are manipulated by methods and acceded in a restricted context. The logic programming paradigm works on two types of entities, the first are qualified by terms and manipulated by clauses, and the second are the own clauses.

The agent-oriented paradigm works mainly on agents, which can execute a bounded amount of actions and can communicate with other agents, considering the guides established in their private mental state.

Our approach for integrating the logic and object-oriented paradigms for agent-oriented programming defines module as the basic component of manipulation. In this context, an object and a method from the object-oriented paradigm are viewed as modules. An object is a module that encapsulates data. A method is a module that encapsulates behavior.

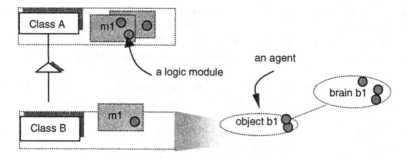

Fig. 1. Scheme of module composition.

The elements manipulated by the logic paradigm are also mapped to modules. Logic modules are defined as a set of Horn clauses following the definition of

O'Keefe [10]. In this way, two algebraic operators are applied for combining logic modules. These operators are named union and overriding union [3].

Figure 1 shows a general scheme of the module composition, highlighting how an agent is built. Logic modules are presented as gray circles. Classes can define part of their methods using logic modules and objects can also define private modules in variables. A simple object associated with another object (that we can call brain), representing a logic language interpreter, composes an agent. The object has the particularity of belonging to a class with the capability of working on logic modules. Finally, the brain also refers to logic modules sent by the object-agent for working on them from that instant.

From here, several interaction constraints among object-oriented and logic modules are defined. These interaction constrains are classified by referring, communication and composition constraints. Referring constraints specify the composition limits of different modules. Communication constraints specify the role of objects in logic modules and the role of logic variables in methods. Composition constraints specify how logic modules can be combined, expressing also the composition of the knowledge base when a query is executed.

3.1   Referring Constraints

The referring constraints establish that logic modules can be located in instance variables and as part of methods. Thus, an agent can be designed as an object with private logic knowledge associated with him. The action capabilities of the agent are represented by methods enabled for using logic knowledge.

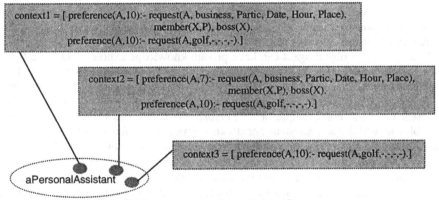

Fig. 2. The private logic modules of an agent.

Figure 2 presents an example of an agent following this multi-paradigm approach. This agent is a personal assistant. This agent is an instance of the *PersonalAssistant* class, which defines the variables named context1, context2 and context3 for recording different preferences about appointment requests.

The fact that an agent records different logic module in variables does not imply that the agent uses all these clauses in the next queries. The agent will only use the logic modules sent to his brain. Thus, several combinations can be made when he is reasoning.

The usage of logic modules into methods is illustrated in Figure 3. This method uses the preferences defined in a logic module referred by the instance variable named context1. A method as usual defines local variables and a particular behavior using the syntax of an object-oriented language. In addition, our methods can use logic modules. The invocation to *userPreferences* enables the clauses into the module logic sent as an argument for the logic language interpreter associated with the receiver object. Moreover, new logic modules can be defined into the own method, which can include queries. Variables like X used in a logic query can also be used in the code of the rest of the method.

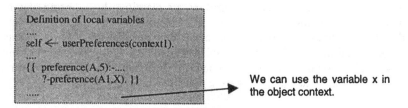

Fig. 3. Logic Modules into Methods.

Simple objects do not have naturally the capability of managing knowledge in a logic format. The possibility that objects manage this type of knowledge will make feasible that these objects combine and infer knowledge without running complex algorithms. By using a logic language interpreter integrated with our objects, this problem has a solution. An instance of a logic language interpreter associated with a particular object allows the definition of object-agents. These object-agents are composed of an object that can manage action and communication messages and a logic interpreter that manages mental attitudes in a logic format.

In this way, an object-agent can have private knowledge expressed in logic form, by means of rules and facts, manipulated through methods of the object-agent class. An object-agent can have zero, one or more instance variables referring logic modules, allowing thus the separation of concepts that the agent wishes to use in different contexts. For example, let a *PersonalAssistant* class that defines instance variables in which each assistant agent can register his different ways for assisting users in, for example, the analysis of appointment requests of other users.

Our approach allows classes to use logic modules as method parts. This enables classes to record facts and rules that represent common knowledge for their instances. The logic modules defined in methods represent common knowledge of the objects of that class. Those logic modules defined in the instance variables of objects represent proper knowledge of each object.

3.2 Communication Constraints

The communication constraints establish that (i) objects can become facts and then they can be part of a logic module, (ii) clauses can use objects as a kind of term, (iii) logic terms used in clauses into a method can be manipulated in all the non-logic parts of the method and vice versa. These constraints specify communication bridges between both object-oriented and logic worlds.

Objects and, particularly, object-agents can become facts when they receive a particular message named *asClause*. Thus, objects can be used during the execution of queries meanwhile these facts are available for the logic interpreter associated with agents. For instance, if an object of Person class receives that message the following clause is generated: person(himself, 'Ann', 33, engineer). The name of this fact is the name of the receiver object class. The first argument is a term of object class (indeed, a person object, the receiver of the method), the other arguments are the contents of the instance variables of the receiver object (name, age and profession of the person).

Clauses can use objects as a kind of term. This characteristic allows the direct usage of objects together with their associated behavior (the methods defined in their class and superclasses) inside logic code. For sending a message to objects from a logic code, a predefined clause named *send* is used. Thus, send(aPerson, age, [], A) into the body of a clause produces the sending of the message *age* to the object *aPerson* without any argument, instantiating the variable A with the number that returns that message.

Logic terms used in clauses into a method can be manipulated in all the non-logic parts of the method and vice versa. Instance variables, class variables, and local variables are available in methods. Logic variables are available in clause as any logic language. Using our approach, when methods are coded in an object-oriented language with some logic module as part of them, it is necessary to define a bridge between both worlds. We specify a bridge in the following way: (i) any variable available in a method can be used as an argument in any clause that is part of a logic module inner to that method; (ii) any variable used in a clause can be used in the method it is part of. This bridge is simply defined because clauses can manipulate objects and any type can be mapped to a class.

3.3 Composition Constraints

The composition constraints treat the limitations in the possibilities of combining logic modules. Three algebraic operators [3] have been applied from two different perspectives. First, modules referred by variables can be directly combined using predefined methods. Second, logic modules as part of a method can be combined by inheritance.

An important point about the usage of variables referring logic modules is that an object-agent can have different instance variables to register different views of the same concept. These views can be used separately or can be combined using operators defined for such goal. For example, the *PersonalAssistant* class mentioned above may have different instance variables (a, b and c) to register different ways for evaluating changes of its schedule from some request. In this way, an assistant agent, in front of a particular situation, can use one of these forms (achieved by one of these variables) or some of its combinations.

The following operators have been defined and implemented for combining logic modules referred by variables:

- re-write: let the logic modules *a* and *b*, "*a reWrite b*" define a logic module that contains all clauses defined in *b* added to the clauses defined in *a* whose head name is not the same as some clause of *b*.
- plus: let the logic modules *a* and *b*, "*a plus b*" define a logic module which contains all clauses of *a* and *b*.

The operator named re-write follows the algebraic definition of overriding union and the operator named plus follows the definition of union.

On the other hand, logic modules can be defined into methods. These logic modules can also be combined using the same operators. Figure 4 shows how these combinations can be made. Each column shows each kind of combination. Both columns expose the method M1 into a class *A* and one subclass *B*.

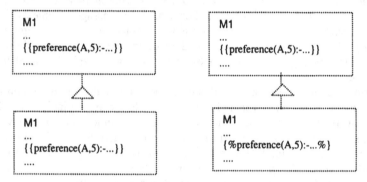

Fig. 4. Combining logic modules by inheritance.

The first column shows the application of the union operator. Each method defines different rules for preferences with a five number as weight. In this case, an object, instance of the class *A*, uses the preference defined between {{ and }} in its queries after the invocation of that method. An object, instance of the class *B*, has two options in terms of the definitions of preferences to be used. The developer has the possibility of invoking explicitly the method *M1* of the superclass, using in this case the addition of both definitions. The place of the invocation defines the sort of the clauses, thus it is important whether the invocation is before or after the definition of the local logic module. The second option is not to invoke the method of the superclass, resulting in a complete redefinition of the method.

The second column exposes the application of the operator overriding union. Here each method also defines different rules for preferences with a five number as weight. An object *A* has the same behavior as that exposed in the first column. But an object *B* has the option of combining the logic modules defined in the method *M1* of the superclass and its own logic modules in a particular way. The marks {% and %} indicate that with logic modules of the superclass and the subclass, the method re-write, materialization of the overriding union operator, is used.

This integration approach allows us the combination of the syntax of object-oriented and logic languages in the definition of behavior. Thus, we can express declarative knowledge in declarative form and operational behavior in procedural form. However, both forms of programming share the same world. For this reason, both forms can access to the same information. Therefore, objects can work with clauses and clauses can work with objects.

3.4 General Issues

We have presented the use of logic modules in the context of agent-oriented programming. This approach integrates two worlds maintaining the conventions of each of them.

In the logic world, objects and methods can be manipulated. Objects can be used as terms in the argument of a clause or can be directly a fact. Methods can be invoked in the body of a clause.

In the object world, we have the possibility that objects manipulate clauses. This manipulation is made through logic modules. It can be located in variables and methods, accepting their combinations by specific methods and special treatment of inheritance, respectively.

Both worlds are connected by the connection of an object with a logic interpreter. The next section introduces JavaLog, a particular integration of the logic and object-oriented paradigms that follows this multi-paradigm approach.

4 JavaLog

This approach has been materialized first integrating Smalltalk and a Prolog and second integrating Java and a Prolog. In this paper, we use the Java-Prolog integration for exposing details of our approach. This integration has been named JavaLog and it is available as free software.

In this section, we expose examples of agents implemented in JavaLog of the concepts introduced in the previous section. Moreover, some details of the design of JavaLog are presented.

JavaLog integrates Java and a particular implementation of Prolog. We developed this implementation of Prolog on the own Java language for enabling extensions of the Prolog interpreter. This characteristic allows us special extensions of Prolog for managing mental attitudes developed as a simple specialization of a set of classes.

Our Java-Prolog integration allows us to define logic modules into Java variables or inside methods. To clarify the presentation, we introduce an example, a salesman agent. It has the ability to select and buy items based on user preferences. *CommerceAgent* is a class defined for implementing this type of agent.

In order to allow flexibility on the approaches of article selection, preferences are represented by Prolog clauses. For instance, the following clauses express the preferences of a user to buy a vehicle.

```
preference(car,[ford, Model, Price]) :-

    Model > 1998, Price < 200000.

preference(motorcycle, [yamaha, Model, Price]) :-
```

```
Model >= 1998, Price < 9000.
```

Below, we present the code of the *CommerceAgent* class written in JavaLog.

```
public class CommerceAgent {

        private PlLogicModule userPreferences;

        public CommerceAgent( PlLogicModule userPreferences ) {

            this.userPreferences = userPreferences;

        }

        ....

        public boolean buyArticle( Article anArticle ) {

            userPreferences.enable();

            if ( ?-send(#anArticle#,type,[],Type),

                    send(#anArticle#,brand,[],Brand),

    send(#anArticle#,Model,[],Model), send(#anArticle#,price,[],Price),

            preference(Type,[Brand, Model, Price).

    )

            buy( anArticle );

            userPreferences.disable();

    } }
```

In the example, it is defined the variable *userPreferences*, which contains a logic module with Prolog clauses representing user preferences. To decide if it is better for a user to buy an article, its user preferences are analyzed. The *buyArticle* method first places the *userPreferences* logic module as available for the Prolog interpreter. Then, an embedded Prolog query is used to test if it is acceptable for the user to buy the article. The Prolog query is introduced by "?-", following a Prolog term as usual. To evaluate *preference(Type,[Brand, Model, Price)*, the clauses into *userPreferences* are used. The query refers the name of a Java variable enclosed into "#". This allows us to use existing Java objects inside a Prolog clause. In the query, *send* is used for sending a message to a Java object from a Prolog program. For instance, *send(#anArticle#,brand,[],Brand)* in Prolog is equivalent to *Brand = anArticle.brand()* in Java. Finally, the method ends disabling *userPreferences* logic module. This operation deletes the logic module from the JavaLog database.

In the example, we have shown how to define Java methods using embedded Prolog, how to use knowledge (specified by Prolog clauses) referenced by a Java variable and how to use Java objects inside a Prolog query.

Now we show how to define logic modules embedded in Java programs. For creating an instance of the *CommerceAgent* class, for example, we have to use its constructor with a logic module as argument.

```
CommerceAgent anAgent = new CommerceAgent(

{{ preference(car,[Brand, Model, Price]) :-

           Brand = ford, Model > 1998, Price < 200000.

   preference(motorcycle, [Brand, Model, Price]) :-

           Brand = yamaha, Model >= 1998, Price < 9000.}}

);
```

In this fragment of program, we have defined a logic module, placing between "{{" and "}}" a group of Prolog clauses. Such a module contains common preferences of that type of user.

JavaLog treats logic modules inside methods through a preprocessor that translates a Java program with embedded Prolog into a pure Java program. As a result, the embedded Prolog is rendered into calls to the JavaLog API.

5 Related Work

Several languages have been proposed for programming agents [6,11,14]. Some of them use some object-oriented concepts in a logic context For example, Metatem [6] is based on temporal logic, encapsulating a set of rules.

Most agent languages (i.e. [11,14]) are based on object-oriented concepts without any consideration about the logic fundamentals of mental attitudes. This lack could be solved using some practical views of architectures on mental attitudes, but the effort of materializing those practical approaches would have a high cost.

Our approach tries to take advantage of both kinds of proposals, defining an integration of both paradigms.

6 Conclusions

In this article, an approach for the development of intelligent agents from the programming point of view has been presented. This approach is based on the fact that the object-oriented paradigm has relevant characteristics for programming agents but it presents some problems in the manipulation of mental attitudes. The problem of the manipulation of mental attitudes, usually treated on specific logic formalisms, is solved by the use of logic programming. In short, we present a multi-paradigm approach for programming agents. This approach is materialized by JavaLog based on Java and Prolog.

This particular approach and its materialization on the JavaLog language present several advantages related to flexibility on components of design. One of them is based on the fact that our Prolog interpreter has been implemented on the proper Java language allowing thus extensions to this interpreter. These extensions can support, for example, some particular management of mental attitudes and time.

JavaLog has been used in several developments showing cost advantages in some points of the use of the integration. For example, an agent applies a least commitment planning algorithm [13]. The main part of the algorithm was developed using Prolog but an object modeled the graph of causal links. This implementation was contrasted with a first implementation completely made on Prolog. This analysis, considering these particular implementations, shows that the planning algorithm using the integration runs ten times more quickly than the pure use of Prolog. The difference is based on the analysis of the graph, which in the integration version is made on Java.

We are still developing new agents based on JavaLog. Now, for example, we are testing an agent for analyzing electronic newspaper pages [4].

References

1. A. Amandi and A. Price. Object-Oriented Agent Programming through the Brainstorm System. In *Proceedings of PAAM'97, Practical Applications of Intelligent Agents and Multi-Agents Conference*. London, April, 1997.
2. A. Amandi and A. Price. Building Object-Agents from a Software Meta-Architecture. In *Advances in Artificial Intelligence*, Springer, 1998. (LNAI 1515).
3. M. Bugliesi, E. Lamma and P. Mello. Modularity in Logic Programming. *Journal on Logic Programming*, 19(20), 1994.
4. D. Cordero, P. Roldan, S. Schiaffino and A. Amandi. Intelligent Agents Generating Personal Newspapers. In *Proceedings of International Conference on Enterprise Information Systems*, Portugal, 1999.
5. K. Fukunaga and S. Hirose. An Experience with a Prolog-Based Object-Oriented Language. *Sigplan Notices (Proc. of OOPSLA '86 Conference)*, Nov, pages 224-231, 1986.
6. M. Fisher. Representing and Executing Agent-Based Systems. In *Proceedings of the* ECAI-94 *Workshop on Agent Theories, Architectures, and Languages,* pages 307-323, Aug. 1994.
7. Y. Ishikawa, M. Tokoro. A Concurrent Object-Oriented Knowledge Representation Language Oriente84/k: It's features and implementation, *SIGPLAN Notices*, 21(11):232-241, 1986.
8. P. Mello and A. Natali. Objects as Communicating Prolog Units. In *Proceedings of ECOOP'87 European Conference on Object-Oriented Programming*, pages 181-191, Jun. 1987
9. P. Marcarella, A. Raffaetà, and F. Turini. Loo: An Object-Oriented Logic Programming Language. In *Proceedings of Italian Conference on Logic Programming (GULP '95)*, Sep. 1995.

10. R. O'Keefe. Towards an Algebra for Constructing Logic Programs. In J. Cohen and J. Conery (eds), *Proceedings of IEEE Symposium on Logic Programming*, IEEE Computer Society Press, New York, pages 152-160, 1985.

11. A. Poggy. Daisy: an Object-Oriented System for Distributed Artificial Intelligence. In Proceedings of *ECAI-94 Workshop on Agent Theories, Architectures, and Languages,* pages 341-354, Aug. 1994.

12. J. Vaucher, G. Lapalme, and J. Malenfant. Scoop: Structured Concurrent Object-Oriented Prolog. In *Proceedings of ECOOP'88 European Conference on Object-Oriented Programming*, pages 191-211. Springer-Verlag, August 1988.

13. D. Weld. An Introduction to Least commitment Planning. *AI Magazine*, 15(4):27-61, 1994.

14. D. Weerasooriya, A. Rao, K. Ramamohanarao. Design of a Concurrent Agent-Oriented Language. In Wooldridge, M.; Jennings, N. (Eds.). *Intelligent Agents*. Berlin: Springer, pages 386-401, 1995. (LNAI 890).

An Efficient Argumentation Framework for Negotiating Autonomous Agents

Michael Schroeder

City University, London
msch@soi.city.ac.uk
www.soi.city.ac.uk/homes/msch

Abstract. Argumentation is important for agent negotiation. In this paper, we develop an efficient framework for multi-agent argumentation. We identify aspects of classical argumentation theory that are suitable and useful for artificial agents and develop an argumentation framework around them. In the framework, we distinguish cooperation and argumentation and introduce skeptical and credulous agents. We develop an operational, goal-driven top-down proof procedure for the argumentation process and evaluate an implementation of our framework for an example of a BT business process.

1 Introduction

Negotiation is fundamental to autonomous agents. In a negotiation process, a group of agents communicates with one another to come up with a mutually acceptable agreement. In many application, such a process may be the exchange of prices between a buyer and seller according to a particular protocol; in others, negotiation involves a more complicated process of argumentation to determine and change the beliefs of agents. In the context of negotiation, argumentation theory has recently attracted increasing interest [11,8].

In this paper, we set out to develop an efficient framework for multi-agent argumentation and evaluate it in the domain of business process management. We review classical argumentation theory as studied in philosophy and rethorics and identify aspects that are suitable and useful for artificial agents and develop an argumentation framework around them. Driven by practical needs, we introduce cooperation as counterpart to argumentation. In the former, an agent, which does not know anything about a certain literal, cooperates with others, which help out and provide the knowledge; in the latter, an agent believes in something and argues with other agents to determine whether this belief is valid or has to be revised. When arguing we can distinguish skeptical and credulous agents which accept more or less, respectively, arguments as valid attack to their beliefs. One of our main objectives is to build an operational argumentation system. Usually, the semantics of such a argumentation process is defined bottom-up and therefore lacks goal-directness. To design an efficient system, we define a top-down, and therefore goal-directed, proof procedure to compute the argumentation process. Finally, we round out the picture by modelling an example of a BT business process in our argumentation framework.

2 Argumentation in Philosophy

Since Leibniz's 1679 *calculus raciocinator*, researchers have been investigating how to automate argumentation. A problem is that many figures of arguments cannot be described formally. The Encyclopedia Brittanica lists for example the following figures: Arguing by example, authority, or analogy, arguing from the consequences, a pari (arguing from similar propositions), a fortiori (arguing from an accepted conclusion to an even more evident one), a contrario (arguing from an accepted conclusion to the rejection of its contrary), undercut (Attacking premisses), or rebut (Attacking conclusions) The first three are semantical and the rest syntactical figures.

The syntactical figures can be formally described by their form, i.e. syntax, and can therefore be easily automated. Although semantical figures such as arguing by authority may be formalised for particular domains (see e.g. [15]), they do not appear to be formalisable as evidenced by the limited success of projects such as CYC. This should not put us off, because it turns out that the syntactical figures of undercut and rebut are already sufficient to define the semantics of logic programs, which - in turn - makes logic programming the implementation language of choice for argumentation tools (see also [8]).

The relevance of an argument, i.e. should an agent accept it or immediately reject it, is an important issue in classical argumentation. Copi and Cohen [3] list, for example, 17 fallacies of relevance of arguments, only three of which can be expressed formally: 1. An *argument from ignorance* argues that a proposition is true simply on the basis that it has not been proved false, or that it is false because it has not been proved true. 2. *Begging the question* - also called *circular argumentation* - assumes the truth of what it seeks to prove in the effort to prove it. 3. *Division* assumes that what is true as a whole must be true in its parts and vice versa.

Interestingly, these three examples of fallacies involve all non-monotonic reasoning and require two kinds of negation: Implicit negation *not a* to express the lack of evidence for a; explicit negation $\neg a$ to state that there is an explicit proof for $\neg a$. The two negations are related in that $\neg a$ implies *not a*. With the two kinds of negation we can express the three fallacies mentioned above: Arguments from Ignorance have the form $a \leftarrow not \neg a$ or $\neg a \leftarrow not a$. Begging the question has the form of a positive loop, e.g. $a \leftarrow a$ or $a \leftarrow not a$ in its most reduced form. Division requires non-monotonic reasoning (NMR) and contradiction removal. A typical example dealt with extensively in the NMR literature is a contradiction between flying birds and not-flying penguins.

Bearing in mind the above knowledge representation, we want to develop a framework and implement a system for argumentation and apply it to examples such as business process management. We motivate this example in the next section and then turn to the framework and system.

3 Motivating Example

The example is derived from the ADEPT project [7], which developed negotiating agents for business process management. One such process deals with the provision of customer quotes [15] for networks adapted to the customers' needs (see Figure 1).

Four agents are involved in this process: the customer service division (CSD), which makes the initial contact with the customer and delivers the quote eventually, the vet customer agent (VC), which determines whether the customer is credit-worthy, the design department (DD), which does the design and costing of the requested network if it is not a portfolio item, and the surveyor department (SD), which may has to survey the customer site for the design department.

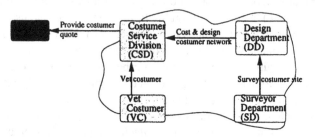

Fig. 1. BT's business process to provide customer quotes.

The process works as follows. Initially, a customer issues a request. The CSD gathers some data for this request such as the requirements, the equipment already installed at the customer site, and how important the client is. Before any action is taken, the CSD asks the VC to vet the customer. If the customer is not credit-worthy the process terminates and no quote is issued to the customer. If it is credit-worthy, the CSD checks whether the required network is a portfolio item so that a previous quote exists. If positive, this quote is send to the customer, otherwise the design department is contacted. The DD develops its design and costing based on the information of given equipment held by the CSD. In many cases, however, this information may be out of date or not available at all, so that the site has to be surveyed. In this case, the DD contacts the surveyors to do a survey. After the survey is done, the DD can design and cost the network and the CSD can finally provide the customer quote.

The above scenario involves two fundamental types of interactions: argumentation and cooperation. If the DD wants to do its task it needs information held by the CSD. Therefore they cooperate. The CSD should not quote if the customer is not credit-worthy which it should assume by default. But the VC may counter-argue and give evidence for the credit-worthiness of the customer. Therefore VC and CSD argue. When arguing it is advisable to distinguish the credulousness of agents. The CSD and VC should be skeptical when arguing about giving a quote, while the other two are credulous. It is important to note that not all agents communicate with each other which would lead to a tremendous amount of messages exchanged, but each agent maintains a list of agents that it cooperates with and that it argues with. Besides knowing these partners, the agents know the partners domains so that they bother their partners only with requests relevant to them. Before we formally model and implement these aspects of the above business process we have to develop the theory underlying our argumentation framework.

4 Single-Agent Argumentation

The argumentation framework is closely related to the semantics of logic programs [4,2]. Well-founded semantics [6] turned out to be a promising approach to cope with negation by default and subsequent work extended well-founded semantics with a form of explicit negation and constraints [12,1].

Definition 1. An *extended logic program* is a (possibly infinite) set of rules of the form $L_0 \leftarrow L_1, \ldots, L_l, not\ L_{l+1}, \ldots, not\ L_m$ $(0 \leq l \leq m)$ where each L_i is an objective literal $(0 \leq i \leq m)$. An *objective literal* is either an atom A or its explicit negation $\neg A$. Literals of the form *not* L are called *default literals*.

Definition 2. Let P be an extended logic program. An *argument* for a conclusion L is a finite sequence $A = [r_n, \ldots r_m]$ of ground instances of rules $r_i \in P$ such that 1. for every $n \leq i \leq m$, for every objective literal L_j in the antecedent of r_i there is a $k < i$ such that L_j is the consequent of r_k. 2. L is the consequent of some rule of A; 3. No two distinct rules in the sequence have the same consequent. [1] A sequence of a subset of rules in A being an argument is called subargument. A rule $r \in P$ is called *partial argument*.

Two argumentation types are fundamental: undercuts and rebuts.

Definition 3. Let A_1 and A_2 be two arguments, then A_1 *undercuts* A_2 iff A_1 is an argument for L and A_2 is an argument with assumption *not* L, i.e. there is an $r : L_0 \leftarrow L_1, \ldots, L_l, not\ L_{l+1}, \ldots, not\ L_m \in A_2$ and a $l + 1 \leq j \leq m$ such that $L = L_j$. A_1 *rebuts* A_2 iff A_1 is an argument for L and A_2 is an argument for $\neg L$. A_1 *attacks* A_2 iff A_1 undercuts or rebuts A_2.

From a computational perspective rebuts can be reduced to undercuts:

Proposition 4. *A rebut to an argument* $[L \leftarrow Body; \ldots]$ *is an undercut to* $[L \leftarrow Body, not\ \neg L; \ldots]$.

Proof: A rebut to $[L \leftarrow Body, \ldots]$ has by definition 3 the form $[\neg L \leftarrow Body', \ldots]$, which is by definition 3 an undercut to $[L \leftarrow Body, not\neg L, \ldots]$.

Definition 5. An argument is *coherent* if it does not contain subarguments attacking each other.

The core of the argumentation framework is an acceptability definition: An agent accepts an argument if it is able to defeat all possible attacks to the argument in question.

Definition 6. Let A_1 and A_2 be two arguments, then A_1 *defeats* A_2 iff A_1 is empty and A_2 incoherent or A_1 undercuts A_2 or A_1 rebuts A_2 and A_2 does not undercut A_1. A_1 *strictly defeats* A_2 iff A_1 defeats A_2 but not vice versa. A_1 is *acceptable* wrt. a set *Args* of arguments iff each argument undercutting A_1 is strictly defeated by an argument in *Args*.

---

[1] Otherwise undercuts to the argument may have no impact at all.

Now we can define the semantics of a program by iteratively accumulating all acceptable arguments.

Definition 7. Let P be an extended logic program and S be a subset of arguments of P and $F_P(S) = \{A \mid A \text{ is acceptable wrt. } S\}$. Then A is *justified* iff A is in the least fixpoint of F_P. A is *overruled* iff A is attacked by a justified argument. A is *defensible* iff A is neither justified nor overruled.

The above semantics gives a declarative definition for an argumentation process of a single agent. Being a fixpoint semantics it is computed bottom-up which can be very inefficient if one is not interested in all justified conclusions. To compute the process in a goal-directed, top-down manner, one can use the proof procedure developed in [1] since the argumentation semantics is equivalent to the well-founded semantics [14].

In the next section, we extend the initial definitition into several directions. First of all, we are interested in *multi-agent* argumentation to model scenarios such as the BT business process. Second, we want to define an efficient goal-driven argumentation algorithm. Third, we want to be able to define skeptical and credulous agents. Forth, we want to develop different methods to select the best argument.

5 Multi-Agent Argumentation

An agent is a tuple consisting of its arguments, its domain, a flag indicating whether it is skeptical or credulous, and lists of its argumentation and cooperation partners.

Definition 8. Let $n > 0$ be the number of agents and $0 \le i \le n$ an index for an agent. Let P_i be an extended logic program, $F_i \in \{s,c\}$ be a flag indicating a skeptical or credulous agent, $Arg_i \subset \{1,\dots n\}$ and $Coop_i \subset \{1,\dots n\}$ be sets of indices[2] , and Dom_i a set of predicate names defining the agent's domain of expertise. Then the tuple $Ag_i = \langle P_i, F_i, Arg_i, Coop_i, Dom_i \rangle$ is called *agent*. A set of agents $\mathcal{A} = \{Ag_1,\dots,Ag_n\}$ is called *multi-agent system*.

Given a multi-agent system we define a top-down inference operator. The inference operator has three parameters M, LA, and GA, where M is either t or tu indicating that we want to prove verity (t) and non-falsity (tu), respectively. This corresponds to computing justified (t) or defensible (tu) arguments. The local and global ancestor lists LA and GA detect negative and positive loops which lead to inference of non-falsity and failure, respectively. The lists allow us to reject circular arguments. To deal with cooperation we define that agent i can derive a literal L if one of its cooperation partners whose domain covers L can do so (see 3. in Def. 9). Argumentation, or more precisely undercutting, is handled as follows: An agent i proposes *not L* successfully if all argumentation partners whose domain covers L agree, otherwise they have developed a justified counter argument and disagree (see 4. in Def. 9). Finally, agents have to select an argument and here we can distinguish credulous and skeptical agents: A skeptical

---

[2] Note, that an agent not necessarily cooperates and argues with itself, i.e. we do not require $i \in Coop_i, i \in Arg_i$. However, in most cases it is sensible to impose this requirement.

agent allows for rebuts and makes use of proposition 4 and adds the implicitly explicit negation $not \neg L$ of a rule head L to the body (see 5. in Def. 9). Formally, the inference procedure looks as follows:

Definition 9. $\models_i$ Let $\mathcal{A} = \{Ag_1,...,Ag_n\}$ be a MAS and $Ag_i = \langle P_i, F_i, Arg_i, Coop_i, Dom_i \rangle$. Let M' be the opposite mode of M.

    1. *(Init)* $\mathcal{A} \models_i L$ iff $\mathcal{A}, 0, 0, t \models_i L$
    2. *(True)* $\mathcal{A}, LA, GA, M \models_i true$
    3. *(Coop)* $\mathcal{A}, LA, GA, M \models_i (L_1, L_2)$ iff
                 $\exists j \in Coop_i$ s.th. $L_1 \in Dom_j$ and
                  $\mathcal{A}, LA, GA, M \models_j L_1$ and
                  $\mathcal{A}, LA, GA, M \models_i L_2$
    4. *(Arg)* $\mathcal{A}, LA, GA, M \models_i not\ L$ iff
                  $\nexists j \in Arg_i$ s.th. $L \in Dom_j$ and
                  $M = t$ and $\mathcal{A}, 0, GA, tu \not\models_j L$ or
                  $M = tu$ and $\mathcal{A}, GA, GA, t \not\models_j L$
    5. *(Select Arg)* $\mathcal{A}, LA, GA, M \models_i L$ iff
                  $L \notin LA$ and $L \leftarrow Body \in P_i$ and
                  $\mathcal{A}, LA \cup \{L\}, GA \cup \{L\}, M' \models_i Body$ and
                  if $F = s$ then $\mathcal{A}, LA \cup \{L\}, GA \cup \{L\}, M' \models_i not \neg L$

To compare multi-agent and single-agent argumentation, we define the latter by integrating all agents into a single agent.

Definition 10. $\models^{s/c}$ Let $\mathcal{A} = \{Ag_1,...Ag_n\}$ be a mutli-agent system with $Ag_i = \langle P_i, F_i, Arg_i, Coop_i, Dom_i \rangle$. Let $F'_1 \in \{s, c\}$ and $Ag'_1 = \langle \bigcup_{i=1}^{n} \{P_i\}, F'_1, \{1\}, \{1\}, \bigcup_{i=1}^{n} \{Dom_i\} \rangle$ then $\mathcal{A} \models^{F'_1} L$ iff $\{Ag'_1\} \models_1 L$.

For consistent programs the above inference operator yields the same results as the argumentation process:

Proposition 11. $\mathcal{A} \models^c L$, iff L is a conclusion of a justified argument. [3]

The above proposition is very important since it connects the argumentation-theoretic semantics to the operational top-down proof procedure. The former cannot be computed efficiently; the latter can, since it is goal-directed. The proposition also yields an important complexity issue, since justified arguments are equivalent to WFSX citesch98i, which has quadratic complexity.

Multi-agent and single-agent semantics are not equivalent, i.e. $\models^{c/s} \not\equiv \models_1$, but if an agent has a complete definition of a literal it is.

Definition 12. Let $\mathcal{A} = \{Ag_1,...,Ag_n\}$ be a MAS. Ag_i *defines* L *partially* iff $L \in Dom_i$. Agent Ag_i *defines* L *completely*, iff Ag_i is the only agent defining L partially.

---

[3] With acceptability as defined in [13], one gets equivalence to the $\models^s$ operator. For proofs see [9].

Proposition 13. *Let Ag_i be an agent that defines L completely, then $\mathcal{A} \models^{F_i} L$ iff $\mathcal{A} \models_i L$.*
Let $\{a_1,\ldots,a_m\}$ be all indices of agents partially defining L, then $\mathcal{A} \models^{F_j} L$ iff ex. j
such that $\mathcal{A} \models_{a_j} L$.

Before we model the business process described in section 3 in the above framework, we consider different strategies for an agent's argument selection.

6 Preferences

In general, the order of arguments exchanged between agents does not affect the overall result. However, a good choice can reduce the number of messages exchanged considerably. In this section, we describe various strategies how an agent may select an argument.

There are three levels of complexity for such strategies: The simplest and computationally least expensive is a fixed order of partial arguments (1). At design time an agent's partial arguments are listed ordered by their importance. At run-time the agent considers these arguments in the given pre-defined order. Computationally more expensive is a choice based on *all* its own partial arguments (2) or even more expensive one based on all full arguments (3) whose computation will involve other agents. Given the agent has gathered a potential set of arguments, the agent has to decide whether it wants to judge the arguments according to the involved assumptions only or to all literals. Furthermore, it could reduce the assumptions and literals considered further by taking into account only those that are part of the argumentation partner's domain.

Then there are three possible selection criteria to determine the best argument. 1. Minimal by cardinality: It could choose the shortest argument in size because it offers the smallest target for the other agent to counter-argue. 2. Minimal by set-inclusion: If one argument is a super-set of another one, the agent selects the latter. 3. Minimal by impact: The agent assigns impact factors in the range of 0 to 1 to literals and assumptions to allow it to distinguish important from unimportant literals. The impact factor of an argument is obtained by multiplying the impact factors of all its literals. This is the most fine-grained choice but has to be traded-off with finding suitable impact factors.

In the current system we have implemented the least expensive fixed choice scheme.

7 Evaluation

To model the example in section 3 we define CSD, VC, DD, and SD.

Ag_1: CSD. Consider the customer service division CSD. It knows about the customer's equipment and its requirements and in the example we assume that the customer has requirement 2 and 3 and equipment 2 and 3. Furthermore, CSD knows that the customer is important. Besides these facts about a particular customer, CSD has some general rules such as requirements 1, 2, and 3 together make up a portfolio and can be quoted if a previous quote exists. Otherwise, the design department has to prepare the quote. CSD does not provide a quote if the client is not credit-worthy, which is assumed by default.

$$P_1 = \quad requ2.$$
$$requ3.$$
$$equ3.$$
$$equ2.$$
$$important.$$

$$portfolio \leftarrow requ1, requ2, requ3.$$
$$\neg quote \leftarrow not\ credit\_worthy.$$
$$quote \leftarrow portfolio, previous\_quote.$$
$$quote \leftarrow quote\_DD.$$

CSD's domain Dom_1 covers all predicates occuring in P_1 and CSD will argue about credit-worthiness with the vet customer agent VC so that $Arg_1 = \{2\}$ and is skeptical in this respect so that $F_1 = s$. It cooperates on quotation with the design department and hence $Coop_1 = \{3\}$. So, $Ag_1 = \langle P_1, F_1, Arg_1, Coop_1, Dom_1 \rangle$.

Ag_2: VC. The vetting agent VC knows that the client is credit-worthy. Its domain is the credit-worthiness of a client which is important because the VC has to be consulted about credit-worthiness independent about such a fact being around. In fact, if not, this is treated as the client being not credit-worthy. The VC is skeptical but does not argue or cooperate with any other agent because it has the full competence. All in all $Ag_2 = \langle \{credit\_worthy\}, s, \emptyset, \emptyset, \{credit\_worthy\} \rangle$

Ag_3: DD. The design department knows that there is no need to survey the client site if the client has equipment 1, 2, and 3. In general, the DD assumes that the survey department does a survey unless it is busy. The quote of the DD is either obtained by the simple design costs provided there was no need to survey or by the complex design costs otherwise.

$$P_3 = \quad \neg need2survey \leftarrow equ1, equ2, equ3.$$
$$survey\_SD \leftarrow not\ busy\_SD.$$
$$quote\_DD \leftarrow \neg need2survey, simple\_design\_cost.$$
$$quote\_DD \leftarrow survey\_SD, complex\_design\_cost.$$
$$simple\_design\_cost.$$
$$complex\_design\_cost.$$

The domain of DD is only $Dom_3 = \{quote\_DD\}$ because all other predicates are internal. DD cooperates with CSD to obtain the customer's equipment, it arguments with SD to do a survey, and it is credulous: $Ag_3 = \langle P_3, c, \{1\}, \{4\}, \{quote\_DD\} \rangle$

Ag_4: SD. The knowledge base of SD is fairly simple: Its domain is its own busyness and since it is lazy it derives that it is busy unless the customer is important. CSD knows about this and therefore SD and CSD argue on SD's busyness: $Ag_4 = \langle \{busy\_SD \leftarrow not\ important\}, c, \emptyset, \{1\}, \{busy\_SD\} \rangle$

Trace. If CSD is asked for a quote, an argumentation process starts where CSD finally provides the quote; formally: $\{Ag_1, \ldots, Ag_4\} \models_1 quote$. The full trace can be viewed as text or 3D animation at www.soi.city.ac.uk/homes/msch/cgi/aca (see Figure 2).

8 Comparison

The work presented in this paper is related to work by Dung [4,5], Bondarenko et al. [2] and Prakken and Sartor [13] on argumentation. Dung and Bonderenko et al. define

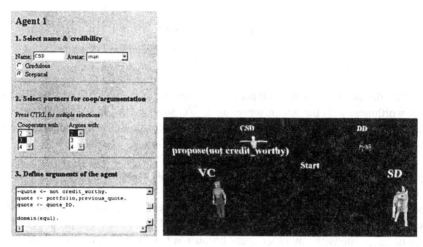

Fig. 2. An HTML form to define an agent and a screenshot of the animated argumentation trace generated.

declarative semantics for extended logic programs using the metaphor of argumentation; Prakken and Sartor are motivated by legal reasoning. Our work continues these lines of research in that we extend their single-agent approaches to a multi-agent one, which deals with both argumentation and cooperation.

Kraus, Sycara, and Evenchik [8] developed argumentation for BDI agents and Parson, Jennings, Sierra, and Noriega [10,15,11] developed a high-level argumentation framework for agent negotiation. In [11] they instantiate their abstract framework with BDI agents closely related to [8] and in [15] they model the BT business process including persuasion, and power hierarchies. Their framework is on a higher level than ours since they do not commit to a particular language. In contrast, our work aims at a theoretically sound, yet implemented, system that is able to deal with figures such as arguments from ignorance, circular arguments, and division.

9 Conclusion

In this article, we described a declarative argumentation framework for a single agent which can be computed bottom-up. We extended this basic framework in several directions: we introduced multi-agent argumentation and cooperation and allow agents to be credulous or skeptical. We showed how to realise this distinction conceptually by allowing undercutting and rebutting, and technically by rewriting arguments and just using undercuts. Most important, we developed a top-down proof procedure for the MAS argumentation process. The proof procedure facilitates a goal-driven implementation of the argumentation process. Furthermore, we briefly described various strategies how agents may select their arguments and discussed their strengths and weaknesses. Finally, we developed our framework guided by an example of a BT business process. The developed system is online and can be visited at www.soi.city.ac.uk/homes/msch/cgi/aca .

Currently, the system does not include updates and observations of the environment. To incorporate these issues, it may be implemented using vivd agents, as done with a simple system in [14].

Acknowledgement I'd like to thank Iara Mora and Jose Julio Alferes for many fruitful discussions and the anonymous referees for their valuable comments.

References

1. J. J. Alferes and L. M. Pereira. *Reasoning with Logic Programming*. (LNAI 1111), Springer-Verlag, 1996.
2. A. Bondarenko, F. Toni, and R. Kowalski. An assumption-based framework for nonmonotonic reasoning. In *Proc. of LPNMR*, pages 171–189. MIT Press, 1993.
3. I. M. Copi and C. Cohen. *Introduction to Logic*. Prentice Hall, 1994.
4. P. M. Dung. An argumentation semantics for logic programming with explicit negation. In *Proc. of ICLP*, pages 616–630. MIT Press, 1993.
5. P. M. Dung. On the acceptability of arguments and its fundamental role in nonmonotonic reasoning, logic programming and n-person games. *Artificial Intelligence*, 77(2):321–357, 1995.
6. A. Van Gelder, K. Ross, and J. S. Schlipf. Unfounded sets and well-founded semantics for general logic programs. In *Proc. of SPDS*, pages 221–230. Austin, Texas, 1988.
7. N. R. Jennings, et al. Agent-based business process management. *Intl. J. of Cooperative Information Systems*, 5(2&3):105–130, 1996.
8. S. Kraus, K. Sycara, and A. Evenchik. Reaching agreements through argumentation: a logical model and implementation. *Artificial Intelligence*, 1998. To appear.
9. Iara Móra, José Julio Alferes, and Michael Schroeder. Argumentation and cooperation for distributed extended logic programs. *Submitted*, 1999. Submitted.
10. S. Parsons and N. Jennings. Negotiation through argumentation-a preliminary report. In *Proc. of ICMAS*, pages 267–274, Kyoto, Japan, 1996.
11. S. Parsons, C. Sierra, and N. Jennings. Agents that reason and negotiate by arguing. *J. of Logic and Computation*, 8(3):261–292, 1998.
12. L. M. Pereira and J.J. Alferes. Well founded semantics for logic programs with explicit negation. In *Proc. of ECAI*, pages 102–106. John Wiley & Sons, 1992.
13. H. Prakken and G. Sartor. Argument-based extended logic programming with defeasible priorities. *J. of Applied Non-Classical Logics*, 7(1), 1997.
14. M. Schroeder, I. Móra, and J.J. Alferes. Vivid agents arguing about distributed extended logic programs. In *Proceedings of EPIA97*. LNAI 1323, Springer–Verlag, 1997.
15. C. Sierra, N. Jennings, P. Noriega, and S. Parsons. A framework for argumentation-based negotiation. In *Proc. of ATAL*, pages 167–182. Springer-Verlag, 1997.

Negotiating Service Provisioning

Mihai Barbuceanu

Enterprise Integration Laboratory
University of Toronto
4 Taddle Creek Road, Rosebrugh Building
Toronto, Ontario, Canada, M5S 3G9
mihai@ie.utoronto.ca

Abstract. The international telecommunications system is the largest distributed computing system in the world, composed of many autonomous subsystems with different ownership over resources and activities. To provide services to customers, these subsystems have to agree on joint activities and on the use of resources. But reaching such agreements is often hampered by unexpected and undesired interactions among the service features preferred by the various parties. These delay the introduction of new features to the market, complicate development and maintenance and cause dissatisfaction among users. In this paper we show how simple and clear models of interaction and behavior can be combined in a generic negotiation architecture able to automate the agreement reaching process between parties that have different preferences and different authority over resources and activities. The architecture integrates a conversational component, enforcing and ensuring the well-formedness of the interaction, a representation of action formalizing agents' authority to set obligations and interdictions upon other agents and a constraint optimization reasoning component allowing parties to deliberate over behaviors and outcomes to decide on their next move.

1 Introduction

When ownership over resources and activities is distributed among the members of a group, agents have to *negotiate* with each other in order to achieve their goals. Negotiation allows agents to discover socially acceptable goals that satisfy their individual needs and to plan and execute them through joint work with other agents.

In this paper we build on the idea that what influences most the interactions and agreements reachable through negotiation are the *authority relations* existing among agents. These derive from agents depending on each other for resources and activities for which they have different ownership and needs. This is in particular true of telecommunications service provisioning applications where multiple levels of national and international carriers, resellers, institutional and private users participate with their own networks and systems on which they run their own policies and preferences.

We believe this simple idea provides a foundation for multi-agent systems able to negotiate the execution of a complex range of business processes in domains like telecommunications service provisioning. To show how this can be done we formalize the following representations and reasoning models and we build a *negotiation shell* that integrates the components and interfaces implementing them.

1. A *process* component, that deals with the structure of the interactions taking place among parties, ensuring the well-formedness of the dialogue. Parties *request, propose, accept reject*, etc. goals and behaviors according to a process following shared social conventions, until some agreement is reached or some failure condition holds. We support this by means of *conversational mechanisms* that provide the descriptive and execution framework for communicative action based structured interactions.

2. A *behavior representation* component, allowing agents to represent their own goals and behaviors, as well as model the others' goals and behaviors. In this context we model authority relations by representing the *obligations* and *interdictions* that agents in given *roles* can dynamically place upon each other, and by quantifying these in terms of costs and rewards associated with the execution or non execution of actions.

3. A *reasoning and decision making* component, allowing parties to deliberate about goals, behaviors and outcomes. To know what to propose, accept or reject agents need to determine, understand and quantify the consequences of given actions and behaviors on both their own and others goals. We support this by means of a *constraint optimization engine* that searches in behavior spaces dynamically generated based on previous knowledge and on knowledge obtained through interactions. This provides *guarantees* for the optimality of the behaviors adopted by agents.

The paper starts with presenting the components of the architecture, namely behavior representation, the search engine and the conversational interaction support. Then we show how this can be applied to negotiate service provisioning in telecommunications by dynamically detecting and solving feature interactions. We end with related work and concluding remarks.

2 Describing Behavior

Syntax and Semantics. Agents act and thus we first need a language to describe and reason about agent behavior. Our language contains two types of actions, *composed* and *atomic*. Composed actions consist of other (sub)actions, while atomic actions do not. Both types of actions have [earliest-start, latest-end] execution time intervals within which they must be executed (discrete time assumed). Atomic actions have specified finite durations. We allow three kinds of compositions.

- *Sequential* compositions, $a = seq(a_1, a_2, ...a_n)$ denote that all component actions a_i must be executed in the given order, inside the time interval of a (their super-action), without temporal overlapping.

- *Parallel* compositions, $a = par(a_1, a_2, ...a_m)$ denote that all component actions must execute within the time interval of a, but with temporal overlapping allowed.

- *Choice* compositions, $a = choice(a_1, a_2, ...a_p)$ denote execution of only a non-empty subset of sub-actions within the time window of the super-action, also with overlapping allowed. *Exclusive choices* (*xchoice*) also require the execution of at most one component action.

From the execution viewpoint, choices have *or* (*xor* for xchoices) semantics in that a choice g is 'on' - meaning will be executed and written $On(g)$ - iff at least one component is on (only one for xchoices) and 'off' - meaning will not be executed and written $Off(g)$ - iff all components are off. Sequences and parallels both have *and* semantics - 'on' iff all components are on, and 'off' otherwise. The difference is that sequences also require *ordered* execution of subgoals, while parallels don't. We address this in a manner that is logically equivalent to breaking any sequence with more than two elements into several two element (binary) sequences and by introducing specific inference rules for the binary sequences. For example, the sequence $s = seq(a_1, a_2, a_3)$ is treated as if it were defined as $s = par(seq(a_1, a_2), seq(a_2, a_3))$. Then, if $On(s)$ that means we must have $On(a_1, a_2)$ *and* $On(a_2, a_3)$. ($On(a, b)$ obviously means a is executed before b). As a specific inference rule, $On(a_i, a_{i+1}) \supset Off(a_{i+1}, a_i)$. From this we also derive that if a sequence is 'on', all its subsequences are also 'on', and if a subsequence is 'off' then all its super-sequences are also 'off'. E.g., $Off(a_1, a_3) \supset Off(a_1, a_2, a_3)$.

Obligation and Interdiction. Setting obligations and interdictions is the way by which agents use power upon each other. There are two ways of obliging or forbidding an action. An obligation can be created by imposing a cost if the action is not done or by giving a reward if it is done. Similarly, an interdiction can be created by imposing a cost if the action is done or giving a reward if it is not done. We use the notation $O_-(g, c)$ to express that g is obliged with cost c, $O_+(g, r)$ for g being obliged with reward r and similarly for interdictions, $F_-(g, c)$ and $F_+(g, r)$. In terms of the on-off state, if an action is on, then all interdiction costs are paid and all obligation rewards are accumulated, while if it's off all obligation costs are paid and all interdiction rewards are accumulated.

Controllable and non-controllable actions. An action is under an agent's control if the agent has discretion over its execution (owns the action). Often, non-controllable actions are part of an agent's plans. In such cases, the agent has to obtain the commitment of the agents controlling these actions about the execution or non-execution of these actions. Obtaining such commitments is the purpose of negotiation.

Roles. The representation of roles specifies, for each role an agent can play or interact with, the goals that can be obliged or forbidden and possibly the range of costs and rewards that the role has authority to use - in other words the *norms* of the organization. These are needed because obligations and interdictions set by other agents can not be accepted at face value, their legality has to be checked first. In our system each agent has such a representation and performs these checks when appropriate. Alternatively, these verifications could be delegated to an external trusted agent, especially if this is also going to be used as an arbiter, mediating disputes about rights and authorities.

Non-power utilities. Obligations and interdictions justified by the norms of the organization are *hard constraints* on agents, their violation incurring an actual loss of utility. When norms do not allow requesting agents to set obligations and interdictions, they may simply quantify their own preferences about goals, the other agent having discretion to decide if the request will be satisfied or not, without any loss no matter what it chooses. *Cooperative* agents may try to satisfy such *soft constraints* as much as possible. For example, $u(g, v)$ quantifies the utility of $On(g)$ as v (with g negated it would be the utility of $Off(g)$) from the viewpoint of some requesting agent, without explicitly setting any obligation or interdiction w.r.t. g.

3 Searching for Optimal Behaviors

Terminology. Let $G = \{g_1, ...g_n\}$ be a goal (action) network. An on-off labeling of the network is mapping $L : G \rightarrow \{on, off\}$ associating either 'on' or 'off' labels to each action in G. A labeling is *consistent* iff the labels of each composed node and of its subgoals are consistent with the node's execution semantics, e.g. if a parallel goal is 'on', then all its subgoals are also 'on' or if a choice goal is 'off', then all its subgoals are 'off', etc. Consistent labelings thus define *executable* behaviors.

Let $C = \{c_1, ...c_m\}$ be a set of constraints, where each c_i is a constraint of the form $On(g_j)$, $Off(g_k)$ or an implication on both sides of which there are conjunctions of on-off constraints. For example, $On(OnSiteService) \supset On(PayOnSiteService)$ is an implication.

Let $P = \{p_1, ...p_k\}$ be a set of obligations and interdictions. Each p_i is one of $O_-(g_i, c_i)$, $O_+(g_i, r_i)$, $F_-(g_i, c_i)$ or $F_+(g_i, r_i)$. This is the set of 'power arguments' currently considered. Given a set P and a consistent labeling L of G, we can compute $Cost_{L,P}(G)$ as the sum of all interdiction costs for 'on' goals and all obligation costs for 'off' goals and respectively $Reward_{L,P}(G)$ as the sum of all interdiction rewards for 'off' goals and all obligation rewards for 'on' goals. (We will drop subscripts where clear). Having both rewards and costs gives system developers more flexibility in expressing how agents influence each other. But for the purpose of the search for optimal behaviors (see next), rewards and costs are just utilities (negative for costs, positive for rewards), same as the non-power utilities, and used in the formulation of the optimization criterion. This also relies on the assumption that costs and rewards are measured with the same unit across the system. For this reason qualitative costs and rewards may be useful to investigate in the future as a better basis for ensuring this uniformity.

Finally, $U = \{u_1(g_1, v_1)...u_l(g_l, v_l)\}$ is a set of (non-power) utilities, communicated by another agent. Given a set U and a consistent labeling L of G we can compute $Util_{L,U}(G)$ as the sum of all (non-power) utilities for the labeled goals in G.

Searching for Behavior. Our main method of reasoning about behavior uses a search method to find a consistent labeling (or behavior) L over G that satisfies all constraints in C and optimizes or satisfies a given *criterion* formulated in terms of the elements of P and U: $Search(G, C, P, U, criterion) = L$.

The criterion is formulated by the agent in response to a request from another agent or to its own needs and reflects the social attitude that the agent adopts vis-a-vis the request or its own situation. Normally, a *social* agent would maximize its own $Reward(G) - Cost(G)$ while seeing to it (to the extent possible) that others' $Util(G)$ are still above some threshold. More cooperative agents may at times want to maximize others' $Util(G)$ while keeping their $Reward(G) - Cost(G)$ above some threshold. In the latter case, if the cost incurred for maximizing the requester's utility is too high, the agent may demand a compensation from the requester, in the form of another action that the requester should achieve. This leads to the creation and exchange of arguments of the type 'I'll do X for you if you'll do Y for me'. To find an appropriate 'Y', an agent can look at its outstanding goals over which the other agent has control. Otherwise, 'Y' can always be 'Pay me something', with the amount to be paid being dynamically computed from the difference between $Cost(G)$ and $Reward(G)$.

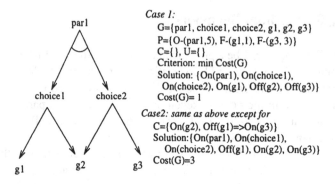

Fig. 1. Behavior Search

We can also represent 'deviant' attitudes, like: (1) *Devoted*: maximize $Util(G)$ regardless of $Cost(G)$ and $Reward(G)$, (2) *Selfish*: maximize $Reward(G) - Cost(G)$ regardless of $Util(G)$, (3) *Anti-social*: minimize $Util(G)$ or (4) *Self-destructive*: minimize $Reward(G) - Cost(G)$ regardless of $Util(G)$.

The search method is illustrated in figure 1 (`choice1` and `choice2` are choices, `par1` is a parallel, the rest are atomic, and `g2` occurs negated in `choice2`). In the first case, without constraints and rewards and minimizing $Cost(G)$, the optimal behavior has cost 1, incurred by $On(g_1)$ that violates $F_-(g_1, 1)$. In the second case, with constraints, the min cost behavior has cost 3, due to $On(g_3)$ which violates $F_-(g_3, 3)$.

Algorithms. In the general framework described, consistent on-off labeling of arbitrary goal networks with constraints is intractable (being equivalent to satisfiability) and so is the associated optimization problem. The main search algorithm we use is a complete *branch-and-bound* backtracking search method. This guarantees that the best behavior will be found, and has acceptable performance for moderate size networks.

4 Managing the Process

To support the process dimension of negotiation we use our previous conversational technology [2]. As this is described elsewhere, we only review here a few elements needed for the understanding of this work. The major elements of our conversational technology are *conversation plans, conversation rules, actual conversations* and *situation rules*. Briefly, a conversation plan is a description of both how an agent *acts locally* and *interacts* with other agents by means of communicative actions. The specification of conversation plans is largely independent from the particular language used for communication for which we currently use a liberal form of KQML [5]. A conversation plan consists of states (with distinguished initial and final states) and rule governed transitions together with a control mechanism and a local data base that maintains the state of the conversation. The execution state of a conversation plan is maintained in *actual conversations*. To decide which conversations to instantiate and to update the agent's data base when events take place, we provide *situation rules*. The top level control loop of an agent activates all applicable situation rules (suggesting conversations to initiate) and then executes new or existing conversations as appropriate.

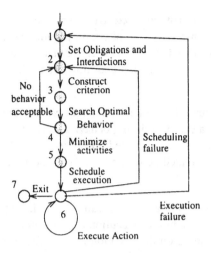

Fig. 2. Basic plan searching and executing behaviors

A top level behavior for an agent may simply consist of the agent setting its relevant obligations and interdictions, deciding on a search criterion and applying it to search for the optimal behavior. If this behavior contains goals that require cooperation with other agents, new sub-conversations are spawned to negotiate the other agent's commitment. The initial conversation is suspended until the sub-conversations terminate, after which is resumed. The conversation plan in figure 2 shows one possible incarnation of this scheme. It shows how:

1. An agent receives utilities representing obligations, interdictions and other preferences that another agent requests it to satisfy (state 1). These are translated, verified and installed in its own goal network (state 2).

2. Decides on its attitude vis-a-vis the request and constructs the search criterion (state 3). Then runs the search engine (state 4).

3. Minimizes the actions to be executed in the optimal behavior. This is done by computing subsumption relations $(On(a) \supset On(b))$ among actions and then applying a min-cover algorithm. The purpose is to avoid executing actions that are implicitly achieved by other actions. (state 5).

4. Schedules the required actions (state 6). Scheduling determines the final order of actions that satisfies all sequencing and resource constraints (we allow these on actions too) as well as the time windows in which each action has to be executed, and is provided by means of a constraint based scheduler. Scheduling failures determine a rerun of the search method with a different criterion.

5. Executes the scheduled actions (by rule `execute-action` in `state 6`). If during action execution new constraints are posted, propagations will be redone. The action execution service is carried out by an executive that makes sure the real time is within the time window for each action and monitors the success or failure of each action.

6. If no execution failure occurs, the plan ends in state `execution-ok`, otherwise it ends in `execution-failed`. If during behavior search the agent determines that it can not satisfy some of the requested constraints, or if actions can not be scheduled or planned, the violated constraints may be sent back to the sender for revision.

This also illustrates our basic approach of providing tools like behavior search, action translation, minimization, scheduling, execution etc. as *services* that may or may not be used by an agent, depending on the situation it is in. These services are made available to the agent through a *Behavior API*.

5 Negotiating Telephone Agents

Most of the value delivered by telecommunication systems to their users comes from allowing users to tailor the telecommunication system's behavior according to their needs [3]. These include aspects like which users to include in calls, where to route calls, what to do when parties are unavailable, which resources to use, etc. But these needs often conflict. A user may not want to be connected to certain numbers, but when she calls another subscriber her call may be forwarded to one of the undesired numbers. Or a user may not want to accept calls from certain numbers, but if she was unavailable when a call from one of these numbers arrived, the automatic recall service may later call back the unwanted number. The telecommunication industry currently solves these interactions in a centralized manner inside multi-million lines of proprietary software. This has severe problems. Service providers must determine how combinations of features will behave, including combinations with other providers features. Maintaining and extending the feature management software when new features are being added is very hard, especially since the correct support of features often depends on the intentions behind their use by various parties. A better solution is thus to have decentralized agents programmed by users handle the interactions by run time negotiation [7]. This would enable users to specify their individual policies involving calls, without being aware of others policies.

To evaluate the power of our negotiation technology, let us now show how it can be used to build such a solution. We start with a few basic examples of the features that are usually available (see [3] for a classification of features):

- *Incoming Call Screening*: the calee will refuse all calls from callers in an incoming call screening list.

- *Call Forward*: the calee will forward the incoming call to another number.

– *Retry*: if the calee is busy, either the caller or the callee will try to establish the connection later.

– *Outgoing Call Screening*: the caller does not allow to be connected to some specified directory numbers.

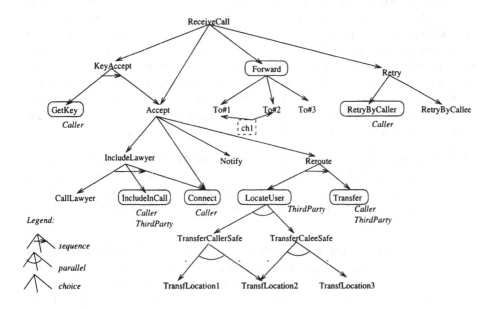

Fig. 3. Call processing behaviors.

As discussed, the feature interaction problem arises from combinations of features that interact in undesired ways, affecting or obstructing the intended functionality of the provided services. *Incoming Call Screening* and *Retry* may conflict if *Retry* is done without checking that the number belongs to the incoming call screening list - we shouldn't call back numbers that are not accepted in the first place. Similarly, *Call Forward* and *Outgoing Call Screening* may conflict if a caller is forwarded to a number that it does not wish to be connected to.

Assume now A and B are agents responsible for establishing voice connections amongst their users. Figure 3 shows the goal structure used by agent B when receiving a call from A. Note that the boxed goals in the figure are non-controllable, they can only be achieved by obtaining the commitment of the agents playing the roles attached to the boxes.

Scenario 1: Basic feature interaction. A has *Outgoing Call Screening* for numbers #1 and #2, and B has *Incoming Call Screening* with A in its incoming call screening list (B does not want to talk to A directly). The set of constraints that A sends to B is

```
{(O_ Take-my-call 5)
  (F_ ch1 9)
  (define-choice
     ch1 Forward-to-Moldova Forward-to-Hong-Kong)}.
```

When receiving this message, B first translates, verifies and installs inside its own context the requested behavior. Goal `Take-my-call` is translated to `ReceiveCall`, while goals `Forward-to-Moldova` and `Forward-to-Hong-Kong` are translated to `To#1` and `To#2` respectively and a new goal, `ch1` is installed among B's goals (in interrupted lines in figure 3). As A is on B's screening list, B will also post it's own interdictions for `Accept` and for `Retry`. The search engine is run and finds a behavior that does not violate any of the stated obligations, namely one where A is forwarded to `To#1`, because the other two possible forwarding numbers are forbidden by A and both `Accept` and `Retry` are forbidden by B. This behavior is immediately executable as it does not violate any constraint. Alternatives to this scenario include:

1. A has `Outgoing Call Screening` to all of #1, #2 and #3. In this case it is not possible to satisfy all requests, but if A has different violation costs for the three numbers, B can forward to the smallest cost one. This may be done automatically by B or with A's approval, in which case the negotiation cycle is extended to include this step.

2. A does not want B to know that it does not want to be forwarded to #1 and #2. In this case, A does not send the corresponding interdiction, but requires B to confirm any forwarding. B replies by informing A about all three possible numbers to forward to and A either calls one of these directly (so that B doesn't know which it is) or asks to be forwarded to a specific one (so that it is not clear which number was avoided).

Scenario 2: Protecting against unwanted calls. Assume now that B has a *Key Protection* feature that requires that certain callers input a key before being connected to B. If A is among these callers, B will place an obligation for `KeyAccept`. Assuming also that A is not one of the callers whose call is accepted only in the presence of a lawyer (see next) and that B is not away, interdictions will be also placed on `IncludeLawyer` and `Reroute`. Again, this has a zero violation behavior consisting of A entering the key and, if successful, being connected to B.

A more sophisticated form of protection is allowing calls from some callers only if the callee's lawyer is also included in the call. This is an example of a *custom* service that some subscribers may create themselves. Assume that A is among those callers whose call is only taken in the presence of B's lawyer. Detecting this forces B to place an obligation on `IncludeLawyer`. The zero violation behavior in this case has B try first call his lawyer and, if successful, take A's call. If the lawyer is not available, her agent may schedule a future time for the call. This time will be communicated to B who in turn will counter propose it to A. If agreed, A will know when to call next time to be able to talk to B.

We note that forbidding or obliging various goals depends on checking a variety of conditions about the agents' state, including agents' own databases that contain screened out callers, callers required to enter valid keys, or even callers for whom a lawyer's presence is required. We provide several ways in which these verifications can take place, including situation rules, conversation rules or specific rules attached on goals that determine if the current situation warrants posting obligations or interdictions on the goal.

Scenario 3: Security concerns. This deals with security concerns when transferring calls to the user's current location (the `Reroute` goal). When a user is at a location considered insecure either by the user or by a caller, the call processing agent must make sure that the call does not take place. As neither the callers' insecure locations nor how much risk they are willing to accept can be known in advance, they have to be communicated dynamically. This happens by allowing callers to include in their initial request definitions for the `TransferCallerSafe` goal as, e.g., parallel compositions where the disallowed goals appear negated. The strongest way to ensure that the called party will not ignore these security requirements is to set costs for the interdictions associated with the insecure locations, under the assumption of power relations allowing callers to charge called parties if their security requirements are ignored:

```
{(parallel TransferCallerSafe
   (- TransfLocation1) (- TransfLocation2))
 (F_ TransfLocation1 9)
 (F_ TransfLocation2 5)}
```

The called party's agent will set to 'on' the `TransfLocationj` goal corresponding to the actual location of the user and search for a *minimum* cost `AcceptCall` behavior. If this cost is greater than zero because of violating caller interdictions, it will be communicated to the caller. If the caller is willing to take the risk expressed by the cost, it will explicitly require so, acknowledging that the called party is not responsible for this cost anymore. Otherwise, only a notification will be sent to the user. This is a clear example of how the dialogue is driven by the exercise of the power that parties have been endowed with.

6   Conclusions

The distribution of ownership over resources and activities creates power relations among the members of a society. When appropriately balanced and distributed, these power relations encourage negotiation as the means for agents to achieve their goals. In this paper we have shown how these relations can be modeled and applied to construct a negotiation architecture that, we believe, faithfully exhibits a complex range of practically relevant negotiation behaviors through the processing of a simple and clear underlying representation.

Historically, game theory has been the major formalization of negotiation phenomena. Recent work in this direction [10] has produced interesting results concerning lying and deceit. However, others [6] have pointed out the limited nature of game theoretic formalizations as they focus exclusively on self-interest and on problem formulations with static valuations completely known in advance. Negotiation, they argue, is a more complex phenomenon, including dialogue, argumentation, planning, focusing, reformulation. Our work is an attempt to address this complexity by creating and integrating components that address its main facets.

Another attempt is [9], whose purpose is to support argumented negotiation by having agents reason internally by formal argumentation. Technically, this relies on free theorem proving in multiple modal logics. This is general in principle, but the practical difficulty of direct implementation by theorem proving, which they imply, is not dealt with. More importantly, we differ from them with respect to what we consider to be the basis of argumentation. Their approach is to have an agent accept an argument of another party if the agent can not logically contradict it. For example, they illustrate a case where an agent A gives a tool T1 to an agent B when B successfully argues that A can also do its job with another tool T2. We believe that in reality even if B can use T2, this does not necessarily mean that he has to accept the request to give T1 *unless* there is some *utility* to be gained (or lost) if he does it (or respectively if he doesn't). In other words, we believe that at the foundation of argumentation lies an evaluation of the *utility* the agent stands to gain or loose and not logical refutability *per se*. In particular, we can easily conceive negotiations where agents may accept arguments even if logically they may appear incorrect, if coming from agents exercising enough power - like when an employee acts to satisfy the CEO's request, even if he does not agree with its logic.

One can argue that reasoning and building arguments about this utility can itself be encoded in the logical language(s) of the agent and thus make the refutability approach applicable in this case as well. This is true, but it leaves the construction of the actual mechanism for reasoning about utility entirely on the shoulders of agent designers. We have tried to remove this burden by providing such a general mechanism. This makes agents easier to construct and provides *guarantees* about the optimality of their behavior.

On the feature interaction front, [7] presents a negotiation approach that shares many intuitions with ours. Where we differ is in the higher level of formality and inference power offered by our negotiation solver and in the richer infrastructure that we offer. This work defines the notions of abstraction and composition for complex action specification. These appear similar to our choice and sequence types, but their meaning seems to come more from the underlying Prolog implementation than from a separate formal specification. Similarly, the inference power of their method is not clear and neither is the complexity of reasoning (although they imply their reasoning is tractable).

As to the role of obligations in collective behavior, [4] and [11] among others have made strong cases for the insufficiency of accounts based solely on joint goals or intentions and for the need to include obligations in any such account. We have previously done work on using deontic logic in coordination [1], proposing an arc-consistency propagation method to infer the consequences of given obligations and interdictions. The price for tractability was a less expressive action language, the apparent impossibility to consider constraints and very limited querying capabilities. This experience has shown that deontic logic is too limited in the range of behaviors it can describe. Thus, we have taken the opposite route, removing these limitations at the price of higher complexity. We believe that realistic negotiation can not do without these extended capabilities.

A first limitation that we are working on comes from the computational cost of systematic search as done by our search engine, which may become problematic as we increase the size of goal networks. Given the equivalence of on-off labeling to satisfiability, we are building a local search engine based on satisfiability methods, with heuristics biasing the solution toward improving the given criterion. This can be used either stand alone, or to provide a good initial upper bound for the complete *branch-and-bound* method.

Second, we know that for goals that require another's agent participation, the commitment of the other agent must be negotiated first, and this negotiation may fail. There is a danger that agents may spend too many resources trying to negotiate behaviors that seem advantageous to them but don't have enough chances to succeed (like trying to negotiate a long distance call free of charge). The cause of this is the failure to consider the *probability* of achieving such goals. We are addressing this by using Bayes networks [8] to represent agents' causal models of actions and to compute the probabilities of actions that agents don't control completely from observations and assumptions about the actions that agents do control. These probabilities are used to calculate more informed *expected* costs, rewards and utilities which are then used by the search engine to determine the best course of action.

7 Acknowledgements

This research is supported, in part, by Materials and Manufacturing Ontario, Mitel Corp., Communications and Information Technology Ontario, Natural Science and Engineering Research Council, Digital Equipment Corp., Micro Electronics and Computer Research Corp., Spar Aerospace, Carnegie Group and Quintus Corp.

References

[1] Barbuceanu, M. 1998. Agents that work in harmony by knowing and fulfilling their obligations. *Proc. of AAAI-98*, Madison, WI, 1998.

[2] Barbuceanu, M. and Fox, M. S. 1997. Integrating Communicative Action, Conversations and Decision Theory to Coordinate Agents. *Proceedings of Automomous Agents'97*, 47-58, Marina Del Rey, February 1997.

[3] Cameron, E.J., N.D. Griffeth, Y.J. Lin, M.E. Nilson, W.K. Schnure, and H. Velthuijsen. 1996. A Feature Interaction Benchmark for for IN and Beyond. In L.G. Bouma and H. Velthuijsen, editors, *Feature Interactions in Telecommunication Systems*, 1-23, Amsterdam, IOS Press.

[4] Castelfranchi, C. 1995. Commitments: From Individual Intentions to Groups and Organizations. *Proceedings of ICMAS-95*, AAAI Press, 41-48.

[5] Finin, T. et al. 1992. Specification of the KQML Agent Communication Language. The DARPA Knowledge Sharing Initiative, External Interfaces Working Group.

[6] Loui, R.P. and Moore, D.M. 1998. Dialogue and Deliberation. Cognitive Science, submitted.

[7] Griffeth, N. and Velthuijsen, H. 1993. Win/win negotiation among autonomous agents. *Proc. of 12th Workshop on Distributed Artificial Intelligence*, Hidden Valley, PA, 187-202.

[8] Pearl, J. 1988. Probabilistic Reasoning in Intelligent Systems, Morgan Kaufmann.

[9] Parsons, S., Sierra, C., and Jennings, N. 1998. Agents that Reason and Negotiate by Arguing. *Journal of Logic and Computation*, 8(3), 261-292.

[10] Rosenschein, J. and Zlotkin, G. 199. Rules of Encounter, MIT Press, Cambridge, MA.

[11] Traum, D.R. and Allen, J.F. 1994. Discourse Obligations in Dialogue Processing. *Proceedings of the 32th Annual Meeting of the ACL*, Las Cruces, NM, 1-8.

Cooperative Plan Selection Through Trust

Nathan Griffiths and Michael Luck

Department of Computer Science, University of Warwick, Coventry, CV4 7AL, UK
Email: {Nathan.Griffiths, Michael.Luck}@dcs.warwick.ac.uk

Abstract. Cooperation plays a fundamental role in multi-agent systems in which individual agents must interact for the overall system to function effectively. However, cooperation inherently involves an element of risk, due to the unpredictable nature of other's behaviour. In this paper, we consider the information needed by an agent to be able to assess the degree of risk involved in a particular course of action. In particular, we consider how this information can be used in the process of plan selection in BDI-like agents.

1 Introduction

BDI agent architectures represent an important class of system that has been used in an increasing number of applications. Based on the folk-psychology mental notions of belief, desire and intention, they are also distinctly popular among the plethora of existing agent architectures. Apart from the intuitive understanding of the BDI model, this popularity may be due to the successful practical application of BDI systems such as PRS [8] and dMARS [5] to diverse areas including malfunction handling on the space shuttle and air traffic control, for example.

Though BDI architectures occupy an an important place in the design of intelligent agents, the limitation of the approach is that it is typically focussed on what might be called *standard* task planning and execution for individual agents. In contrast, our work is concerned with the *extension* of a BDI-like architecture to include those higher-level control strategies and other modifications so that domain properties of multi-agent environments can be used to hone agent behaviour. In this paper, we consider how to augment the process of plan-selection in such agents to provide a richer and potentially more effective mechanism.

We begin by reviewing key components of the target architecture, including the basic control cycle and details of the actions and plans that form the basis of this work. Then we describe the problem of plan selection and examine some of the relevant factors that may be used in multi-agent domains, and proceed to develop a detailed model of plan selection. Before finally assessing the value and contribution of this work, a mechanism for the critical application of the model to partial plans is presented.

2 The Base Architectural Model

The basic operation of BDI agents is based around their beliefs, desires and intentions. An agent has beliefs (about itself, others and the environment), desires (in terms of the states it wants to achieve in response) and intentions as adopted plans. In addition, agents also maintain a repository of available plans, known as the *plan library*. Agents respond to changes in their goals and beliefs, resulting from perception, by selecting appropriate plans from the plan repository and then instantiating one of these plans as an intention. Intentions comprise actions and subgoals to be achieved, with the latter giving rise to the addition of new subplans to that intention.

This control cycle, while proving generally effective and useful in many domains, does not, however, relate to the specific issues that arise in multi-agent scenarios where cooperation among multiple interacting agents is either necessary or desirable. For example, the questions of who to cooperate with, and how, are not addressed at all. In this paper, we are specifically concerned with the impact of multi-agent plans on the plan-selection process in this kind of architecture. However, before considering plan selection itself, we must describe the nature of such plans.

For an agent situated in a multi-agent environment to take advantage of others, its plans must include a means for it to interact with those others. Cooperation may take the form of an agent performing an action on behalf of another, a group of agents performing an action together or set of actions performed at the same time. Thus there are three distinct types of action that a plan may include, described below.

Individual actions are those performed by an individual agent, without the need for assistance from others. An individual action may be executed by the agent owning the plan in which it is contained, or by another agent on its behalf.

A *joint action* is a composite action, made up of individual actions that must be performed together by a group of agents. Each agent involved in executing a joint action makes a simultaneous *contribution* to the joint action, corresponding to the component action that it performs. For example, if agents α and β perform the joint action of lifting a table, then α must make the contribution of lifting one end of the table simultaneously with β lifting the other.

Concurrent actions are those that can be performed in parallel by different agents, without the need for synchronisation (except at the beginning and end of a set of concurrent actions). As with joint actions, the action an agent performs as part of a set of concurrent actions is its *contribution*. For example, if agents α and β each write a chapter for a book, and they perform their actions in parallel, then α and β perform concurrent actions where each agent's contribution is the action of writing the appropriate chapter.

Our definitions of joint and concurrent actions are related to the notions of strong and weak parallelism described by Kinny *et al.* [9]. The key difference is that while we consider the component actions, or contributions, that make up a joint action, Kinny represents joint actions as a "black-box" without explicit contributions. These are primitive actions from which others can be constructed. Thus, related and dependent actions that do not fit directly into these categories can be built up from them.

In the BDI model, the plans in a plan library are *partial plans* in that they are incomplete, and contain subgoals in addition to actions. We do not consider the arguments for and against such a choice of representation here, since it is has been addressed elsewhere, but note that this is one standard form of organisation [1].

We thus define a plan as sequence of steps, where a step is either an individual action, a joint action, a set of concurrent actions, or a subgoal. In addition, since plans apply only to particular situations, they must also have preconditions.

3 Cooperative Plan Selection

In the BDI model, an agent's actions are determined by its intentions. When an agent forms an intention to achieve a given goal, it does so by committing to a plan to achieve that goal. However, for any particular goal there may be several plans to achieve it that are *applicable* in the current situation, since their preconditions are satisfied. Some of these plans may contain actions beyond the agent's capabilities (or joint or concurrent actions) which, if chosen, require assistance from another agent.

Thus, an agent's choice of plan determines whether it must cooperate to achieve its goal. If all the applicable plans for a goal contain actions that cannot be performed by the agent alone, cooperation is *necessary*. If there is a choice between plans that are performable alone and those that are not, then cooperation is *optional*. If choosing to cooperate in this case, there must be some inherent advantage to the cooperation, for example by minimising effort, since it can also be achieved by the agent alone.

In existing work, several researchers have considered the situation where cooperation is necessary. For example, Castelfranchi *et al.* have developed a model of cooperation based upon the notion of *dependence*, where an agent is dependent on another for an action if it is unable to perform that action itself [3]. However, the issues involved in determining why an agent might choose to cooperate when this is optional, have been largely unaddressed. One exception is Wooldridge and Jennings' [15] formalisation of cooperative problem solving, in which they argue that it begins with an agent recognising the potential for cooperation, either because it is unable to achieve its goal alone (and cooperation is necessary), or because it prefers assistance (and cooperation is optional). Since their work is relatively high level, though, many details such as *why* an agent might prefer assistance are not considered. The approach to plan selection described in this paper is an attempt to answer this question.

3.1 Plan Selection Criteria

The problem of plan selection amounts to choosing the best plan — the plan that is most likely to be successful, with least cost in terms of time and resources, and the least *risk*. (While in some circumstances, such as gambling, the influence of these factors may be contradictory, requiring an agent to make a trade-off between the two, we assume that in general an agent's high-level desires are likely to be such as to attempt to minimise both the risk and the cost of its actions.) When the plans involved do not involve other agents, standard plan selection criteria (or planning heuristics) can be used to assess cost. However, when one or more of the agent's plans do involve others, an element of *risk* is introduced by the inherent uncertainty of interaction. In addition to a measure of the cost of a plan, therefore, we need to be able to assess the likelihood of finding an agent (or agents) for actions that are required for successful plan execution; the likelihood that once such agents are identified they will agree to cooperate; and the likelihood that once a commitment has been given, the agents concerned will fulfill their commitments.

We identify four primary factors relevant in comparing plans in respect of risk: knowledge of other's capabilities, risk from others, knowledge of view of self, and knowledge of other's preferences. Certainly, risk may be introduced for any number of other reasons, but these are the key domain-independent general issues.

Agent Capabilities Knowledge of others' capabilities helps to determine which agents might perform the required actions. If many agents are known to have the target capabilities, then successful execution of the plan is more likely than if fewer or no agents do so. However, in line with the motivating concerns of dynamic environments and uncertain and incomplete knowledge, we cannot assume that an agent's knowledge of others faithfully represents them, and success at execution time may be possible even if it is not at evaluation time, just as failure is also possible. In general, though, we assume that there is sufficient stability for this to be useful in assessing plans prior to execution.

Risk from Others Once potential cooperating agents are identified, they may be evaluated in terms of the risk involved in interacting with them. Plans involving agents with whom interaction is more likely to be successful, should be rated higher than those involving interactions less likely to be successful.

Risk from view of Self Knowledge of the view of oneself in the eyes of others in terms of risk of interaction may also be useful in assessing plans. It can provide a measure of the likelihood that another agent will agree to cooperate, since an agent is more likely to cooperate with another if it has confidence in the success of that interaction. Thus, the agents identified in competing plans can be evaluated in respect of their view of the risk involved in cooperating with the planning agent. It is, however, difficult to maintain an assessment of how one is viewed by others.

Agent Preferences It might also be possible to assess plans in relation to the higher-level motivations of the agents involved in them, and whether cooperation would be likely. This would require a detailed model of the motivations and goals of other agents, however, which is unlikely to be accurate.

3.2 Trust

How then to assess risk in interaction? Fortunately, as recognised by several researchers [2, 4, 7, 10, 11], this has a relatively simple solution in the form of *trust*. The risk of whether to cooperate and with whom, may be determined by, among other things, the degree of confidence or *trust* in other agents. Despite the notion of *trust* being commonplace in our everyday interactions, there are few formal definitions. However, it is generally accepted that trust implies some form of risk, and that entering into a trusting relationship is choosing to take an uncertain path that can lead to either benefit or cost depending on the behaviour of others [12].

In this paper, we view trust as one of the means available to an agent for estimating the risk involved in cooperation, in terms of an estimation of the degree of expectation that others will do what they agree to do, i.e. an *expectation of risk*. This is a synthetic notion of trust since, unlike Deutsch [4] and Luhmann [10], for example, we are not concerned with how trust operates in humans, but with how the concept of trust can be used in relation to cooperation between artificial agents. We are also primarily concerned with *how* an agent can use the degree of trust it has in another in reasoning about cooperation, rather than how an agent determines this degree of trust in the first place.

4 A Model of Cooperative Plan Selection

4.1 Plan Ratings

The problem of plan-selection is essentially the same as that of finding effective heuristics for plan construction. In that sense, we can apply standard domain-independent heuristics for evaluating plans which perform a valuable, if limited, service. These heuristics include, for example, the length of a plan as the number of its actions, the cost based on the cost of the actions it contains, and the duration of plan execution based on the duration of individual actions. We will not consider this further in this paper, since these issues are well addressed by textbooks (for example [14]), but suffice it to state that any such heuristics may be used to arrive at an assessment of a plan in terms of its *standard rating*.

This evaluation of a plan does not, however, address our key concerns of assessing plans in relation to the dynamic multi-agent nature of the environment. If one or more of the plans available to an agent requires interaction with another, the *standard rating* is inadequate, since this interaction introduces an element of risk. A second rating is therefore necessary in these terms, which we call the *cooperative rating*.

4.2 Trust

The perceived risk of cooperating with a particular agent is determined by that agent's reliability, honesty, etc., embodied by the notion of *trust*. Thus an agent can use its trust in others as a means of assessing the risk involved in cooperating with them. Describing *trust* in terms of *risk* allows us to consider the limits of trust more precisely, and to quantify it. An agent with a high trust value is more trusted than an agent with a low trust value, and represents less risk in terms of cooperation, for example. This suggests an inverse relationship between trust, T, and risk, R, as follows.

$$R = \frac{1}{T} \tag{1}$$

An agent's trust of another is dependent on a variety of factors, including the other's believed reliability, honesty, veracity, etc. However, modelling all such potentially relevant factors is excessive, and can add to the complexity of the solution, when typically they will not be needed. Consequently, we base our model of trust upon Marsh's formalism [11] and the work of Gambetta [7], and define the trust in an agent α, to be a value from the interval between 0 and 1: $T_\alpha \in [0, 1]$. The numbers merely represent comparative values, and are not meaningful in themselves. Values approaching 0 represent complete distrust, and those approaching 1 represent complete, blind trust. In this paper we are not concerned with how an agent should update its trust of others, but Marsh [11] describes a possible approach that will suffice. This representation of trust corresponds to Marsh's notion of *general trust*. However, Marsh also introduces *situational trust*, where an agent's trust in another is dependent on the importance of the situation being considered. For example, while an agent may trust another to extract product information from a database, it might not trust it to determine which product represents the best value for money. Although conceptually this situational trust is a more powerful mechanism that general trust, the computational overhead involved in identifying trust in *tasks* can be prohibitive, and we do not consider it further.

4.3 Agent Models

In order to choose between plans that may require cooperation for their execution, an agent needs some knowledge about the other agents that it may cooperate with. Durfee [6] notes that in order to cooperate effectively an agent may need to know certain information about others, about themselves, about how they view others and are viewed themselves and so on. However, since an agent's reasoning is resource bounded, if taken to an extreme, the amount of knowledge an agent possesses to facilitate its cooperation might overwhelm its limited reasoning capabilities. Thus agents need just enough knowledge to coordinate well, and no more, since any additional knowledge may simply hinder the reasoning process of the agent.

An agent has a *model* of each other agent with which it may interact, that contains its knowledge of the other's capabilities and the degree to which it is trusted. These agent models form part of the agent's wider knowledge base, or beliefs. The conceptual form such models may take in an agent's knowledge base is shown in Figure 1, which represents an agent's models of two others, α and β. For each agent, the model contains a set of capabilities, and the degree of trust in that agent.

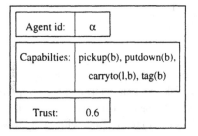 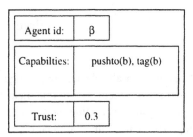

Fig. 1. Example agent models

4.4 Assessing Actions

In assessing the merit of a plan, an agent must make a judgement about the risk attached to each action in the plan requiring cooperation, by examining the trust value in its model of each of the possible cooperating agents. Suppose that an agent knows of n others, $\alpha_1, \alpha_2, \ldots, \alpha_n$, with the required capabilities for performing a given action, and ordered such that $T_{\alpha_{x-1}} \geq T_{\alpha_x}$, where T_{α_x} denotes the trust in α_x. Several possibilities for assessing the risk involved in cooperating with others are discussed below.

We might only consider trust in the *most trusted* agent involved so that the risk of a particular action would be as follows.

$$R_{\text{action}} = \frac{1}{T_{\alpha_1}} \tag{2}$$

Though simple, the problem with this approach is that this most trusted agent might not be the actual agent involved in the cooperative action, for any number of reasons. In particular, the autonomous nature of agents underlying this model suggests that it is impossible to determine the behaviour of another agent in advance. As a consequence, cooperation with less trusted others may be needed, and this must be factored into the measure of risk. Alternatively, then, we might consider the additive total of trust in all agents in the set of potential agents for the action.

$$R_{\text{action}} = \frac{1}{\sum_{i=1}^{n} T_{\alpha_i}} \tag{3}$$

This avoids the problem of only considering the most trusted agent, and considers all agents to an equal extent, but does not address the decreased likelihood of cooperation with less trusted agents. An agent would first try to cooperate with α_1 and, if unsuccessful, would then try α_2, and so on, but for each successive agent, the likelihood of success decreases. To address this, we can adjust the formula to increase the significance of more trusted agents, by dividing the trust of successive agents by a correspondingly increasing factor.

$$R_{\text{action}} = \frac{1}{\sum_{i=1}^{n} \frac{T_{\alpha_i}}{i}} \tag{4}$$

Thus, trust in all relevant agents is considered, but in relation to the likelihood of cooperation with them. Using this measure of risk, we can determine the *cooperative rating* of a plan by summing the risk associated with each action in it. Thus a plan with few high risk actions may be rated better (or less risky) than a plan with many low risk actions. For a plan with m actions, $a_1, a_2, \ldots, a_m$, the cooperative rating C for that plan is given by the following equation.

$$C = \sum_{i=1}^{m} R_{a_i} \tag{5}$$

4.5 Plan Quality

Once both the *standard* and *cooperative* ratings of a plan have been determined, they must be combined to form an overall measure of plan quality to select between alternative applicable plans. It would not be sensible simply to add the two values together, since one measures the *cost* of the plan, and the other the *risk* involved in it, and the relative importance of these may vary for each agent. We therefore include a weighting for these ratings for a particular agent in the overall quality measure, Q, as follows, where w_s and w_c represent the influence weighting applied to the *standard rating*, S and *cooperative rating*, C, respectively.

$$Q = (w_s * S) + (w_c * C) \tag{6}$$

Different agents may use different weightings, the values used reflecting, in part, an agent's predisposition, since agents that place greater importance on the *standard rating* are inclined to minimise the cost of achieving their goals, whether or not this requires cooperation. Conversely, agents that place most importance on the *cooperative rating* are predisposed to minimising the risk involved in cooperating with others, even if this increases the cost involved in achieving their goals. Thus agents that place more importance on the standard rating are more inclined to take risks associated with cooperation in order to minimise the cost of their plans, when compared to agents that place more importance on the cooperative rating. The values of the weighting that provide the best selection of plans depends on an agent's environment.

5 Cooperation in Partial Plans

5.1 Plan Evaluation

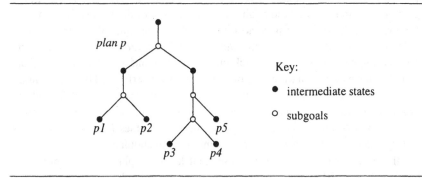

Fig. 2. Example plans

Figure 2 shows a graphical representation of a plan that includes all possible elaborations, where the edges represent actions, solid bullets correspond to intermediate states between actions, and outline bullets correspond to subgoals. For each subgoal in the plan, there are a set of applicable plans, each of which forms a branch of possible elaboration from that subgoal. The set of plan elaborations is the set of paths from the root of the graph to the leaves. Thus, for plan p possible elaborations are paths from the root to the nodes labelled $p1$, $p2$, $p3$, $p4$, and $p5$. If this set has been determined, the alternatives can be evaluated in respect of the criteria developed for fully elaborated plans, and an appropriate plan selected.

A naive solution would thus be to require an agent to fully elaborate each of its applicable plans in order to choose between them. While this would indeed allow direct use of the criteria described above, it also requires a premature commitment to a particular plan. Such a requirement would negate the benefit of using partial plans in the possibility of interleaving execution and deliberation to cope with the environmental change that is typical of multi-agent scenarios. More importantly, it demands a search through the entire tree of plans so that the quality of each possible path solution can be measured. This is prohibitively expensive to be performed in real-time.

We assume, for reasons of simplicity, that plans are not recursive, meaning that a plan should not contain a subgoal that is the same as the top-level goal that plan achieves.

5.2 Pre-Execution Plan Assessment

If we are to avoid constructing the entire search tree at the time of plan selection, we must be able to make a choice based on a limited number of alternatives, such as the top-level applicable plans. An informed choice at this level is only possible, however, if we have some measure of the value of plans in terms of the standard and cooperative ratings, but clearly, this is not possible to do on the fly. Instead, we perform an off-line *pre-execution assessment* of the plan library in which all of the plans in it are evaluated in a coarse fashion with respect to the agents required for successful execution. This approach represents a compromise between the desire to minimise the computational overhead and that of maximising the quality of any measure of the value of a plan.

Starting with the plans that require no further elaboration, since these are the only ones which can be directly evaluated, the *standard* and *cooperative* ratings are determined. These ratings must then be fed back into the other plans as values for subgoals within them. For each plan containing actions that cannot be performed by the planning agent, the set of all agents known to have the relevant capability is generated through inspection of its agent models, so that these ratings can be calculated as described earlier. There are two possible approaches to incorporating these values for fully elaborated plans into the larger partial plans of which they might form subplans.

Firstly, these values can be used in subsequent levels of plans in the library for which the plans *best* satisfy subgoals, and so on until each plan has an overall quality measure. This quality measure is an assessment of the *best-case* solution.

An alternative solution is to take into account *all* possible elaborations and calculate a *mean* rating for competing plans, so that there is less reliance on one individual plan that may not be possible at execution time. This provides a less sensitive measure, but one which is more likely to be useful in a dynamic environment, since it might still be relevant. The balance between the *best-case* and *mean* ratings amounts to a trade-off between an agent trying to find the best final plan and minimising the chance of the final plan being poor due to environmental change (in terms of these ratings). These best-case and mean ratings for agent plans will need periodic reassessment as the agent's knowledge of other's capabilities (and its trust in them) changes.

The *best-case advantage* (BCA) of one plan over other applicable plans is the advantage of that plan over others if its final elaboration has the best quality rating. Thus, for two applicable plans, p and q, with best-case ratings of $Q_b(p)$ and $Q_b(q)$ respectively the BCA is equal to the difference between the quality rating for p and that for q, $|Q_b(p) - Q_b(q)|$. If there are more than two applicable plans, as is typical, then the BCA is equal to the difference between the minimum and maximum best-case ratings. Thus with applicable plans $p, q, \ldots, z$ the BCA is determined by the following equation.

$$BCA = max\{Q_b(p), Q_b(q), \ldots, Q_b(z)\} - min\{Q_b(p), Q_b(q), \ldots, Q_b(z)\} \quad (7)$$

The *mean-case advantage* (MCA) of one plan over other applicable plans is the typical (or mean) extra advantage. This is a general case measure that incorporates more information, since it takes into account all possible elaborations of the applicable plans. With mean ratings for p and q of $Q_m(p)$ and $Q_m(q)$, the MCA is equal to $|Q_m(p) - Q_m(q)|$. As above, if there are more than two applicable plans, the MCA is equal to the difference between the minimum and maximum mean ratings. Thus with plans $p, q, \ldots, z$ the MCA is as follows.

$$MCA = max\{Q_m(p), Q_m(q), \ldots, Q_m(z)\}$$
$$-min\{Q_m(p), Q_m(q), \ldots, Q_m(z)\} \quad (8)$$

Selecting between partial plans There is a trade-off between maximising the best-case advantage and the mean-case advantage. If the best-case advantage of a plan p over another, q, outweighs the mean-case advantage of q over p, then p should be selected, but if the mean-case advantage of q over p is greater than the best-case advantage of p over q, then q should be selected.

More generally, the advantage should be maximised, regardless of whether it is best case or mean-case. If $BCA > MCA$ then the best-case rating should be used to select plan x, such that $Q_b(x) < Q_b(p) \wedge Q_b(x) < Q_b(q) \wedge \ldots \wedge Q_b(x) < Q_b(z)$. Alternatively, if $MCA > BCA$ then the mean-case rating of the applicable plans should be used.

Certainly, more sophisticated mechanisms involving the likelihood of elaboration of individual plans are possible, but these require much more extensive knowledge of the relationship of plans and environments, and the nature of change in environments, as well as significantly more costly computation. Given that the environment is largely unpredictable, there is unlikely to be any significant advantage, however.

This approach is suited to situations in which the likelihood of the environment and the agent models remaining the same is high so that plan elaboration at execution time is likely to reflect the plan quality values determined in advance for the overall partial plan concerned. Reassessment of these quality measures will be required periodically to ensure they are consistent with the changes in trust of others. Although we do not address

action	effect and cost	performable by
$pickup(b)$	pick up box b, (cost 2)	α_1
$putdown(b)$	put down box b, (cost 2)	α_1
$carryto(l,b)$	carry box b to location l, (cost 2)	α_1
$pushto(l,b)$	push box b to location l, (cost 4)	α_2
$shelve(b)$	put box b on the nearest shelf, (cost 2)	α_3
$tag(b)$	put a tag on box b, (cost 1)	α_1, α_2

plan p_1 — $[tag(box), pushto(long\_term\_storage, box)]$
plan p_2 — $[tag(box), pickup(box), carryto(standard\_storage, box), goal(stored(box))]$
plan p_3 — $[putdown(box)]$
plan p_4 — $[putdown(box), shelve(box)]$

Fig. 3. Actions and plans in the warehouse domain

this issue in this paper, a simple strategy is for an agent to perform this reassessment when it is not otherwise occupied, or when the change in its trust of others exceeds some threshold. Although there will be some significant computation involved, it is limited in the number of capable agents, the number of plans and the the numbers of actions in those plans. Moreover, since assessment is carried out in a *pre-execution* strategy combined with periodic reassessment, the overhead placed on an agent for plan selection at run time is relatively low, especially if computation relating to plan reassessment is performed when the agent is idle.

6 Warehouse Example

To illustrate this scheme, consider the example of a warehouse domain, comprising three agents α_1, α_2, and α_3. The warehouse has three areas: a delivery area, a standard storage area, and a long term storage area, such that boxes arrive in the delivery area and must be moved to one of the storage areas. On the arrival of a box it is unknown how soon it will be needed, and whether it should be put in standard or long term storage. Boxes in the standard storage area can be kept on the floor or on shelves, with the only constraint being that a box cannot be placed on top of another, to allow easy access. Thus, if an agent wishes to store a box in the standard storage area, and the floor is full, it must be stored on the shelves. In the long term storage area boxes can be stored on the floor or on other boxes. The possible actions, the agents that are able to perform them, along with an example set of plans, are shown in Figure 3. Each action has an associated cost, shown in parentheses, corresponding to its standard rating.

The warehouse requires that once boxes arrive in the delivery area they are moved to one of the storage areas, and that the first agent to perceive a box in the delivery area should adopt the goal to move the box. Suppose that agent α_1 notices a box in the delivery area, and forms the goal of the box being placed in a storage area. Now, it has two applicable plans for this goal, p_1 and p_2. Plan p_1 is fully elaborated and can be executed without further elaboration, while p_2 is partial and requires elaboration before it can be fully executed. There are two plans, p_3 and p_4, that can be used to elaborate p_2. Which of these plans will be used for elaboration depends on the circumstances at the time of elaboration. For example, if there is sufficient floor space in the standard storage area then p_3 can be used, but if there is no free space then p_4 must be used. We use the notation $p_{2(3)}$ to refer to p_2 when elaborated with p_3, and $p_{2(4)}$ when with p_4. Note that agent α_1 has sufficient capabilities to execute $p_{2(3)}$ by itself, but it must cooperate to execute both p_1 and $p_{2(4)}$.

The *standard rating* for the possible plans can be determined from the cost of the actions, and is equal to 5 for p_1, 7 for $p_{2(3)}$ and 9 for $p_{2(4)}$. However, since agent α_1 is unable to execute p_1 without assistance, and may be unable to execute p_2 without assistance (depending on how it is elaborated), it must consider the plan's *cooperative rating*. Suppose that α_1 has a trust value of 0.8 for both agent α_2 and α_3. The only agent capable of performing the action required for p_1, $pushto(l, b)$, is α_2, so the *cooperative rating* for plan p_1 is equal to $\frac{1}{0.8} = 1.25$. For p_2, if the agent elaborates the plan with p_3 then cooperation is not needed, so the rating is 0. However, if elaborated with p_4, the agent must cooperate with α_3, so the rating is $\frac{1}{0.8} = 1.25$.

If we suppose for simplicity that the weighting used in combining the *standard* and *cooperative* rating (i.e. w_s and w_c) are both equal to 1, then the overall rating for the plans can be determined. Since p_1 is fully elaborated the rating is simply arrived at from the formula $(w_s * S) + (w_c * C)$, i.e. $5 + 1.25 = 6.25$. The rating for p_2 depends on the ratings for each of its possible elaborations, $p_{2(3)}$ and $p_{2(4)}$. The rating for $p_{2(3)}$ is equal to $7 + 0 = 7$, and similarly $9 + 1.25 = 10.25$ for $p_{2(4)}$. Thus the best-case rating for p_2 is 7, while the mean rating is $\frac{7+10.25}{2} = 8.625$. In this example the best-case advantage is $7 - 6.25 = 0.75$, and the mean-case advantage is $8.625 - 6.25 = 2.375$. The mean-case advantage is greater so the agent should use the mean rating in plan selection. Since p_1 has the lowest mean-rating, it should be selected by the agent.

Alternatively, if α_1 has a trust value of 0.2 for agent α_2, the best-case, and mean, rating for p_1 becomes $5 + \frac{1}{0.2} = 10$. Here, the best-case advantage outweighs the mean-case advantage, so the best-case rating is used to select the best plan, in this case p_2.

7 Conclusions

In this paper we have presented a mechanism for plan selection in BDI-like agents that takes into account the inherent risk involved in cooperation. We describe how an agent can assess the risk for a given plan in the light of its knowledge of others' capabilities, and its trust in them. Plans are judged both in terms of the risk they involve and their cost according to standard criteria. However, computational constraints mean that a full analysis of plans is not possible at execution time and a pre-execution assessment is performed instead, allowing an agent to make an informed selection between plans.

The work described in this paper is part of a wider effort investigating the process of cooperation with respect to BDI-like agents. As part of this, several questions remain open with respect to the mechanisms described in this paper. Firstly, we might consider how to incorporate the notion of an agent's *rights* [13] to perform actions, both in terms of an agent not having right to perform an action and so needing to cooperate, and also when assessing the risk involved in a plan in relation to the rights of other. Secondly, as Marsh [11] points out, an agent's trust in another is dependent on the action being considered. This would provide a richer basis for plan selection if incorporated into the assessment of plans, but at a cost of increasing the overhead of modelling others. In order to take further advantage of the dynamic multi-agent nature of the environment further exploration of these and other issues will be required. Nevertheless, in this paper we propose an effective mechanism for cooperative plan selection that moves us a step forward towards to better exploiting the potential benefits of the multi-agent domain.

Acknowledgements Thanks to Kevin Bryson and the anonymous referees for many heipful comments.

References

1. M. E. Bratman, D. Israel, and M. Pollack. Plans and resource-bounded practical reasoning. *Computational Intelligence*, 4:349–355, 1988.
2. C. Castelfranchi and R. Falcone. Principles of trust for MAS: Cognitive anatomy, social importance, and quantification. In *Proceedings of the Third International Conference on Multi-Agent Systems*, pages 72–79, 1998.
3. C. Castelfranchi, M. Miceli, and A. Cesta. Dependence relations among autonomous agents. In E. Werner and Y. Demazeau, editors, *Decentralized AI 3*, pages 215–227. Elsevier Science Publishers, 1992.
4. M. Deutsch. Cooperation and trust: Some theoretical notes. In M. R. Jones, editor, *Nebraska Symposium on Motivation*, pages 275–319. University of Nebraska Press, 1962.
5. M. d'Inverno, D. Kinny, M. Luck, and M. Wooldridge. A formal specification of dMARS. In Singh, Rao, and Wooldridge, editors, *Intelligent Agents IV*, pages 155–176. Springer, 1998.
6. E. H. Durfee. Blissful ignorance: Knowing just enough to coordinate well. In *Proceedings of the First International Conference on Multi-Agent Systems*, pages 406–413, 1995.
7. D. Gambetta. Can we trust trust? In D. Gambetta, editor, *Trust: Making and Breaking Cooperative Relations*, pages 213–237. Blackwell, 1988.
8. M. P. Georgeff and A. L. Lansky. Reactive reasoning and planning. In *Proceedings of the Sixth National Conference on Artificial Intelligence*, pages 677–682, 1987.
9. D. Kinny, M. Ljungberg, A. Rao, E. Sonenberg, G. Tidhar, and E. Werner. Planned team activity. In *Proceedings of the Forth European Workshop on Modelling Autonomous Agents in a Multi-Agent World*, pages 227–256, 1992.
10. N. Luhmann. Familiarity, confidence, trust: Problems and alternatives. In D. Gambetta, editor, *Trust: Making and Breaking Cooperative Relations*, pages 94–107. Blackwell, 1988.
11. S. Marsh. *Formalising Trust as a Computational Concept*. PhD thesis, University of Stirling, 1994.
12. S. Marsh. Trust in distributed artificial intelligence. In C. Castelfranchi and E. Werner, editors, *Artificial Social Systems*, pages 94–112. Springer, 1994.
13. T. J. Norman, C. Sierra, and N. R. Jennings. Rights and commitments in multi-agent agreements. In *Proceedings of the Third International Conference on Multi-Agent Systems*, pages 222–229, 1998.
14. S. Russell and P. Norvig. *Artificial intelligence: A modern approach*. Prentice Hall, 1995.
15. M. Wooldridge and N. R. Jennings. Formalizing the cooperative problem solving process. In *Proceedings of the Thirteenth International Workshop on Distributed Artificial Intelligence*, pages 403–417, 1994.

Extending Social Reasoning to Cope with Multiple Partner Coalitions

Nuno David[1], Jaime Simão Sichman[2], and Helder Coelho[3]

[1] ISCTE/DCTI, Department of Information and Technology Sciences, Lisbon, Portugal
Nuno.David@iscte.pt
[2] LTI/PCS/EP/USP, University of São Paulo, São Paulo, Brazil
jaime@pcs.usp.br
[3] DI/FC/UL, University of Lisbon, Lisbon, Portugal
hcoelho@di.fc.ul.pt

Abstract. We present a utility-driven rationality and a complementary-driven rationality based model, relative to multiple partner coalitions, motivated by relations of dependence and instrumental goal adoption. For this purpose, we analyze social dependency patterns and its corresponding dependency networks. The networks are used as a source of quantitative and qualitative information with which an agent is able to choose the best set of partners and adequate proposals to form coalitions. An e-commerce example is presented, showing the usefulness of the mechanism in real world multi-agent systems.

1 Introduction

In some classes of multi-agent systems (MAS), the notion of autonomy usually suggests that agents do not necessarily attempt to do what is requested of them. This so-called non-benevolence assumption is frequently undertaken from two divergent points of view: (1) a quantitative utility oriented perspective, from which the most obvious examples are game theoretic models (e.g. [9]), or (2) a socio-psychological perspective, from which we may refer to the theory of dependence and social power [1][2]. Common to both perspectives is the problem around the choice of partners and proposals for coalition formation. With respect to the first approach, choice of partners and proposals has been fundamentally associated with the classic principle of economic rationality (maximizing the agent's expected utility as suggested by decision theory, (e.g. [3])). As for the second approach the literature is not so extensive. Sichman and his partners [5][6] adopt a pure complementary-driven rationality and propose a taxonomy of *dependency situations* as a criterion for choosing partners susceptible to accept proposals of coalitions. Nevertheless, the latest research does not consider multiple partner coalitions and the taxonomy is solely based on the agents' goals, beyond the set of possible plans, actions and its corresponding costs, which are required for an effective proposal of coalition.

In this paper, we extend the *social reasoning mechanism* [6] and present both a utility-driven rationality (quantitative) and a complementary-driven rationality (dependence) based model, relative to multiple partner coalitions, motivated by relations of dependence and instrumental goal adoption [1][2]. To achieve this aim, we analyze social dependency patterns and model its corresponding dependency networks with the concepts of *and-* and *or-dependencies* [1] and *inverse dependence relations*. Such networks are utilized as a source of quantitative and qualitative information with which an agent is able to decide about the best set of partners and adequate proposals in order to form multiple partner coalitions. Specifically, we advocate that a preliminary selection of adequate offered goals, plans and actions with respect to a proposal is intimately related to qualitative notions of dependency situations between partners. On the other hand, the final selection of actions to be effectively proposed to the partners depends closely on quantitative measures of dependence between partners. We conclude with a practical example in the field of e-commerce in the Internet. The example involves coalitions of companies in the software industry, where the adoption of each other's "service packages" for software reuse is a strategic advantage.

2   The Social Reasoning Mechanism

The social reasoning mechanism allows an agent to reason about the capabilities of others in order to answer such questions as whether his goals and plans are feasible and/or to assess how he stands in relation to other agents in the agency. Consequently, an agent must have a data structure where this information about the others is stored. Such data structure is called an *external description* - a private data structure that holds for every agent, including himself, a corresponding entry describing the *goals* an agent wants to achieve; the *actions* an agent is able to perform; the *resources* an agent is able to use; and the *plans* an agent wants to execute, making use of any actions and resources in order to achieve a certain goal.

We start by assuming a finite set of agents Ag. The agent $ag_o \in Ag$ is a generic agent, designated *object* agent, whose social properties are going to be analyzed by a *subject* agent. It is quite often the case when the subject and the object of social reasoning analysis are one and the same, and we will consider this fact hereinafter, i.e., the agent ag_o represents both the *subject* and *object* agents. The external description of the object *agent* ag_o, regarding some third party *agent* ag_t, **entry**, is defined as follows: $Ext_{ag_o}(ag_t) =_{def} \{G_{ag_o}(ag_t), A_{ag_o}(ag_t), R_{ag_o}(ag_t), P_{ag_o}(ag_t)\}$, where $G_{ag_o}(ag_t)$ is a set of goals, $A_{ag_o}(ag_t)$ is a set of actions, $R_{ag_o}(ag_t)$ is a set of resources and $P_{ag_o}(ag_t)$ is a set of plans (we do not analyse resources dependencies but see [6] for a preliminary analysis). A plan $p=(id_{goal}(p), I(p))$ that supposedly achieves some goal given by its goal identity $id_{goal}(p)$ comprises a set of instantiated actions $I(p)$, each one of them $i \in I(p)$ corresponding to some action given by its instantiated action identity $id_{action}(i)$. These actions needed by a plan do not necessarily belong to every agent's set of controlled actions and thus an agent may *depend* on others in order to carry out a plan and attain a particular goal.

In the present work, we use two quantities in the external description: the importance given by the *third party* agent ag_t to each one of his goals $g \in G_{ag_o}(ag_t)$, denoted by $w_{ag_o}(ag_t, g)$, and the cost given by the *third party* agent ag_t to each one of his controlled actions $a \in A_{ag_o}(ag_t)$, denoted by $c_{ag_o}(ag_t, a)$. Notice that the expected cost for each instantiated action in a plan depends on the set of costs given by all agents that are able to execute the action in the agency. From the point of view of the *object* agent ag_o, an action is said to be *available* if there is, at least, one *third party* agent ag_t represented in his external description Ext_{ag_o} that is able to perform it (maybe the object agent himself). The predicate $feasible_{ag_o}(p)$ is true if for every instantiated action in the plan p the corresponding action is available. If a plan is feasible, some needed actions and the corresponding costs may be controlled by some agents but not by others. Therefore, plan expected costs are calculated dynamically and are not explicitly represented in the external description. If a plan is not feasible its expected cost will be undefined.

2.1 Inverse dependence relations

We adopt a definition of dependence based on the notion of *action-dependencies*. Let E_{ag_o} be the set of all agents represented in the external description Ext_{ag_o} of *object* agent ag_o. We say an *object* agent ag_o has an *action-dependency* relative to a plan p and an action a, if the *object* agent ag_o is not able to perform the action but there is one other *third party* agent ag_t member of E_{ag_o} who is able to perform it:

$$a\_dep(ag_o,p,a) \equiv_{def} \exists (i \in I(p)) (id_{action}(i)=a \wedge a \notin A_{ag_o}(ag_o) \wedge \exists (ag_t \in E_{ag_o}) (a \in A_{ag_o}(ag_t))). \qquad (1)$$

An *object* agent ag_o has a dependency on a *third party* agent ag_t, in regard to a specific goal g, according to the plans the *object* agent thinks the *source* agent ag_s has, iff (1) the *object* agent ag_o has the goal g in his set of goals $G_{ag_o}(ag_o)$; (2) there is a plan for goal g in the set of plans $P_{ag_o}(ag_s)$ that the *object* agent thinks the *source* agent ag_s has, and (3) the *object* agent ag_o has, at least, one action-dependency corresponding to some instantiated action in the plan for which the action is available in the set of actions $A_{ag_o}(ag_t)$ that the *object* agent thinks the *third party* agent ag_t has, i.e. the *third party* agent is able to perform the action according to the *object* agent's beliefs:

$$dep\_on(ag_o,ag_t,g,ag_s) \equiv_{def} \exists (g \in G_{ag_o}(ag_o), p \in P_{ag_o}(ag_s)) \qquad (2)$$
$$(id_{goal}(p)=g \wedge \exists (i \in I(p), a \in A_{ag_o}(ag_t)) (a\_dep(ag_o,p,a) \wedge a=id_{action}(i))).$$

Dependency situations (dep-sits) are based on the distinction between social cooperation and social exchange [2] and local and non-local believed dependencies [6]. An object agent ag_o is Mutually Dependent on a third party agent ag_t for some goal g, according to the plans the object agent thinks the source agent ag_s has, if the object agent and the third party agent depend on each other for goal g, according to the plans the object agent believes the source agent has. While a Mutual Dependency between the object agent ag_o and the third party agent ag_t interprets a bilateral dependency concerning the same goal g, a Reciprocal Dependency translates a bilateral dependency in regard to two different goals g and g':

$$MD(ag_o,ag_t,g,ag_s) \equiv_{def} dep\_on(ag_o,ag_t,g,ag_s) \wedge dep\_on(ag_t,ag_o,g,ag_s). \qquad (3)$$
$$RD(ag_o,ag_t,g,g',ag_s) \equiv_{def} dep\_on(ag_o,ag_t,g,ag_s) \wedge dep\_on(ag_t,ag_o,g',ag_s) \wedge g \neq g'.$$

Moreover, if the object agent ag_o concludes there is a mutual dependency with the third party agent ag_t for goal g, according to his own set of plans, but he can not reach the same conclusion using the set of plans he believes the third party agent has, then there is a Local Believed Mutual Dependency: $LBMD(ag_o,ag_t,g) \equiv_{def} MD(ag_o,ag_t,g,ag_o) \wedge \neg MD(ag_o,ag_t,g,ag_t)$. However, if the object agent also reaches the same conclusion using the plans he believes the third party agent has, he will infer a Mutual Believed Mutual Dependency (MBMD).

Table 1. Dependency situations as seen by the subject/object agent. Column headers indicate dependencies inferred according to the object agent's set of plans and line headers according to the plans the object agent thinks the third party agent has: Mutual Believed Mutual Dependencies, Local Believed Mutual Dependencies, Mutual Believed Reciprocal Dependencies, Local Believed Reciprocal Dependencies and Unilateral Dependencies.

$P_{ag_o}(ag_o)$ $P_{ag_o}(ag_t)$	$MD(ag_o,ag_t,g,ag_o)$		$RD(ag_o,ag_t,g,g',ag_o)$		$dep\_on(ag_o,ag_t,g,ag_o)$		$\neg dep\_on(ag_o,ag_t,g,ag_o)$	
$MD(ag_o,ag_t,g,ag_t)$	MBMD	(1)	LBRD	(2)	UD	(3)	IND	(4)
$RD(ag_o,ag_t,g,g',ag_t)$	LBMD	(5)	MBRD	(6)	UD	(7)	IND	(8)
$dep\_on(ag_t,ag_o,g,ag_t)$	LBMD	(9)	LBRD	(10)	UD	(11)	IND	(12)
$dep\_on(ag_o,ag_t,g,ag_t)$	LBMD	(13)	LBRD	(14)	UD	(15)	IND	(16)
$\neg dep\_on(ag_t,ag_o,g,ag_t)$	LBMD	(17)	LBRD	(18)	UD	(19)	IND	(20)

As shown in the table, the referred taxonomy of dep-sits is a very general one. A detailed analysis on the referred set of dep-sits may look for further composition of local dependencies. Suppose that some object agent finds himself in situation number eleven (11). He will infer a Unilateral Dependency (UD) with the third party agent. Yet, the third party agent is also unilaterally dependent on him according to the plans he believes the third party agent has. This may as well be an incentive for cooperation or social exchange. Even though the object agent and the third party agent plans must be necessarily different (considering $E_{ag_o}(ag_o)=E_{ag_t}(ag_o) \wedge E_{ag_t}(ag_t)=E_{ag_o}(ag_t)$) each agent thinks that he depends on the other according to his own plans. The crucial point to note is that a single third party agent dependency on the object agent, inferred according to the plans the object agent thinks the third party has, assigns some sort of social (strategic) power to the object agent over the third party agent as well. In fact, if the object agent finds some sort of dependence on the third party agent, according to his own plans, he might be open to influence the third party agent to collaborate by using his power over what he thinks the third party agent beliefs are. Note that even if one or both agents do not believe that the other's plans are right (e.g. do not achieve the intended goals), they might be open to collaborate in order to attain their own goals. This does not necessarily breaks a principle of sincerity assumption: both agents may be aware of the fact; still, they believe the other party beliefs are wrong and theirs are right.

We call a third party agent dependency on the object agent inferred according to the plans the object agent thinks the third party has, a Remote Believed Inverse Dependency: $RBID(ag_o,ag_t,g) \equiv_{def} dep\_on(ag_t,ag_o,g,ag_t)$. Conversely, we call a third party agent dependency on the object agent, inferred according to the object agent's set of plans, a Local Believed Inverse Dependency: $LBID(ag_o,ag_t,g) \equiv_{def} dep\_on(ag_t,ag_o,g,ag_o)$.

3 Dependency and Strategic Reasoning

Usually, after a proposal, there may be three subsequent basic outcomes: the potential partner accepts the proposal without further demands; rejects the proposal; or makes a counter-proposal in order to reach an agreement, which may partially satisfy all parties involved. In effect, the principal vehicle for carrying out negotiation activities is the exchange of proposals and counter-proposals. Moreover, to reject an offer and not to make a counter-proposal may well lead the other party to break off negotiation [4]. The initial choice of potential partners should, therefore, be viewed in *strategic* terms. Not only should the proponent have in hands a first valuable proposal, sufficiently strong to lead the potential partner to collaborate, but also be able to control other alternative propositions, which may be needed to deal with the potential partners' further counter-proposals.

Most of existing work in strategic reasoning in MAS has been exclusively based on pure decision utility-based models (e.g. [8]). However, when reasoning about coalition formation in cognitive domains, the commitment to a minimal cost solution associated with a certain set of possible partners does not necessarily contributes to the proponent's predicative power on their intentional decisions and thus their susceptibility to accept proposals of coalition. For this end, prior reasoning on the third party agents' goals and dependencies is needed (social power/bargaining). Assume that some object agent ag_o is pursuing some goal g_e and commits to some feasible plan p_e that we call the object agent's *engaged goal* and *engaged plan*, respectively. If the engaged plan is feasible then all action-dependencies expected costs can be computed since all actions and its corresponding set of costs are available in the agency. In reality, plan choices to achieve a specific goal may depend on a number of criteria such as plan feasibility conditions, number of action-dependencies, and/or instantiated actions (expected) costs. Analogously, two classes of criteria for selection of multiple partners relative to some engaged goal $g_e \in G_{ag_o}(ag_o)$, and engaged plan $p_e \in P_{ag_o}(ag_o)$ are identified, namely, complementary (C) and utility (U) oriented choices:

(C1) Number of action-dependencies the third party agent originates on the object agent's chosen plan. Conjunctive dependencies or *and-dependencies* [1] augment the degree of power/dependence between agents. We call *multi-action and-dependencies* to a set of actions if every action makes the same agent dependent on another relative to the same plan. In purely complementary terms, the higher is the number of action-dependencies that make the object agent dependent on the third party agent with reference to the engaged plan, the more the object agent depends on the third party agent. On the other hand, such condition may decrease the number of expected partners in the coalition and thus the overall communication flow.

(C2) Number of goals that make the third party agent dependent on the object agent. Prior effective planning and preparation are among the most critical elements to achieve further negotiation objectives. This requires an effort from the proponent agent, not only to specify his objectives and goals, but also to understand the possible partner's perspective and identify his needs and goals. This point is crucial for social exchange, where the object agent must find which third party agent goals originate reciprocal dependencies if coupled with the object agent's engaged goal. The higher is the number of goals that are identified, the larger will be the set of possible alternative proposals. We call the goals that may be offered to a third party agent the object agent's *offered-goals*. Offered goals are captured by the notion of *multi-goal and-dependencies* - the third party agent depends on the object agent for multiple goals. Offered goals comprise any goal g in the set of goals that the object agent thinks the third party agent has $G_{ag_o}(ag_t)$, which make the third party agent ag_t dependent on the object agent ag_o, respectively, according to the object agent's set of plans or the set of plans the object agent thinks the third party agent has, i.e., local or remote believed inverse dependencies:

$$Off\text{-}Goals_{ag_o}(ag_t) \equiv_{def} \{g \in G_{ag_o}(ag_t) \mid LBID(ag_o, ag_t, g) \vee RBID(ag_o, ag_t, g)\} . \tag{4}$$

(C3) Number of available plans for each offered goal *Multi-plan or-dependencies* result from multiple action-dependencies within different plans that make the third party agent dependent on the object agent for the same goal. The set of all possible *offered plans* comprises any plan p in the object agent's set of plans $P_{ag_o}(ag_o)$ or in the set of plans that the object agent thinks the third party has $P_{ag_o}(ag_t)$, that may contribute to any offered goal:

$$Off\text{-}Plans_{ag_o}(ag_t) \equiv_{def} \{p \in (P_{ag_o}(ag_o) \cup P_{ag_o}(ag_t)) \mid \exists (g \in Off\text{-}Goals_{ag_o}(ag_t))(id_{goal}(p)=g)\}. \tag{5}$$

Interestingly, the existence of *multi-plan or-dependencies* may be a strategically advantage for all parties involved, enriching the range of available solutions, and consequently the possible existence of satisfactory proposals for both parties.

(C4) Number of actions controlled by the object agent and not controlled by the third party agent for each offered plan. The set of *offered actions* comprises any action a in the object agent's set of controlled actions $A_{ag_o}(ag_t)$ that make the third party agent ag_t dependent on the object agent ag_o for any offered plan:

$$Off\text{-}Actions_{ag_o}(ag_t) \equiv_{def} \{a \in A_{ag_o}(ag_o) \mid \exists (p \in Off\text{-}Plans_{ag_o}(ag_t))(a\_dep_{ag_o}(ag_t, p, a))\} . \tag{6}$$

Notice that there is the case of *multi-plan or-dependencies* with respect to a same offered goal, where for each offered plan there is a **distinct** offered action, and the case where a set of offered plans for a same offered goal hold one **same** offered action. The latest situation is highly valuable since the object agent may offer a number of alternative solutions to the third party agent with a single offered action. Moreover, a unique offered action can also contribute to accomplish multiple offered non-parallel goals, yielding a strong influencing power over the third party agent.

(U1) The cost each third party agent assigns to each object agent's action-dependency in the object agent's engaged plan. The choice of a plan has inherently attached an individual internal commitment to the object agent: finding a set of preferred partners, each one chosen from the set of possible partners associated with each action-dependency. For each action-dependency and from the corresponding set of possible partners, the third party agent assigning the lowest cost to the action is chosen among the ones who share the highest degree of dependence. Indeed, even though a proposal may be rejected because of misleading beliefs involving one or both parties or simply disagreement of proposals and its costs, the proponent may hold other alternative possible partners for his action-dependency.

(U2) The cost of the offered actions. May be used as a function regulator to the third party agent degree of dependence on the object agent. Suppose the third party agent holds a great amount of dependence on the object agent but the object agent costs for executing his *offered actions* are expected to be very high. Consequently, it may not turn out to be a strategic advantage to collaborate, at least, from the object agent's point of view.

(U3) **The importance of the offered goal(s)**. A prioritization of the partners' goals shall be considered. Once again, this situation is more relevant for reciprocal dep-sit cases, as there may be several alternative goals to offer. Here, the strategic value rests, essentially, on which goals to offer when in the first stages of coalition proposal, beyond partner selection activities.

Frequently, negotiation fails to set clear objectives. Hence, when something has to be given, or the other party makes a proposal that rearranges the elements in a settlement, they are not in a position to evaluate new possibilities quickly and accurately [4]. Beyond the search for the best potential partners, there is equally a need to reason around the most adequate corresponding proposals to be sent. For this purpose, a specific social dependency network is established holding all possible offered actions and their costs to every possible offered plan, all possible offered plans to every possible offered goal, all possible offered goals and their importance to every possible partner, and all possible partners for each action-dependency and its corresponding expected cost. The result is a structural network of alternatives that can be used to reason about workable proposals and feasible arguments. Furthermore, when picking up the possible partners with the *highest* and *strongest* dep-sit, there is a good chance of achieving a quick agreement. The *highest* dep-sit is calculated with reference to a partial ordered set of dep-sits (e.g. see [5]). The *strength* accounts for an assessment on the number of the possible partner's *and-* and *or-dependencies* on the proponent. What we need is to quantify the *dimension* of the dependency network.

Different offered actions assign different degrees of power over an agent and thus contribute differently to each possible partner's strength of dependence. We define a function for every third party agent ag_t represented in the object agent's external description and for every action a available in the set of offered actions, adding value to actions contributing to a significant number of plans and goals. We call this function (offered) action strength:

$$\text{action-strength}_{ag_o}(ag_t, a) =_{def} (\Sigma_i\ N_{plans}(g^a_i) \cdot w_{ag_o}(ag_t, g^a_i)) / c_{ag_o}(ag_o, a)). \tag{7}$$

Here, g^a_i is any offered goal for which the offered action a contributes, $w_{ag_o}(ag_t, g^a_i)$ is the goal importance as given by the external description third party agent entry, $N_{plans}(g^a_i)$ is the number of offered plans for which the offered action a contributes and $c_{ag_o}(ag_o, a)$ is the cost of the offered action as given by the external description object agent entry. The third party agent ag_t dependence strength on the object agent ag_o is defined as the sum of all object agent's possible offered action strengths:

$$\text{dep-strength}_{ag_o}(ag_t) =_{def} \Sigma\ a \in \textbf{\textit{Offer-Actions}}_{ag_o}(ag_t)\ \text{action-strength}_{ag_o}(ag_t, a). \tag{8}$$

The first formula considers criteria C2, C3, U2 and U3, adding value to actions that contribute to a high number of offered plans and offered goals. The last criterion acts as a denominator, regulating the third party agent's dependency links importance and number, against the cost of the offered action. Finally, the notion of dependence strength considers the number of possible offered actions, i.e. criterion C4, and ponders and integrates their strength. While the latter definition identifies the most dependent possible partners on the proponent, the former is able to identify the partners' most valued needed actions with respect to selection of adequate proposals.

4 Multiple Partner Coalitions

Let $Action\text{-}Dep_{ag_o}(p_e)$ be the set of all object agent's action-dependencies with reference to his engaged plan p_e. For every action-dependency a^d in $Action\text{-}Dep_{ag_o}(p_e)$ there is a set of possible partners represented in the external description that are able to perform it. Furthermore, each possible partner will probably originate different dependence conditions. We want to find a set of ordered pairs (a^d, ag_t) – action-dependency / best possible partner – where for each action-dependency a^d in $Action\text{-}Dep_{ag_o}(p_e)$ there is one third party agent ag_t in the corresponding set of possible partners $Pos\text{-}Partners_{ag_o}(p_e, a^d)$ for which the object agent ag_o sends him a proposal of coalition. This is the problem of multiple partner coalitions associated with criterion C1, which may not be a mere generalization problem from two partner coalitions if communication flow is a critical problem in the system.

4.1 Choice of partners

At this point, we define a new strategy to identify third party agents that are susceptible to accept coalition proposals, while trying to decrease the proponent's costs and communication flow. The strategy assumes a sequence of priorities but any other sequence or composition of weighed functions could be used.

Let $highest\text{-}dsit_{ag_o}:(superset(E_{ag_o}), G_{ag_o}(ag_o), P_{ag_o}(ag_o)) \rightarrow superset(E_{ag_o})$ be a function where, given a set of agents in the object agent's external description, the object agent's engaged goal g_e and engaged plan p_e, returns the subset of agents with the highest inferred dep-sit using the set $\{p_e\}$ as the object agent's set of plans. Also, the function $n\text{-}adep_{ag_o}:(E_{ag_o}, P_{ag_o}(ag_o)) \rightarrow N$ returns the number of action-dependencies in a given engaged plan p_e that make the object agent dependent on a third party ag_t. Assume that the plan p_e is feasible. Then for each action-dependency a^d in the engaged plan p_e there is a non-empty set of possible partners $PPartners$ that are able to perform it.

Definition 1 If $ag, ag' \in PPartners$ then $ag' \leq_{partner} ag$ iff:

- $ag'=ag$, or
- $ag' \notin highest\text{-}dsit(PPartners, g_e, p_e) \wedge ag \in highest\text{-}dsit(PPartners, g_e, p_e)$,
- $ag', ag \in highest\text{-}dsit(PPartners, g_e, p_e) \wedge dep\text{-}strength(ag') < dep\text{-}strength(ag)$,
- $ag', ag \in highest\text{-}dsit(PPartners, g_e, p_e) \wedge dep\text{-}strength(ag')=dep\text{-}strength(ag) \wedge c(ag', a^d) > c(ag, a^d)$,
- $ag', ag \in highest\text{-}dsit(PPartners, g_e, p_e) \wedge dep\_strength(ag')=dep\text{-}strength(ag) \wedge c(ag', a^d) = c(ag, a^d) \wedge n\text{-}adep(p_e, ag') < n\text{-}adep(p_e, ag)$.

The relation $\leq_{partner} \subseteq PPartners \times PPartners$ is reflexive, anti-symmetric and transitive and thus a partial ordered set of possible partners. Let S_{max} be the set in which all of its elements are major elements of $S^c_{max} = PPartners - S_{max}$ and hence also maximal elements in S_{max}, that is, (i) if $ag \in S_{max}$ and $ag' \in S^c_{max}$ then $ag' \leq_{partner} ag$ and; (ii) for all ag

$\in S_{max}$ and $ag' \in S_{max}$, if $ag' \leq_{partner} ag$ then $ag'=ag$. The choice of a partner is defined as follows: $decision_{a-partner}=_{def} random(S_{max})$.

In conclusion, for each action-dependency $a^d \in Action\text{-}Dep_{ag_O}(p_e)$ in the engaged plan p_e, the preferred partner is chosen from the corresponding set of possible partners $Pos\text{-}Partners_{ag_O}(p_e,a^d)$ among the ones originating the highest dep-sit, with the highest dependence strength, with the lowest action-dependency cost, inducing the highest number of action-dependencies in the engaged plan. If two third party agents share the same dependence conditions and costs, the one who is potentially able to execute the highest number of action-dependencies in the engaged plan is chosen, i.e., partner choices will try to decrease communication flow, still preventing weak dependent agents from overcoming strong dependent ones.

4.2 Choice of Proposals

4.2.1 Offered Goals
Suppose that the object agent infers a mutual dependency (locally or mutually believed) with the preferred partner. A logical and immediate proposed offered goal is the one that originates the mutual dependency. In reality, except for unilateral dependencies, the set of chosen offered goals for the preferred partner ag_t, engaged goal g_e and plan p_e results from offered goals that originate the dep-sit:

$$C\text{-}OGoals(ag_t,g_e,p_e)\equiv \qquad\qquad (9)$$

$$\{g_e\} \qquad\qquad\qquad\qquad if\ dep\text{-}sit\ (ag_t,g_e,p_e)=MBMD\ or\ LBMD$$

$$\{g' \in Off\text{-}Goals(ag_t) \mid LBID(ag_o,ag_t,g') \wedge RBID(ag_t,ag_o,g')\} \qquad if\ dep\text{-}sit(ag_t,g_e,p_e)=MBRD$$

$$\{g' \in Off\text{-}Goals(ag_t) \mid LBID(ag_o,ag_t,g')\} \qquad\qquad if\ dep\text{-}sit(ag_t,g_e,p_e)=LBRD$$

$$\{g' \in Off\text{-}Goals(ag_t) \mid RBID(ag_o,ag_t,g')\} \qquad\qquad if\ dep\text{-}sit(ag_t,g_e,p_e)=UD$$

$$\varnothing \qquad\qquad\qquad\qquad\qquad if\ dep\text{-}sit(ag_t,g_e,p_e)=IND$$

Notice in the Unilateral Dependency (UD) case that all chosen offered goals result necessarily from the set of plans the object agent thinks the preferred partner has, i.e., Remote Believed Inverse Dependencies (RBID). If there are no such dependencies, this set may be empty, meaning that the preferred partner has zero dependence strength on the object agent. If that is the case, then the object agent holds little or no influencing power over the preferred partner, which illustrates the possible existence of different degrees of influencing power for a same dependency situation.

4.2.2 Offered Plans
Beyond the intended effects on the preferred partner, proposed offered plans also play an important role on the proponent's needs, depending on the type of inferred dep-sit. For example, being a mutual dep-sit case, both parties are necessarily pursuing the same and identical goal. Therefore, the offered plan should be feasible in order to meet the proponent's goals, which are also the preferred partner's goals. Notice, however, that the existence of a single plan believed by both parties and originating a Mutual Believed Mutual Dependency (MBMD) implies two conditions: (i) there is a single plan for each set of plans in the external description that originate a mutual dependency; (ii) the two plans are identical. Being this case an exception rather than a

rule, proposed offered actions should mostly result from mutually or locally believed plans so as to influence the preferred partner towards the proponents' goals and plans. On the contrary, if there is but a Unilateral Dependency (UD) then all offered plans are necessarily calculated according to the set of plans the object agent thinks the third party agent has. Such plans have little or no impact on the proponent mainly if his engaged goal g_e differs from all goals associated with the set of offered plans.

Let the set $C\text{-}OPlans(ag_t,g_e,p_e)_l$ be a subset of all offered plans $Off\text{-}Plans(ag_t)$, calculated according to the set of chosen offered goals $C\text{-}OGoals(ag_t,g_e,p_e)$, i.e., $C\text{-}OPlans(ag_t,g_e,p_e)_l \equiv \{p \in Off\text{-}Plans(ag_t) \mid \exists (g \in C\text{-}OGoals(ag_t,g_e,p_e))(id_{goal}(p)=g)\}$.

Definition 2 If $p1, p2 \in C\text{-}OPlans(ag_t,g_e,p_e)_l$ then $p1 \leq_{plan} p2$ iff:

- $p1 = p2$, or
- $feasible(p1)=false \wedge feasible(p2)=true$, or
- $feasible(p1)=feasible(p2)=true \wedge p1 \notin (P_{ag_0}(ag_0) \cap P_{ag_0}(ag_t)) \wedge p2 \in (P_{ag_0}(ag_0) \cap P_{ag_0}(ag_t))$, or
- $feasible(p1)=feasible(p2)=true \wedge p1,p2 \notin (P_{ag_0}(ag_0) \cap P_{ag_0}(ag_t)) \wedge p1 \in P_{ag_0}(ag_t) \wedge p2 \in P_{ag_0}(ag_0)$.

The set $(C\text{-}OPlans(ag_t,g_e,p_e)_l, \leq_{plan})$ is an ordered set by $\leq_{plan}$. Assume the set of chosen offered plans $C\text{-}OPlans(ag_t,g_e,p_e)$ to be the set in which all of its elements are major elements of $C\text{-}OPlans(ag_t,g_e,p_e)^C = C\text{-}OPlans(ag_t,g_e,p_e)_l - C\text{-}Oplans(ag_t,g_e,p_e)$. The best feasible offered plans are the ones believed by both agents. Local believed plans are also preferred to non-local believed plans.

4.2.3   Offered Actions

Let $C\text{-}OActions(ag_t,g_e,p_e)_l$ be the subset of all offered actions associated with the set of chosen offered plans, i.e,
$C\text{-}OActions(ag_t,g_e,p_e)_l \equiv \{a \in Off\text{-}Actions(ag_t) \mid \exists (p \in C\text{-}OPlans(ag_t,g_e,p_e))(\exists (i \in I(p))(id_{action}(i)=a))\}$.
Assume that $max\text{-}strength_a$ is the maximum action strength value in $C\text{-}OActions(ag_t,g_e,p_e)_l$. The set of chosen offered actions $C\text{-}OActions(ag_t,g_e,p_e)$ are those members of $C\text{-}OActions(ag_t,g_e,p_e)_l$ that share the highest action strength.

In conclusion, the preferred offered action is chosen from the object agent's set of controlled actions associated with (1) offered goals originated by the highest dep-sit; (2) feasible and a convenient source set of plans; (3) the maximum observed action strength. The final proposal for each preferred partner ag_t, relative to the object agent's engaged goal g_e and engaged plan p_e is therefore:

$$decide_{prop}(ag_t,g_e,p_e) =_{def} \qquad\qquad\qquad\qquad\qquad\qquad\qquad (10)$$

$$
\begin{cases}
undef & \text{if } C\text{-}OActions(ag_t,g_e,p_e)=\varnothing \\
(a, P(a), G(P(a))) & \text{if } C\text{-}OActions(ag_t,g_e,p_e)\neq\varnothing
\end{cases}
$$

where,

$a = random(C\text{-}OActions(ag_t,g_e,p_e))$
$P(a) = \{p \in C\text{-}OPlans(ag_t,g_e,p_e) \mid \exists (i \in I(p))(id_{action}(i)=a)\}$
$G(P(a)) = \{g \in C\text{-}OGoals(ag_t,g_e,p_e) \mid \exists (p \in P(a))(id_{goal}(p)=g)\}$

5 Example: Multi-Agent Contracts for Software Reuse

Experimentation was the way to evaluate our ideas about the social reasoning mechanism and to check the relevance of the hybrid decision rationality. Since we have limited space we present a piece of a small experiment concerning coalition formation for software reuse. Here a company has a set of projects (goals) and different alternative configurations (plans) of packages (actions) to build its software products. Each project is associated with a given importance and each package with its cost. Companies may be willing to set up a strategically agreement with the others, instead of building service packages from scratch. Suppose there are two agents known to Company A. The external description of Company A is the following:

```
Identity:   <CompA luke.somewhere.org 1090>           Goals:    SecureBrowser (90) / WordProc (100)
Actions:    EnglishThesaurus (10) / MultiLingThesaurus (12) / TCPPack (32)
Plans:      WordProc:= MultiLingThesaurus, HtmlEditPackS1.1, GraphEditPack.
            WordProc:= EnglishThesaurus, HtmlEditPackP, GraphEditPack.
Identity:   <CompB zeus.compB.org 1094>               Goals:    EMailClient (55)
Actions:    GraphEditPack (23) / HtmlEditPackS1.1 (25), SEditor (9)
Plans:      EMailClient:= TCPPack, SEditor.
Identity:   <CompC compC.org 1095>                    Goals:    SecureBrowser (110) / DBaseClient (65)
Actions:    SQLPack (4) / HtmlEditPackS1.1 (23)
Plans:      WordProc:= MultiLingThesaurus, HtmlEditPackS1.1, GraphEditPack.
            DBaseClient:= MultiLingThesaurus, SQLPack.
```

The agent CompA will adopt WordProc as his active goal and choose the plan with the least expected cost set of actions. He then builds his dependency networks:

```
The engaged goal is: WordProc (100), my dependency network with reference to goal <WordProc> is:
<CompA>
--------- WordProc (100)
       |-------- WordProc:= MultiLingThesaurus, HtmlEditPackS1.1, GraphEditPack. (Feasible EC:59.0)
       |       |--------- HtmlEditPackS1.1 (EC:24.0)
       |       |*******  <CompB 1094> (25.0)
       |       |         | <CompC 1095> (23.0)
       |       |         |---------
       |       | GraphEditPack (EC:23.0)
       |       |*******  <CompB 1094> (23.0)
       |       |         |---------
       |-------- WordProc:= EnglishThesaurus, HtmlEditPackP, GraphEditPack. (Feasible EC:66.0)
               |--------- HtmlEditPackP (EC:33.0)
               |*******  <CompC 1096> (33.0)
               |         |---------
               | GraphEditPack  (EC:23.0)
               |*******  <CompB 1094> (23.0)
                         |---------
The chosen plan is <WordProc:= MultiLingThesaurus, HtmlEditPackS1.1, GraphEditPack.>.
(. . .)
My possible partners, offered goals, plans and actions for my action-dependencies are:
 HtmlEditPackS1.1 and GraphEditPack
|------
    |<CompB zeus.compB.org 1094> /dep-sit: UD / dep-strength: 1.7 / dep-action cost: 25.0 and 23.0
    |------
      |EMailClient (55) (RBID)
      |--------
          |EMailClient:= TCPPack, SEditor. (NonLocalSource)
          |---------
              |TCPPack (32)
HtmlEditPackS1.1
|------
    |<CompC compC.org 1095> / dep-sit: MBMD / dep-strength: 25.6 / dep-action cost: 23.0
    |------
      |WordProc (110) (MBMD)
      |--------
      |   |WordProc:= MultiLingThesaurus, HtmlEditPackS1.1, GraphEditPack. (BothSources)
      |   |---------
      |   |    |MultiLingThesaurus (12)
      |   |    |------
      |   |WordProc:= EnglishThesaurus, HtmlEditPackP, GraphEditPack. (LocalSource)
      |   |---------
      |        |EnglishThesaurus (10)
      |        |------
      |DBaseClient (65) (RBID)
      |------
          |DBaseClient:= MultiLingThesaurus, SQLPack. (NonLocalSource)
          |---------
              |MultiLingThesaurus (12)
The selected partner(s) and proposal(s) are (dep-sit > dep-strength > action-cost > na-deps) :
| Needed action: <HtmlEditPackS1.1>          Chosen Partner: <CompC CompC.org 1095>
```

```
Offered action: <MultiLingThesaurus>          Offered goals: <WordProc> / <DBaseClient>
I Needed action: <GraphEditPack>              Chosen Partner: <CompB zeus.compB.org 1094>
  Offered action: <TCPPack>                   Offered goals: <EMailClient>
Sending proposals of coalition to <CompC CompC.org 1095> and <CompB zeus.compB.org 1094> ...
```

There were two possible partners for the object agent CompA's missing package HtmlEDITPackS1.1 and one for GraphEditPack. Even though the agent CompB controls both packages, the object agent chose CompC for the first package in the coalition. In effect, CompA holds a significant flexibility for negotiating with CompC: (1) both agents are pursuing the same project and share a Mutual Believed Mutual Dependence (MBMD); (2) CompC's dependence strength (=25.6) is visibly high compared to CompB (=1.7); (2) in fact, CompA is aware that the package MultiLingThesaurus is an important one to CompC in two of his current projects, contributing to a strong dependence strength (WordProc and DBaseClient); (3) ComC assigns a lower cost than CompB to ComA's action-dependency HtmlEDITPackS1.1. Finally, CompC's missing package MultLingThesaurus belongs to a plan believed by both sources, holds the highest action strength in the network and therefore is chosen as one of the final proposals.

One may notice that CompA holds only a Unilateral Dependency (UD) on CompB. However, the power of CompA over CompB is not insignificant, according to the plans CompA thinks CompB has. In effect, CompA may be able to instrumentalize the Remote Believed Inverse Dependency (RBID) with his proposal involving the offered goal EmailCLient and the offered action TCPPack. Below we partially show CompB's dependency networks. He is in fact dependent on CompA for the proposed action TCPack and goal EMailClient. He also infers that he controls CompA's needed action GraphEditPack, according to the plans he thinks CompA has. Once more, Unilateral Dependencies (UD) do not necessarily mean zero dependence strength and negotiation power. Coalitions may in fact take place with different subjective views of the world. Notice that such situation was possible with consistent beliefs about each other's goals and controlled actions, even though they do not share the same plans.

```
Received a coalition proposal (PROP <CompA luke.somewhere.org 1090> (WordProc/GraphEditPack UD EmailClient/TCPPack))
My dependence network is:      <CompB>
                         ---------- EMailClient (55)
                         |--------- EMailClient:= TCPPack, SEditor. (EC:41.0)
                                   |-------- TCPPack (EC:32.0)
                                   |-------- <CompA 1090> (32.0)
My possible partners, offered goals, plans and actions for my action dependencies are:
 TCPPack
|------
  I<CompA luke.somewhere.org 1090> / dep-sit: UD / dep-strength: 12.8 / dep-action cost: 32.0
  |--------
      IWordProc (100) (RBID)
      |-------
          IWordProc:= MultiLingThesaurus, HtmlEditPackS1.1, GraphEditPack.(NonLocalSource)
          |---------
          I    IHtmlEditPackS1.1 (25)
          I    |------
          I        IGraphEditPack (23)
          I        |------
          IWordProc:= EnglishThesaurus, HtmlEditPackP, GraphEditPack. (NonLocalSource)
          |---------
              IGraphEditPack (23)
(. . .) I will accept the proposal because I do not have a better partner.
```

6   Conclusions

There may be different degrees of influencing power for a same dependency situation. Inverse dependencies are valuable tools for reasoning strategically on the partners' needs and proposals. The network of inverse dependencies establishes a structural network of alternative proposals with relevant qualitative and quantitative information about possible courses of action to the proponent. The dimension of such social dependency network may be used strategically as a quantitative measure for selecting partners and proposals to form coalitions.

Our analysis and experimental results suggests that dependence based choices of partners and proposals are obligatorily integrated issues. Furthermore, while the choice of a goal with respect to a proposal is closely related to the set of observed dep-sits, the choice of relevant actions is related to quantitative measures of dependence. This means that it is essential to make an assessment on the set of available proposals before choosing adequate partners to form a coalition. Such view may be essential on a number of negotiation and brokering protocols involving multicasting (e.g. contract net protocols [7]) and in large and open networks (e.g. the Internet). The proponent is able to concentrate his efforts from the start on the possible partners that are more susceptible to accept his proposals, decreasing the amount of control and content information exchange and, possibly, the time to find the most suitable partners in the agency.

One interesting result concerns the proponent's power of influencing a third party agent to form a coalition even though he may not believe the third party is dependent on him according to his own plans, but only according to the plans he believes the third party has. This is common and fundamental in real world applications, since the other agents' plans play an important role in any negotiating project. For example, one can not imagine two aircraft companies negotiating without considering both companies' carriers in the final coalition.

References

1. Cristiano Castelfranchi, Maria Miceli, Amedeo Cesta, *Dependence relations among autonomous agents*. In Proceedings of MAAMAW'92, Elsevier Science Publishers B. V., Amsterdam, pages 215-227, 1992.
2. Cristiano Castelfranchi, *Social power: a point missed in multi-agent, DAI and HCI*. In Proceedings of MAAMAW'90, pages 49-62, 1990.
3. Steven Ketchpel, *Forming coalitions in the face of uncertain rewards*. In proceedings of AAAI, pages 414-419, Seattle, WA, 1994.
4. Roy Lewicki, Joseph Litterer, *Negotiation*. Irwin, 1985.
5. Jaime Sichman and Yves Demazeau, *Exploiting social reasoning to enhance adaptation in open multi-agent systems*. In: Proceedings of SBIA'95, LNAI 991, J. Wainer and A. Carvalho editors, pages 253-263, LNAI, Springer-Verlag, 1995.
6. Jaime Sichman, Rosaria Conte, Yves Demazeau and Cristiano Castelfranchi, *A social reasoning mechanism based on dependence networks*. In Proceedings of ECAI'94, pages 188-192, 1994.
7. Reid Smith, *The contract net protocol: High-level communications and control is a distributed problem solver*. IEEE Transactions on computers, vol.29 (12), pages 1104-1113, 1980.
8. Park Sunju, Edmund Durfee and William Birmingham, *Advantages of strategic thinking in multiagent contracts (a mechanism and analysis)*. In Proceedings of ICMAS'96, MIT Press, pages 259-266, 1996.
9. G. Zlotkin and J. Rosenchein, *Coalition, cryptograpphy and stability: Mechanisms for coalition formation in task oriented domains*. In Proceedings of AAAI, pages 432-437, Seattle, WA, 1994.

Basic Mental Attitudes of a Collaborating Agent: Cognitive Primitives for MAS

Cristiano Castelfranchi , Rino Falcone

National Research Council - Institute of Psychology
Division of "Artificial Intelligence, Cognitive and Interaction Modelling"

cris@pscs2.irmkant.rm.cnr.it [*]

Abstract. . In this paper, we try to identify the relationships among three main (in our view) proposals of the basic mental attitudes in collaborative problem solving (the Toumela's theory of acting together, in particular the notion of *We-Intention*; the Grosz and Kraus' theory of collaboration, with special attention to the notion of *Intention-that*, and the Castelfranchi and Falcone' theory of Delegation-Adoption). We show several overlaps, convergencies, but also complementarities, contradictions and competitions among these theories. The aim of this paper is some clarification and systematisation of the necessary mental attitudes in agents' mind that characterise acting together and cooperating. We will not consider in this analysis other very important mental ingredients of complex forms of collaboration, like agents' motivations in taking part in collective activity, trust, and normative components: permissions, rights, norms, roles, etc.

1 Introduction

In the last ten years several important works have been done both in AI (particularly in the DAI and MAS domain) and in philosophy for a conceptually well grounded and formalised theory of various forms of collective activity, with particular attention to forms of acting together and collaborating[1] .

This work succeeded in arguing that to model and formalise a team cooperation it is necessary to model the minds of the involved agents: the beliefs of the agents about

---

[*] We would like to thank Maria Miceli and Frank Dignum for their comments. A special thank to Raimo Tuomela for his patient (although perhaps not completely successful) explanations. This research has been developed within the agreement between CNR and Provincia Autonoma di Trento, research project on *"Applicazioni avanzate di informatica"*.

[1] For ex. [Tuomela&Miller, 88; Tuomela, 98; Tuomela, 84; Levesque et al., 90; Grosz&Kraus, 96; Grosz&Kraus, 96; Jennings, 93; Haddadi, 96; Wooldridge&Jennings, 94; Rao et al., 92; Werner, 89&90; Singh, 95].

Very important is also the DAI and Multi-Agent System litterature on coordination, organisation, distributed planning, like: [Von Martial , 92; Malone et al., 88; O'Hare&Jennings, 96; Gasser, 91; Weiss&Sen, 98; Demazeau&Mueller, 90;] Ferber,

each other and the joint plan. However, we think that this approach is not sufficient to account for a group or to a truly cooperative work because a much richer representation of the individual social mind is needed [Conte&Castelfranchi, 95]. In fact in these models there is only a limited account of the individual mental states in cooperation. First, -as we will argue- one should explicitly model not only the beliefs about the intentions and the shares of the others, but also the goals about the actions and the intentions of the others [Grosz&Kraus, 96]: each member not only expects but wants that the others do their job [Castelfranchi&Falcone, 98]. And conversely one should model the social commitment to the others also in terms of delegation of goals/task and of compliance with the others' expectations: i.e. as goal-adoption [Castelfranchi, 91&95].

Moreover, although several of these approaches refer to and compare with each other; we have not really arrived yet to a systematisation of examples and concepts to be accounted for, of theoretical problems to be solved, and of the relationships among the different formal proposals. There are several overlaps and convergences among the different theories but where they are complementary, where contradictory and in competition, where redundant, it is not clear.

The aim of this paper is some clarification and systematisation of part of these problems: those referring to the necessary mental attitudes in agents' mind that characterise acting together and cooperating (in a broad sense). To arrive to this *basic ontology of the collaborative mind*, we will compare some of the competing attempts: our notions of *Reliance/Delegation*, *Coordination*, and *Goal-Adoption*; complex Tuomela's theory of acting together, in particular the crucial notion of *We-Intention*; Grosz and Kraus' theory of collaboration, with special attention to the notion of *Intention-that*. We will argue that

a) each of these theories identifies some of the very important 'primitives' necessary to characterise the mind of an agent in a collaborative activity;

b) they are really complementary.

We will examine also some limits of each approach and their differences. Finally we propose how those contributions should be integrated in a coherent conceptual model to be formalised. We will not discuss all the ingredients postulated by those models (for example, we do not discuss about mutual beliefs or shared plans) since our aim is to focus on the very primitives of the collaborative mind, and on the independent cognitive and practical *roots* of collaboration starting from individual (but social) action and mind [Castelfranchi, 98].

Notice that we do not consider here all or all the most important models of team work and joint plans in AI. We just consider the important approaches which provide us -on our view- some of the very basic, atomic component of a collaborating mind. Other models (for example [Wooldridge&Jennings, 94] or [Dunin-Keplicz&Verbrugge, 96]) take in fact into account some of these points and would not exposed to our criticisms (for example about not explicitly modelling X's goals about Y's actions). However, these advanced models are strongly concerned only with joint plans, and are not particularly interested in argumenting about their basic cognitive ingredients, which are, on the contrary, our focus and what we claim need to be clarified. We mean that there is not a careful theory of the basic forms of reliance, we-intention, goal-adoption, compliance, coordination, etc. and of their relationships, that should be the basis of modelling more complex phenomena like joint plans or social commitments.

We will not consider also in this analysis other very important mental ingredients of complex forms of collaboration, like agents' motivations in taking part in collective activity, trust, and normative components: permissions, rights, norms, roles, etc. Nor we discuss the objective basis of collaboration: the Dependence structure [Conte&Castelfranchi, 95]. What we discuss are just (some of) the basics of collaborative minds.

2 Reliance: making the other realise our goal

A goal-pursuing agent in a MA world is exposed to negative interferences and competition, but it has also a great opportunity: that of exploiting the action of other agents, i.e. of achieving its own goals doing noting (positive interferences). On the one side, this is very important for multiplying the 'powers' [Castelfranchi, 91] of the agent, i.e. augmenting the number of goals it can achieve. In fact agents have limited resources and limited capabilities and they might have not the *power of* realising some of their goals, while other agents might be able to realise them -either alone or together- (Dependence). On the other side, even if the agent would be able to achieve a given goal it might be very profitable to achieve it without spending any resource, thanks to the action of another agent (Weak-Dependence) [Jennings, 93]. This is quite obvious, however usually collaboration theories do not stress and explicitly theorise on this: on the fact that *in any collaboration one exploits the actions of the others.* In particular they do not analyse the mental attitude behind this exploiting position which is given for granted and obvious. We call this attitude 'Reliance' (or *Delegation^2*). Let us now define and model Reliance starting from its weakest and elementary form. Notice that in this perspective (like in Tuomela's one) a Multi-Agent plan is not necessarily a Joint plan. In our model a MA-plan can be just in the mind of one agent exploiting (by promoting it or not) the converging activities of other agents. It is in fact achieving its own goal through the planned (predicted and preferred) concurrent actions of several autonomous agents.

We define Reliance/Delegation as follows [Castelfranchi&Falcone, 98]:

Given two agents A and B and an action α (for a goal state g - $\tau=(\alpha,g)$, where τ is a task), with (α,g) in a plan of A, we will say that A delegates $\tau=(\alpha,g)$ to B if and only if A knows and wants that B performs α so that A can exploit the results of α for its own plan..In other words, A is trying to achieve some of its goals through B's behaviours or actions; thus A has the goal that B performs a given action/behaviour.

Notice that this does not mean that the two agents have the same goal. On the one side B could be a non goal-oriented or regulated agent, but simply a natural force, a material tool. On the other hand even if B would be a goal-regulated agent, with its own goals, A might exploit and rely on some result/action that B does not really 'intend' to

---

^{2} We use also the term 'Delegation' which -at least in English- is more intuitive for the more complex and advanced forms. In fact usually it implies also some asymmetric power and control, and acting "on the behalf of". However we claim that the basic kernel of Delegation is precisely this: reliance on the act of another agent; allocating some action or causal process - useful for our plan- to some entity. We call this 'weak delegation' while 'strong delegation' is closer to common sense and is the basis of the even stronger organisational, institutional and legal notion.

do (some side effect, etc. For ex. A might relying on B amusing people, without any intention of her/him of amusing them and make them laugh). In other terms, not all the results of an action are known or intended by a cognitive agent, and A might exploit precisely those results of B's.

Usually, A is constructing in its mind a *MA plan* and B has a "part", a share in this plan: B's *task*. This is true when A has to do some complementary action to achieve the goal [3]. However, B's action can be sufficient to achieve A's goals, so there is not always a MA plan (except for A's mental action of deciding and Delegating).

Moreover, depending on the kind of delegation B's *task* can be either an action-goal (α) or a state-goal (g). In this case, A just believes that the other will efficaciously do some action able to produce g, i.e. it will in some way bring it about that g. If A knows the specific action thank to whom B will produce g, he believes that B will do it, is able to do it, and there will be the opportunities for a successful execution of it.

When A believes to be (weakly or strongly) dependent on B, there are three possible situations:

- either A *accepts*, permits (in a weak sense), *lets* B doing α (this presupposes that A might prevent B about α);
- or A is happy or in any case accepts (by changing its own plan/decision) the action of B, but he would not be able to prevent it;
- A is himself provoking, inducing B's action in order to obtain g (this implies that B would not perform α without A's intervention, and then A might prevent α).

In all these cases A *wants* B's action, *expects* it, and *relies/counts* on it for achieving g.

As we said it is possible that B's action is sufficient for achieving g, or that A should himself doing something concurrent with B's action α, in order to achieve g. In other words, a M-A plan is necessary (following A) to produce g, part of this plan (sub-goal) is allocated (in A's mind) to B (which might ignore even the existence of A!) while part of this plan is A's own task/share. Now A's *allocation* of α to B, his *expectation*, and *reliance* is identical in the two cases (when A has to do something for g, take actively part in the plan performance; and when everything is allocated and delegated to B). It is precisely *the same mental ingredient*, without and before We-intention (acting together) -in mere exploitation- and in We-intention, where it converges and merges with the intention to do his own share, and constitutes (changing indexicality) the intention that "we do x".

On the basis of the kind of interaction between the delegating agent and the delegated one, it is possible to define various types of delegation. The five basic types of delegation are shown in Table 1 [Castelfranchi, 97].

We call *weak delegation* (line 1, column 1, in Table 1) delegation based on scrounging, on the passive achievement by A of the task. In it there is no agreement, no request or even influence: A is just exploiting in its plan a fully autonomous action of B. In fact, A has only to recognise the possibility that B will realise τ by itself and that this realisation will be useful for A, which "passively" awaits the realisation of τ.[5]

---

[3] This is in fact the case in We-intentions (see later).

[5] These distinctions are still quite coarse. In fact, one should more subtly distinguish between: the situation where B is completely unaware; when it is aware but cannot avoid the

	Unilateral	Acceptance-based [4]
by Exploitation	no mutual belief & passive achievement of τ	mutual belief & passive achievement of τ
by Induction	no mutual belief & active achievement of τ	mutual belief & active achievement of τ
by Agreement		mutual belief & mutual active achievement of τ

Table 1

More precisely,

a) The achievement of τ (the execution of α and its result g) is a *goal* of A.

b) A believes that there exists another agent B that has the *power of* [Castelfranchi, 91] achieving τ.

c) A believes that B will achieve τ in time.

c-bis) A believes that B *intends* to achieve τ in time (in the case that B is a cognitive agent).

d) A *prefers*[6] to achieve τ through B.

e) The achievement of τ through B is the goal of A.

f) A has the goal (*relativized* to (e)) of not achieving τ by itself or by other delegations.

We consider (a, b, c, and d) what the agent A views as a "*Potential for relying on*" the agent B, its *trust*; and (e and f) what A views as the "*Decision to rely on*" B. We consider "Potential for relying on" and "Decision to rely on" as two constructs temporally and logically related to each other.

We call *mild delegation* (line 2, column 1, in Table 1) the delegation based on induction, on the active indirect achievement by A of the task. In it there is no agreement, no request, but A is itself eliciting, inducing in B the desired behaviour in order to exploit it.

We will call *strict delegation* (line 3 in Table 1) delegation based on explicit agreement, on the active achievement by A of the task through an agreement with B. It is based on B's adopting A's task in response to A's request/order. Strict delegation is always connected with strict adoption.

---

exploitation; when it is aware and lets A profit from its autonomous behaviour (passive help); it decides to do *a* also because A needs it; the cases where A understands that B knows about its reliance but B does not understand that A understands; the cases where A is relying on B's understanding and adoption of its goal without any request; the case where there is mutual understanding and some form of tacit agreement. What we call "weak delegation" is not limited to B's anawareness; what is important for us is that A is not inducing that autonomous behaviour (but just exploiting it) and that there is no mutual understanding of this, i.e. some tacit agreement between A and B.

[4] Even more subtle distinctions were needed. For example here we mix up delegation based on a real (implicit or explicit) agreement (mutual belief), with delegation based on the unilateral awareness and acceptance of the delegated/exploited agent (see later).

[6] This means that, either relative to the achievement of τ or relative to a broader goal g' that includes the achievement of τ, A believes to be dependent on B [Sichman et al., 94].

3 Goal-Adoption: to act in order to realise a goal of the other

As claimed in [Castelfranchi, 97]:

Social Goal-Adoption (shortly G-Adoption) would deserve a more detailed treatment, since:

a) it is the true essence of all pro-social behaviours, and has several different forms and motivations;

b) frequently enough its role in cooperation is not understood: either agents are just presupposed to have the same goal [Werner, 89; Haddadi, 96], or the adoption of the goal from the other partners is not explicitly accounted for [Levesque et al., 90]; or the reasons for adopting the others' goal and take part in the collective activity are not explored (benevolence).

In G-Adoption B is changing his mind: he comes to have a new goal or at least to have new reasons for an already existing goal. The reason for this (new) goal is the fact that another agent A wants to achieve this goal: B knows this and decides to make/let her achieve it. If B is cooperating with A, if they have a common plan, B although doing his action for his own pre-existing goal, must also do it *for* A, then for additional reasons, with a different (social) mind.

We will now shortly examine different types of G-Adoption, first in order to have some form of correspondence with the types of Delegation, second, to deeply understand the mental ingredients of the more usual forms of G-Adoption, searching for the subatomic particles of social interaction.

There are several weak forms of G-Adoption, depending on B simply knowing about a favouring consequence of his behaviour, or on B just letting A's doing something he could hinder or prevent.

3.1 Weak and strong forms of G-Adoption

Side G-Adoption. We will use the formal definitions of [Conte&Castelfranchi, 95]. The weakest form of G-Adoption is just the awareness of an objective favour relation: B does α, B believes that one of α's results is g, B believes that (GOAL A g). So B knows that his action will favour A but B does not execute α strictly in order to make A achieve her goal (this is only a side intention) [7]

True G-Adoption. It is when B comes to have the same goal of A, *because* he knows that is A's goal

$(R - GOAL\ B\ g\,(GOAL\ A\ g))$

but not as in simple imitation [8] : here B has the goal that g (wants g be true) in order for A to achieve it:

---

[7] (GOAL B (DOES B act)) 3 (BEL B (((DONE act) 2 g) 3 (GOAL A g))))
but not:
(R-GOAL B (DOES B act) ((DONE act 2 g) 3 (GOAL A g))
which characterises cases of true G-Adoption.

[8] Confusion between mere imitation and true G-Adoption is allowed by other definitions (e.g., [Cohen&Levesque , 90] notion of *helpful goals*).

$$(G-ADOPT \ B \ A \ g) \overset{def}{=} (R-GOAL \ B \ (OBTAIN \ A \ g)(A-GOAL \ A \ g))$$

In words, B *is adopting a goal of A's when B wants A to obtain it as long as B believes that A wants to achieve that goal* [9]. In other words, B has a new goal as a result of goal-adoption. He has it, a) *as long as* he believes that A has it (escape condition), and b) *in order for* A to obtain it. Of course

$$(G-ADOPT \ B \ A \ g) \supset (GOAL \ B \ g)$$

Adoption does not coincide with *benevolence*. A relation of benevolence, indeed, is a form of generalised adoption. This has to do with the motivation for G-Adoption.

Motivation for adoption and other kinds of G-Adoption. For us Benevolence is a *terminal* (non instrumental) form of G-Adoption (pity, altruism, love, friendship).

Goal-adoption can be also instrumental to the achievement of selfish goals. For example feeding chickens (satisfying their need for food) is a means for eventually eating them; instrumental G-Adoption also occurs in *social exchange* (reciprocal conditional G-Adoption).

Another motive-based type of G-Adoption (that might be consider also a sub type of the Instrumental one) is *cooperative* G-Adoption: B adopts A's goal since she is co-interested in (some of) A's intended results: they have a common goal.

The distinction among these three forms of G-Adoption is very important, since their different motivational basis (why B adopts) allows important predictions on B's "cooperative" behaviour. For example, if B is a rational agent, in social exchange she should try to cheat, not reciprocating A's adoption. On the contrary, in cooperative adoption B normally is not interested in free riding since they have the same goal that g (not a parallel one) and they are mutually dependent on each other as for this goal: both A's action and B's action are necessary for g, so B's damaging A would damage herself. Analogously, while in terminal and in cooperative adoption it might be rational in many cases to inform A about difficulties, obstacles, or defections [Levesque et al., 90; Jennings, 93], in exchange, and especially in forced, coercive G-Adoption this is not the case.

Passive G-Adoption. Here B has the goal that A obtains what he needs/desires without actively taking part in his plan:

- either, B does not intend to do anything: she will just share A's achievement or A's goal frustration;

- or B just has the goal of *permitting/letting* the other achieve his own goal.

Active G-Adoption or Help. In Active G-Adoption, B decides to do something in order to favour the achievement of the A's goal. So, the goal of doing something is a goal of helping, and the execution of the action for the adopting goal, is actual help [Miceli et al., 95]. We do not consider "help" just to *let* the other achieve his own goal:

$$(DOES-FOR \ B \ \alpha \ (OBTAIN \ A \ g)) \ \text{(help)} \ [10]$$

and

---

[9] Where OBTAIN is defined as follows:

$$(OBTAIN \ A \ g) \overset{def}{=} (KNOW \ A \ g) \wedge (BEFORE \ (A-GOAL \ B \ g)(KNOW \ A \ g))$$

Not only g (the goal of A) has to be true, but also A has to know this. Thus, B's goal that A obtains g implies the goal that g be true and that A believes that g is true (for ex. informing A).

[10] Where (Conte and Castelfranchi, 1995):

$$(DOES-FOR \ A \ \alpha \ g) \overset{def}{=} (R-GOAL \ A \ (DOES A \ \alpha)((DONE \ \alpha) \supset g)) \wedge (A-GOAL \ A \ g)$$

$(G-ADOPT\ B\ A\ (DOES\ B\ \alpha))$ (goal of helping) [11]

Unilateral G-Adoption. Our definition of G-Adoption covers also the unilateral case (another weak form), in which B enjoys or lets A satisfy her goal, or actively helps A, while A is unaware of all this. It is worth noticing that in this case exactly the same MA plan typical of unilateral delegation is in the mind of the unilateral helper. In case of bilateral agreement (acceptance-based delegation + acceptance-based adoption) i.e. "contract" [Castelfranchi&Falcone, 98] they have the same plan, and there is mutual belief about this [Tuomela&Miller, 88].

Strong G-Adoption is active and acceptance-based (A is aware of it), and frequently enough it is on request.

In all types of strong G-Adoption, but especially in exchange, B has not only the goal that g, the goal that A achieves/obtains g, and the goal of doing something for this, he also has the goal that A *knows about his help*. In fact, this is a necessary condition for reciprocation in exchange, and in general for satisfying the commitment and A's expectations. If just A obtains g there is no debt, no satisfaction of possible obligations or commitment, no reciprocation. In strong delegation, request for adhesion, A has also the goal that B lets her know if he accepts/agrees and commits himself to the task and to let her know about its execution and success [Levesque et al., 90; Jennings, 93].

Passive, unilateral, and side G-Adoption are all weak forms of G-Adoption; they can be also combined. True, active, and acceptance-based (and their combination) characterise stronger forms.

Goal-Adhesion or Compliance. Among the various forms of G-Adoption, especially for modelling agreement, contract and team work, a special relevance has *G-Adhesion*. That is when the G-Adoption is due to the other's request (implicit or explicit), to his goal that B does a given action, or better to his goal that B adopts a given goal. It is the opposite of spontaneous forms of G-Adoption. So in *Adhesion/Compliance* B adopts A's goal that he adopts.

$$(G-ADHERE\ B\ A\ g) \overset{def}{=} (G-ADOPT\ B\ A\ (G-ADOPT\ B\ A\ g))$$

G-Adhesion is the strongest form of G-Adoption. Agreement is based on Adhesion; true requests are aimed at obtaining adhesion. In negotiation, speech acts, norms, etc. that are all based on the communication by A of his intention that the other does something, or better adopts his goal (for ex. obeys) G-Adhesion is what really matters.

Let us now explicitly relate Delegation and G-Adoption. In *Strict Delegation*, the delegated agent knows that the delegating agent is relying on it and accepts the task; in *Strict Adoption*, the helped agent knows about the adoption and accepts it (very often both these acceptations are preceded by a process of negotiation between the agents).

In other words, *Strict Delegation requires Strict Adoption, and vice versa*: they are two facets of a unitary social relation that we call "delegation-adoption" or "contract" and implies a Social-Commitment of the delegated agent.

---

[11] A narrow definition of help is proposed in [Miceli et al., 95] where help is not only active goal adoption but is also related to A's Dependence. Help in fact might be conceived as "needed". That is not true for all kinds of G-Adoption.

4 We-Intention

Also We-Intention is an individual social attitude. It characterises the state of an individual's mind (not of the collective, we-mind -if any) merged in a collaborative activity, i.e. intentionally acting together with another agent. We do not analyse Tuomela's very large and subtle theory of different forms of social behaviour [Tuomela&Bonnevier, 97], and all the theory of we-intending. We will just remind the notion of we-intend and its aims, and in particular the notion of weak-we-intention; since our aim is to show that it identifies fundamental components of the collaborating mind but does neither (explicitly) account for reliance nor for goal-adoption, although it accounts for individual agents having in mind and 'intending' a MA plan. Let's cite a recent synthetic text by Tuomela (Tuomela 1998) (we add some underlying and bold):

"Joint and collective intentions in their basic sense apply to a number of agents. Thus a collective intention can be expressed by an (m+1)-place predicate $CI(A_1,...,A_m,X)$ standing for "the agents $A_1,...,A_m$ jointly intend to perform the action X jointly". By analogy the same can be said of joint intentions. I will also speak, in a distributive sense, of <u>a single agent personally having a collective intention</u>. This is the case when the agent is one to which the predicate CI applies, and this entails also that the agent in question endorses or accepts the collective intention in a commitment-generating sense (to be commented on later). As to my technical notions, the notion of we-intention is a social intention that an individual has: $WI(Ai,X)$ standing for "agent Ai we-intends to do X". A group-intention is a we-intention or a disposition to acquire a we-intention. Finally, a group, G, can have an intention to perform something: $I(G,Y)$ standing for "group G intends to perform group action Y" (Y could be "invading the town" or "painting the house"). The weakest kind of collective intention is the kind of intentionality one can find in separate actions performed for the same reason. (...) In the case of a collective intention based on the participants' intention to satisfy its content by acting together, a special condition of "collectivity" applies: Due to the nature of the goal as a common goal and its having being collectively accepted by the participants it is necessarily the case that if the intention content is satisfied for one of the agents, it is satisfied for all the participants. The notion of intention here is one which can be adequately applied to the collective of agents in question. <u>The individual agents cannot normally intend the content in question in the standard sense of the notion of intention, which basically requires that they believe that they by their own action can satisfy the content.</u> They can, however, be said to have the content of the collective intention as their (distant) goal, they can aim at its satisfaction and collectively committed to it, their basic action-commitment being to their own contributions to (or possibly part-performances related to) the goal at hand. I will speak of <u>"aim-intention" and "aim-goal" in such a case in contrast to standard "action-intentions"</u>. A person has an action-intention if he believes that he can satisfy the intention by means of his own action. A participant's intention to perform his part of a joint action is a species of action-intention. A full-blown (viz. plan-based) joint intention is stronger, indeed the strongest kind of collective intention. In its case <u>each agent we-intends ... to perform X jointly with the others</u>. **A we-intention in its analyzed sense basically amounts to one's intention to perform one's part of the joint action.** The intention to perform one's part is an action-intention, but one with a "holistic" content involving joint action. This personal (but still "non-private") intention is based on the joint intention in question. Joint intentions will be regarded as a subclass of collective intentions of the aforementioned more general kind. (...) I will now give a summary analysis of the notion of a *shared intention with a collective content to act together*. The analysis and the explicatory discussion following it is modeled closely after the treatment of the notion of acting together in Tuomela and Bonnevier-Tuomela (1997): (IAT) You and I share the intention to act together in performing an action X if and only if

1) X is a collective action type (in the sense of a "joint action type" Chapter 5 of Tuomela, 1984, viz. an "achievement-whole" divided into A's and B's parts, not necessarily on the basis of an agreement or even a social norm); and this is understood by us.

2) a) I intend to perform X together with you, and on this basis I accordingly intend to participate in the performance of X (or to contribute to X); b) you intend to perform X together with me, and on the basis of this you intend to participate in the performance of X (or to contribute to X);

3) a) I believe that you will participate in the performance of X; b) you believe that I will participate in the performance of X;

4) 2)a) in part because of 3)a), and 2)b) in part because of 3)b).

(...) Clause 2) is a crucial one. It attributes to the participants an intention with the collective content to act together and also, on conceptual grounds, makes this intention a reason for them to intend to participate (take part, perform their parts of, or to contribute to, as the case may be) in the collective action. The locution "on the basis of" is meant to be understood in the following way. The concept of acting together occurs in the analysans in the intention content and should be possessed, at least in a rudimentary sense, by the participants. This notion is the general idea of performing something together, as a collective project, in which the participants take part. Acting together is a primitive notion in my analysis which I do not attempt to give a noncircular analysis of.

It must be emphasized that we are here dealing with personalized intentions with a collective content (viz. acting together). We can accordingly say here that the participants in a weak sense collectively intend, this intention being in part "presuppositionally" based on their beliefs (not necessarily mutual beliefs in a loop-involving sense) that the other will participate. Thus we can say that the intention to act together (or, which we regard as equivalent, to perform X with the others) is conceptually based on the belief that the others will participate and also that belief gives at least a conceptual ground or reason (presupposition-reason) for the agents to maintain their intention (a more realistic formulation would make the belief a probabilistic one). Thus the belief 3) is a presupposition-reason for the intention and the action. How strongly the belief 3) will motivate the participants to form and maintain the intention to act together is a different matter."

5   Overlaps and Complementarity

Our notion of weak-delegation/reliance [Castelfranchi&Falcone, 98] is quite close to Tuomela and Muller' original notion of We-intention. Their notion has been introduced within the orison of the theory of collective intentionality, to explain group intentions, and joint activity, and in a sense in a top-down approach by analysing and deconstructing the social and collective mind/action.

We arrived to our notion in the opposite direction (let say bottom-up) trying to understand individual action (and plans) in interference and dependence situation [Castelfranchi, 97] and the transformation of an individual or abstract plan into a MA plan [Castelfranchi&Falcone, 94; Falcone&Castelfranchi, 96]. By proceeding in two opposite directions eventually (and happily) we converge and arrive to very similar results and to very close but not completely overlapping mental ingredients.

It seems to us that it is not clear whether the Intention that 'we do ....' formally entails the goal (or aim-intention) that the other does its part/share[12] . This is not clear also conceptually given the definition of acting together as a non analysed primitive (" Acting together is a primitive notion in my analysis which I do not attempt to give a noncircular analysis of.").

Anyway, our claim (one of the difference and complementarity of our approach) is that an explicit and analytic theory of this goal (that the other does its part/share) and of its basis is absolutely necessary (it cannot be simply tacitly presupposed or implicitly implied). This is because:

- this mental ingredient of the acting together (in all its forms) has an independent origin, its own root: it can be there without any We-Int, while is a necessary ingredient of it; and this independent root to cooperation must be studied;[13]
- this ingredient assumes different forms, role, and strength in different forms of acting together; thus it requires its own theory;
- it is the basis of many relevant aspects of collaborative relations, like expectations about the other's behaviour, disappointment, collaborative coordination (int that), complementarity of roles, conflicts and protests, goal-adoption or compliance in S-Commitment. All this entails or presupposes that A expects (i.e. has not only the belief but also the goal -sub-goal in its plan) that B does something concurrent, complementary to the achievement of the goal.

Let us now a bit clarify these claims and the differences and the common kernel of the two notions, as we see them.

5.1   Relationships between Reliance/Delegation and Weak We-Intention

The main difference between Delegation and We-intention seems to be in the focus of attention. Tuomela focus on the *individual intention* to do its own share (within the view of a MA plan and supported by the *beliefs* that the other agent(s) will do their share). On the contrary, we focus on the complementary part, on the reliance upon the

---

[12] We-intentions are in fact "aim-intentions" about the global action that agents have to perform together. This should imply the intention that the other does its part. However what explicitely We-intentions entail is the participant's action-intention to do his share of the global action.

[13] As we said, the origin, the elementary form of this goal and of this social relation (we call "reliance" or weak delegation") is the idea that an agent can realise a goal of its own doing noting! simply scrounging the results of the action of another agent.

other(s)' action, on *expecting* and *delegating* that part of a MA plan just conceived in the individual mind.

The main specific differences are the following ones.

1. In our notion there is not only the *belief* that the other agent will do but there is the *goal* (*expectation* is the combination of both). [14] In fact, since I include its action in my plan [15], since I need it, since I <u>decide</u> to rely on and depend upon it, not only I believe (predict or observe) that it will do, but I want that it will do (this is also close to the notion of 'intention that' - see later). That the other agent does what is needed in the plan definitively is a goal of mine. I 'delegate' means that I bet on this event, that I renounce (if it has been possible) to do myself that part of the plan, that I renounce to search for other agents doing this job. [16]

2. A second difference concerns the fact that Reliance/Delegation as we conceive it -although we use the notion of MA plan to explain it- *does not necessarily requires an action/intention (a share) of the delegating/relying agent*. This is only usual. But in principle is it possible that only the action(s) of the other agent(s) are necessary and sufficient for achieving my goal and that I completely delegate to them and rely on them for my goal: I do not really have my own share. Consider the case where there is g (ex. to die), and g is the result of the independent activity other agents, and suppose that g is a goal of mine (I desire to die), and that I rely on them to achieve g, and finally suppose that I cannot do anything for personally achieving g (ex. I'm paralysed). In this form of plan (for my goal!) there is no

---

[14] *Expectation* is a belief relative to the future: it is "positive expectation" when the expected event coincides with a goal of the agent

$$(posEXPECT\ A\ \Diamond q) \stackrel{def}{=} (BEL\ A\ \Diamond p) \wedge (BEL\ A\ (p \supset q)) \wedge (GOAL\ A\ \Diamond q)$$

it is "negative" when the event will frustrate a goal of the agent:

$(negEXPECT\ A\ \Diamond q) = (BEL\ A\ \Diamond p) \wedge (BEL\ A\ (p \supset q)) \wedge (GOAL\ A\ \neg \Diamond q)$

[15] Consider Tuomela's nice example: "Suppose I am collecting some trash from our park due to last night's celebration. I can see you entering the other end of the park and starting to do the same thing. I see you and you see me, but neither of us needs to have acquired the belief that the other one has noticed him (or her). Not being acquainted with each other, we just continue with our cleaning without further contact. In a very rudimentary sense we are cleaning the park together. Each is of course doing his or her bit of cleaning intentionally, but there is also some element of collective intentionality involved. It might be that you and I have just separately decided - say, beforehand - to clean a certain small area. Then we would have only a case of separate individual action by the two of us." [Tuomela, 98]. Now, if I intend to clean the park, and I meet sombody else wich is doing the same, I *have to* change my plan, in order to coordinate with the other's activity. Either I must prevent him from doing part of my original plan, or I must 'accept' and include his actions in my plan, then r*elying on* them! (I can even *let* he doing all the job). Notice that at the beginning the two agents do not have the 'same' goal at the level of the action/plan: they have 'parallel goals' [Conte et al., 91]. A has the goal "A cleans the park" while B has the goal "B cleans the park" (at a higher level there is the common goal "the park be clean"). The collective indexicality ('We') make identical A and B' goals that in origin were simply parallel: both A and B have the goal "we clean the park".

[16] Notice that we said that the delegating agent believes and wants that the other 'will do' not that s/he believes and wants that the other 'intend to do'. This is in fact only a special case, and it is not necessary. This is another important difference.

share of mine, no action I have to intend and perform (even the mental action of renouncing to do is excluded).

Thus, weak Reliance/Delegation is both richer than weak We-Intention (because is more that simple beliefs) and poorer (because the other agent might be not an intentional agent, or there might not be a MA plan, and a 'We' agent). In more rich forms of collaborations the two notions are both incomplete and have a large overlap.

5.2 Relationships between Adoption and Weak-We-Intention

Also the complement, the pendant of A's delegation and expectation in B's mind, has been let implicit in We-Intention approach. If B is aware of the fact that A exploits and relies on his doing his action (delegation of τ), he *has to* decide whether to undergo and accept this or not.

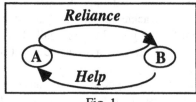

Fig. 1

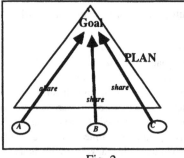

Fig. 2

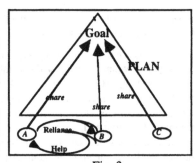

Fig. 3

If he accepts this without changing his original goal/plan we have a form of "passive adoption": B *lets* A to benefit from his action, *permits* this. A achieving her goal in a form of 'side or passive' intention of B, since now B knows and accepts this additional effect of his action. Thus, in fact there is always some modification in B's goals: an additional side intention. If B has to change his goal/plan by adopting A's goal (for ex. under A's request or order) we have an "active help": B does something just because and until this is wanted by A.

In both cases there is *adoption* of A's expectation-goal about B doing his part. B does his part not only for his own reasons but also *for* the other. In collaboration people is helping each other, and the help of B responds to the reliance of A (and vice versa) (Fig. 1).

Can we deeply understand taking part in a collective collaborative activity (group and team action, etc.) simply in terms of (aware) convergence of actions towards a common goal within a common plan (Fig. 2)?

Or have we to explicitly models also the reliance-help between the members (Fig. 3)?

Social-commitment, as we modelled it, is precisely this meeting and match between reliance and adoption. In fact in S-Commitment [Castelfranchi, 95] B is promising to A to do τ, but this presupposes that

- τ (and B doing τ) is a goal of A, and that
- A accepts (wants) to achieve her goal through B's action, i.e. that she *delegates* B.

There is no real, effective promise (but simply offer or intrusion) if there is no delegation on the other side. Strong delegation implies S-Commitment, and vice versa.

Now, in We-Intention also the idea that B is *responding* to A's expectation/reliance and 'helping' her, is not modelled. It seems that he simply has the intention of doing his share, but only for himself, not (also) for the other to respond to her expectations.

6 Coordination

Let us now consider another basic component of acting together and collaborating. This component is so fundamental that it holds even in a socially isolated agent dealing with a dynamic environment: *coordination*. In social interaction -both competitive or collaborative- coordination obviously remains crucial. Which are the elementary aspects of social coordination from the point of view of the agent's mind? Let us analyse some aspects of it that are related to some important ingredients of the collaborative mind that have been postulated (like Grosz and Kraus' Intention that).

6.1 Selfish Coordination

Selfish-Coordination is that elementary form of coordination activity of an agent which is pursuing it own goals by itself dealing with the (positive or negative) interferences by the other agents. In other words, the agent is acting in the world and modifies, adapts its own action (plan) in order to avoid obstacles and damages and to exploit possible opportunities for its own goal. But it does neither induce or modifies the behaviour of the others (this is a different social strategy) nor is adopting (facilitating) the goals of others.

6.2 Collaborative Coordination, and its importance

There are other forms of coordination: A might modify her own behaviour in order to avoid negative interference for the other's action or to create positive interferences. This is *Collaborative Coordination* (CC): A is adapting her behaviour in order to favour B's actions. A perceives that its own action could hinder or favour another action (of B) and modifies it (in time, shape, resources, etc.) in order to avoid negative interference or to favour that action.[17] CC is a form of strong social action [Castelfranchi, 98]. In fact, it is not only based on beliefs relative to the others' mind (like selfish coordination), but is guided by a Social Goal: the goal that the other achieves his goal. It necessarily implies some form of either passive or active goal-adoption.[18]

While Selfish-Coordination is typical of a non-delegating and non-adopting agent[19] , CC *is the form of coordination specifically required by both Reliance/Delegation, and Goal-Adoption*. Both Reliance and Goal-Adoption would be contradictory and self-defeating without collaborative coordination. We will argue later on this while comparing CC with Intention That.

7   Intention-that

Let us directly cite Grosz and Kraus' paper [Grosz&Kraus, 96] to not be misleading:
"Searle [Searle, 90] and Grosz and Sidner [Grosz&Sidner, 90] argued that the propositional attitudes of belief, mutual belief, and individual intention to act were insufficient for representing the mental state of participants in collaborative activity. Collaborative plans were more than a simple combination of individual plans. (...) To address [these] concerns (...), the formalisation introduces the attitude of *intending-that* (...); the definitions require intentions-that toward the overall group action and the actions of others ."(p.333) "Collaborative activity must rest eventually on the actions of individual agents; as a result, the collaborative plans of a group must include as constituents the individual plans of group members. These individual plans may be more complex than accounted for in Pollack's formulation [Pollack, 90]. First, Pollack presumed that an agent had a complete recipe for the action (...). Second, Pollack considered only two types of action relations, generation and enablement; (...) Third agents may 'contract out' to other agents some of the actions to be done. We provide an expended definition of the plan of an individual agent that overcomes these limitations" (p.271).

"IntTo (...) are used to represent an agent's *intention to* do some action; IntTh are used to represent an agent's *intention that* some proposition hold. (...) The commonalty between IntsTo and IntsTh is that both commit an agent to not adopt conflicting intentions.... IntTo commits an agent to means-ends reasoning and, at some point, to acting. In contrast, an IntTh does not directly engender such behavior. IntsTh form the basis for meshing subplans, helping one's collaborator, and coordinating status updates." (p.281).

---

[17] It has been shown that some form of CC is necessary for a good group work [Cannon-Bowers et al., 93]. Of course, the two forms of coordination can be unilateral or bilateral (with serious problems of misunderstandings), and mutual (based on mutual beliefs).

[18] Frequently adoption is *pro-active*: it anticipates B's needs and is not a response to a request or expectation. And frequently it is also 'tutorial', viz. A cares of B's 'interests' beyond B's current goals [Conte&Castelfranchi, 95]. Sometimes this implies Over and Critical Help: I do something more or better than expected.

[19] Although, there may be selfish-coordination also with delegation, when the agent adapts it own action to exploit also the action of another agent, thus to rely on it.

"The key properties of the model are as follows:

(i) it uses individual intentions to establish commitment of collaborators to their joint activity;

(ii) it establishes an agent's commitments to its collaborating partners' abilities to carry out their individual actions that contributed to the joint activity;

(iii) it accounts for helpful behavior in the context of collaborative activity;

(iv) it covers contracting actions and distinguishes contracting from collaboration;

(v) the need for agents to communicate is derivative, not stipulated, and follows from the general commitment to the group activity;

(vi) the meshing of subplans is ensured; it is also derivative from more general constraints.

The attitude of intending-that plays a significant role in establishing several of these properties. It is the basis for agents to avoid adopting intentions that conflict with those that arises from the group's plan [(i) and (ii)], and it engenders helpful behavior [(iii)]. The way in which IntTh is used in Shared Plans captures the difference between agents having a Shared Plan and one agent contracting to another agent [(iv)]. ..... Intentions-that represent [the agent's] responsibilities with respect to the actions of another agents" (pp. 306-7) "Two key characteristics of collaboration derive from IntTh...: (1) agents avoiding the adoption of intentions that conflict with the joint activity; and (2) agents adopting intentions to communicate.... The IntTh explicitly represents each group member's commitment to the group's performance." (p.311)

"The agent may either do all of the subactions [of a given recipe] itself, or may contract out some of them". ..."Contracting [out].. . depends on an agent believing that by doing one action.. it can get a different agent to perform another action; the meta-predicate GTD 'get to do' is used to represent this" (p.288) "Contracting, unlike collaborative plans, does not require reciprocity in [its] commitment; contracting is not in and of itself collaborative. " (p.297)

7.1 "Intention that", Delegation, and Collaborative Coordination

As we understand it Delegation and Collaborative coordination (CC) are the conceptual basis of Grosz and Kraus' (G&K's) social "intention that". Let's argue on this.

We agree with G&K's claim that mutual beliefs and individual intentions are not enough for modelling collaborating agents. They refer for example to Cohen and to Jennings, but what these authors add for modelling team work (the obligation to communicate defection, and conventions about this), or people postulating primitive collective We-intentions (like Searle) does not solve the problem. The crucial point - as we said- are the reciprocal expectations (goals). We believe that G&K grasp precisely this and attempt to capture (part of) this with their "intention that". However, it seems to us that a) this notion is not sufficient; b) it mixes up different things; c) has not clear foundation, as defined.

As for (a) let us say that the 'IntTh' does not entail obligations, rights, resistance in dropping the task, trust, etc. Very crucial aspects in collaboration. However, we do not consider these aspects in this paper.

As for the other points, let us examine more deeply this notion.

If it is assumed as a basic form of intention, the 'IntTh' should be an intention relative to a world state or process (included the action of another agent): I intend that g. It is close to Tuomela's 'aim-intention'. This is the difference between 'IntTh' and 'Intention to' which necessarily is about an action of the intending agent. Thus 'IntTh' would be good for formalising delegation in general (*my goal that you do a given action or achieve a given goal*). We need in fact a logic for expressing this kind of preferred and realisable goal. However, this is not how G&K use their notion. They do not elaborate so much on *A's 'intention' about B's action.*[20] Or better they use 'IntTh' for several things and in particular to express my intention that you be able and in condition to do your job. (Notice that this presupposes my goal that you do your job).

'IntTh' aims at expressing at the same time: reliance/delegation; goal-adoption; and (part of) CC, without clearly distinguishing between them.

What G&K do with their 'IntTh' is quite important and effective: do not hinder the other, help him, inform him, etc.[21] However:

a) On the one hand, a series of properties that are claimed to be typical of the 'IntTh' and specific of MA plans and collaboration [Grosz, 96], are in fact more general and basic. They are present also in Single Agent plans.

b) 'IntTh' is not grounded - as it should be- on the different origins of the goal that you do the task or on the goal that you achieve your goal.

c) 'IntTh' is quite a powerful notion but also quite confuse: it mixes up different collaborative attitudes and situations.

d) Because of (c) the frame is neither clear nor complete: for example there is no "acceptance" of B of the 'IntTh' of A about his activity.

The intention that "B does action α" (or achieves goal g) is different from the intention that "B is able and in condition to do α", which derives from the former and is the true basis of CC (is the goal of CC). Moreover, the goal that "B achieves goal g" (or "does action α") has two completely different origins, which makes quite different predictions: either it comes from delegation (I count on you for my original goal), or from goal-adoption (I adopted your goal and I want that you achieve it). 'IntTh' capture something which is formally in common between the two mental perspectives, but doing this it mixes up two very different and asymmetric scenarios. It transforms collaboration in a symmetric scenario, but collaboration is symmetric only when and because both the agent are at the same time delegating and adopting, clients and contractors, not because the relationship between a client and a contractor

---

[20] For example they do not have a real goal of 'influencing'. In fact the goal ('IntTh') that the other agent does an action, should be translated -when B is a cognitive agent- into the goal ('IntTh') that the agent *intends* to do, which in its turn presupposes the intention that the other agents has the *goal* of doing. In our vocabulary:

(Goal A (Does B α)) => (Goal A (IntendToDo B α)) => (Goal A (Goal B (Does B α))).

[21] In a paper about how to transform an abstract or a SingleAgent plan in a MAplan [Castelfranchi&Falcone, 94] we have shown how and why this requires the introduction of additional actions in the plan: communication actions, monitoring actions, transfer of resources, coordination actions. All this because of my goal that you realises your task. At least for us it is not true that "The possibility of an agent contracting out an action to another agent has not been discussed in previous work on multi-agent plans" (Grosz and Kraus, cited, p.296)

(a delegating and a delegated/adopting agent) is *per se* symmetric. Saying that both have an 'IntTh' about the other, does not clarify the issue. Nature and predictions of delegation-based and of adoption-based 'IntTh' are quite different.

'IntTh' from Delegation. If I have the goal that the other realises my goal, and I trust on it, I will have the goal of not interfering with and preventing its action, or I will have the goal of facilitating it. In sum, I will have the goal of Collaboratively Coordinating my activity with its activity (aimed at my goal). Precisely for the same reasons if I want to rely/delegate or to ask, command, etc. I must also permit (a request or a prescription without permitting is a pragmatic contradiction).

'IntTh' from G-Adoption. If I adopted the other's goal and I want to help it (for any kind of motive), I will have the goal of not interfering with or preventing its complementary actions aimed at that goal, or I will have the goal of facilitating them. In sum, I will have the goal of Collaboratively Coordinating my helping activity with its activity (aimed at that goal).

In both cases collaborative coordination is derived from more basic attitudes.

As for the relationship with CC, let us notice that:

'IntTh' seems to capture only one move of CC: avoiding obstacles and conflicts to the other's action. While our notion would include also actively favouring that action.

Moreover, for us social CC is very close -and derives from- (collaborative) coordination with my-self, i.e. coordination among several actions of mine within a given plan. As I have the goal that my action α_1 does not hinder my action α_2, and I have to solve these conflicts in my own plans, analogously, I should have the goal that my action α_1 does nor hinder action α_2 of another agent, in the same plan and for my goal or for a goal that I have just adopted. Thus, it is not true that this is a specific component of MA plans and collaboration: it is just the 'form' assumed by a more basic component when passing from a SingleAgent-plan to a MAplan [Falcone&Castelfranchi, 96].

As for the relationship between Reliance/Delegation and 'contracting out', they are also very closed. However, 'contracting out'

- first, is only *induced* by an action of A (there is no weak delegation and lucky exploitation), and it is not clear if there is a formal theory of self-realising goals: goals I have nothing to do for;
- second, there is no theory of when and why contracting out (Dependence theory); thus they do not have objective constraints on collaboration;
- third, there is no explicit account of delegation of control and monitoring, and of delegation of meta-action (ex. deciding, searching for a plan, .etc.).
- G&K "distinguish *individual plans* that are formed by individual agents from *Shared Plans* that are constructed by groups of collaborating agents" [Grosz&Kraus, 96: p.273]; what about our notion of a MA plan necessarily holding in an individual mind (not shared) in any basic form of Reliance/Delegation (than in unilateral Contracting out)?
- As they claim, Contracting out does not requires reciprocity and is not in itself collaborative (and this is very closed to Reliance/Delegation); but it is not clear if it is not *collaborative* because it does not require a symmetric contracting out (like in exchange) or because it does not requires adoption by the other. We have weak forms without adoption, and strong forms with adoption but without reciprocity.

Goal-adoption in response to delegation is different from reciprocity and symmetry in helping and delegating.

There is another weak point of this important theory:

- It does not contain an explicit and sufficient theory of *goal-adoption*, and of its motives. They try to bypass Adoption theory thanks to 'IntTh' and its powerful consequences. For this the theory does not seem able even to discriminate between coercion and collaboration [Grosz, 96][22] . For sure it is not able to distinguish between strict cooperation and exchange situations.[23]
- Consequently there is no theory of different levels of help, from the point of view of the helper.

8   Concluding remarks

No group activity, no joint plan, no true collaboration can be established without:

a) the goal of A (member or group) about the intention of B of doing a given action/task α (delegation; intention that);

b) the we-intention of A about doing his own share until he beliefs that it is useful and successful, thanks to the MA plan and the collaborative activity;

c) A's "intention that" B is able and has the opportunity to do α; and in general the "collaborative coordination" of A relative to B's task. This is derived from the necessary coordination among actions in any plan.

d) the *social commitment* of B to A as for α, which is a form of *goal-adoption* or better of adhesion.

Both goal-adoption in collaboration and groups, and the goal about the intention of the other (delegation and influencing) are only implicitly presupposed in many theories. They mainly rely on the agents' *beliefs* about the intentions of the others. On the contrary, we need to model all complete *expectations* and *commitments*.

Moreover, those ingredients of collaboration (strong reliance; help and compliance; intention (commitment) to do my share; reciprocal (selfish and collaborative) coordination) are simply strong forms of more elementary social attitudes and *have their independent roots and forerunners in non-symmetric (social and non-social) action.*

---

[22] In fact, even an abducted or raped person - if worries about the fact that the other can discover and punish his/her opposition or rebellion attempts - has the goal of doing as the other wants and facilitating him (of course neither s/he has a free/spontaneous goal, nor is benevolent, or co-interested in the objective, or over-helper).

[23] [Grosz, 96] explicitly cites it as an example of collaboration. Have I -in exchange- the goal of facilitating you in achieving your goals? Only for that part that concern me and is *for* me (for ex. your giving me the money). But not for that part that is just for you (for example your taking away the goods). Except if you pay me also for this, or I want give you a good impression for future exchanges, or I'm an over-helper, benevolent guy. Thus, one should distinguish between the agent's 'IntTh' to facilitate the action he needs (delegation) from other possible 'IntTh's of a contractor due to other reasons and with different stability, for example over-helping attitudes which are not canonical or rational in exchange, differently than in strict cooperation.

More precisely their origins are: unilateral reliance; unilateral goal adoption and help; intention (commitment) to do my action (in a MA world); coordination: not damaging or favouring my/your actions.

We hope that now the set of useful basic ingredients for modelling the individual mind in MA plans or collective activities, is more clear, a bit more systematic, and more ready for a uniform and expressive formalisation. We believe that the notions of weak we-intention, of weak reliance/delegation, of intention-that, and of collaborative coordination -not forgetting goal-adoption- importantly contribute to this with their overlaps and with their complementarity and focus.

References

1. [Cannon-Bowers et al., 93] Cannon-Bowers, J.A., Salas, E. and Converse, S. (1993) Shared mental models in expert team decision making. In M.J. Castellan (ed.) *Individual and group decision making*, Hillsdale, Erlbaum.
2. [Castelfranchi, 98] C. Castelfranchi, (1998), Modelling Social Action for AI Agents, *Artificial Intelligence*, 103, pp. 157-182.
3. [Castelfranchi, 91] C. Castelfranchi, (1991) Social Power: a missed point in DAI, MA and HCI. In *Decentralized AI*. Y. Demazeau & J.P.Mueller (eds), Elsevier, Amsterdam, 49-62.
4. [Castelfranchi, 97] C. Castelfranchi, (1997) Principles of Individual Social Action. In Tuomela R., & Hintikka, G. (eds.) Contemporary Action Theory. Kluwer.
5. [Castelfranchi, 95] C. Castelfranchi, (1995), Commitment: from intentions to groups and organizations. In *Proceedings of ICMAS'95*, S.Francisco, AAAI-MIT Press.
6. [Castelfranchi&Falcone, 94] Castelfranchi, C., Falcone, R. (1994), Towards a theory of single-agent into multi-agent plan transformation. The *3rd Pacific Rim International Conference on Artificial Intelligence*, Beijing, China, 16-18 agosto.
7. [Castelfranchi&Falcone, 98] Castelfranchi, C., Falcone, R., Towards a Theory of Delegation for Agent-based Systems, *Robotics and Autonomous Systems*, Special issue on Multi-Agent Rationality, Elsevier Editor. Vol 24, Nos 3-4, pp.141-157.
8. [Cohen&Levesque , 90] Cohen, P.R. & Levesque H. J., (1990), Intention is choise with Commitment. Artificial Intelligence, 42, pp. 213-61.
9. [Miceli et al., 95] M Miceli, Cesta A., and P Rizzo (1995) Distributed Artificial Intelligence from a socio-cognitive standpoint: Looking at reasons for interaction,. *AI & Society*, 9, 287-320.
10. [Conte&Castelfranchi, 95] R. Conte & C. Castelfranchi, Cognitive and Social Action (UCL Press, London, 1995).
11. [Conte et al., 91] Conte, R., Miceli, M. C. Castelfranchi. (1991), Limits and levels of cooperation. Disentangling various types of prosocial interaction. In *Decentralized AI-2*, Y. Demazeau, J.P. Mueller (eds), 147-157. Armsterdam: Elsevier.
12. [Demazeau&Mueller, 90] Demazeau, Y. & J.P. Mueller (eds) (1990). *Decentralized AI*. Amsterdam: Elsevier.

13.[Dunin-Keplicz&Verbrugge, 96] Dunin-Keplicz, B., and Verbrugge R., (1996) Collective Commitments, in M. Tokora (editor), Proceedings Second International Conference on Multi-Agent Systems, California AAAI-Press.

14.[Durfee et al., 87] Durfee,E.H., Lesser,V.R., Corkill,D.D. (1987) Cooperation through communication in a problem-solving network. In *Distributed Artificial Intelligence* , M.N. Huhns (ed.), 29-58. San Mateo, CA: Kaufmann.

15.[Falcone&Castelfranchi, 96] Falcone, R., Castelfranchi, C., (1996), Plan Recognition: from Single-Agent to Multi-Agent plans. in J.Perram & JP. Muller (eds.) Distributed Software Agents and Applications, *Lecture Notes in Artificial Intelligence*. Springer-Verlag pg.166-178.

16.[Ferber, 95] J. Ferber. Les Systemes Multi-Agents. InterEditions, Paris, 1995.

17.[Gasser, 91] Gasser, L. (1991). Social conceptions of knowledge and action: DAI foundations and open systems semantics. *Artificial Intelligence, 47*, 107-38.

18.[Grosz, 96] B. Grosz, Collaborative Systems. *AI Magazine* (summer 1996) 67-85.

19.[Grosz&Kraus, 96] Grosz B., and Kraus S. (1996), Collaborative Plans for Complex Group Action, *Artificial Intelligence, 86*, pp. 269-357.

20.[Grosz&Sidner, 90] Grosz B., and Sidner S. (1996), Plans for Discourse. In: Cohen P., Morgan J.L., and Pollack M.E. eds., Intentions in Communication (MIT Press, Cambridge, MA).

21.[Jennings, 93] Jennings. N.R. (1993). Commitments and conventions: The foundation of coordination in multi-agent systems. *The Knowledge Engineering Review*, 3, 223-50.

22.[Haddadi, 96] A. Haddadi, Communication and Cooperation in Agent Systems (the Springer Press, 1996).

23.[Levesque et al., 90] H.J. Levesque, P.R. Cohen, Nunes J.H.T. On acting together. In Proceedings of the 8th National Conference on Artificial Intelligence, 94-100. San Marco, California: Kaufmann. 1990.

24.[Malone et al., 88] Malone T.W. , Fikes R.E. and Howard M.T., (1988), Enterpise: a market-like task scheduler for distributed computing environments, in: Huberman B. A. ed. The Ecology of Computation (North-Holland, Amsterdam), 177-205.

25.[O'Hare&Jennings, 96] O'Hare G. and Jennings N., (1996) Foundations of distributed Artificial Intelligence. Wiley & Sons.

26.[Pollack, 90] Pollack, M., (1990) Plans as complex mental attitudes in Cohen, P.R., Morgan, J. and Pollack, M.E. (eds), *Intentions in Communication*, MIT press, USA, pp. 77-103.

27.[Rao et al., 92] Rao, A. S., Georgeff, M.P., & Sonenberg E.A., (1992). Social plans: A preliminary report. In *Decentralized AI - 3,* E. Werner & Y, Demazeau (eds.), 57-77. Amsterdam: Elsevier.

28.[Searle, 90] Searle J.R., (1990), Collective Intentions and Actions. In: Cohen P., Morgan J.L., and Pollack M.E. eds., Intentions in Communication (MIT Press, Cambridge, MA) Chapter 19.

29.[Sichman et al., 94] Sichman, J, R. Conte, C. Castelfranchi, Y. Demazeau. (1994), A social reasoning mechanism based on dependence networks. In Proceedings of the 11th ECAI.

30. [Singh, 95] M.P. Singh, (1995) Multiagent Systems: A Theoretical Framework for Intentions, Know-how, and Communications. Springer Verlag, LNCS, volume 799.

31. [Tuomela, 84] Tuomela, R. `(1984)``A Theory of Social Action , Reidel Pub., Boston.

32. [Tuomela, 98] Tuomela, R. `(1998)``` Collective And Joint Intention (Forthcoming in the proceedings of the Rosselli Foundation conference "Cognitive Theory of Social Action" held in Turin, June 1998)

33. [Tuomela&Bonnevier, 97] Tuomela, R. `and Bonnevier-Tuomela, M. (1997)`From Social Imitation to Teamwork. In Holmstrom-Hintikka, G. and Tuomela, R. `(Eds.)`` Contemporary Action Theory. Vol. II: Social Action. Kluwer, Boston.

34. [Tuomela&Miller, 88] Tuomela, R. `and Miller, K.(1988)``'We-Intentions'. Philosophical Studies, 53, 115-37.

35. [Von Martial , 92] Von Martial F., (1992) Coordinating Plans of Autonomous Agents. LNAI 610, Springer.

36. [Weiss&Sen, 98] Weiss, G. and Sen, S, (eds.) (1998) Multi Agent Systems - A modern Approach to Distributed Artificial Intelligence. AAAI/MIT Press.

37. [Werner, 89] Werner, E. (1989), Cooperating agents: A unified theory of communication and social structure. In Distributed artificial intelligence, Vol. 2, M. Huhns, L. Gasser (eds), 3-36. London: Kaufmann and Pitman.

38. [Werner, 90] Werner, E. (1990), What can agents do together? A semantics for reasoning about cooperative ability. Proceedings of the 9th European Conference on Artificial Intelligence. London: Pitman.

39. [Wooldridge&Jennings, 94] Wooldridge M. and Jennings N., (1994), Formalizing the cooperative problem solving process, in: Proceedings 13th International Workshop on Distributed Intelligence, Lake Quinalt, WA, 403-417.

Subjective Situations

Antonio Moreno[1], Ulises Cortés[2], Ton Sales[2]

[1] Departament d'Enginyeria Informàtica - Universitat Rovira i Virgili (URV)
Carretera de Salou, s/n. 43006-Tarragona, Spain - amoreno@etse.urv.es
[2] Dep. de Llenguatges i Sistemes Informàtics - Universitat Politècnica de Catalunya
C/Jordi Girona, 1-3. 08034-Barcelona, Spain - {ia,sales}@lsi.upc.es

Abstract. The beliefs of the agents in a multi-agent system have been formally modelled in the last decades using *doxastic logics*. The *possible worlds model* and its associated *Kripke semantics* provide an intuitive semantics for these logics, but they commit us to model agents that are *logically omniscient*. We propose a way of avoiding this problem, using a new kind of entities called *subjective situations*. We define a new doxastic logic based on these entities and we show how the belief operators have some desirable properties, while avoiding logical omniscience. A comparison with two well-known proposals (Levesque's *logic of explicit and implicit beliefs* and Thijsse's *hybrid sieve systems*) is also provided.

1 Introduction

In the last decade *doxastic modal logics* have been considered the most appropriate formal tool for modelling the beliefs of the agents composing a multi-agent system ([1]). The standard way of providing a meaning to the modal formulas of these logics is to use the *possible worlds model* ([2]) and its associated *Kripke semantics* ([3]). This semantics is quite natural and intuitive, but it is well known that the agents modelled in this framework are *logically omniscient* ([4]). Therefore, this semantics is unsuitable to model the beliefs of realistic, non-ideal agents. The aim of our work is to provide a plausible way of modelling the beliefs of non-logically omniscient agents, while keeping the essence and the beauty of the possible worlds model and the Kripke semantics.

This article[3] is structured as follows. In section 2 we give an intuitive explanation of our approach to the logical omniscience problem, which is based in a new kind of entities called *subjective situations*. In a nutshell, a subjective situation is the perception that an agent has of a certain state of affairs. These situations, as will be explained below, will take the role of possible worlds. In section 3, a formalization of subjective situations in the framework of doxastic propositional logic is made. Section 4 is devoted to a study of the behaviour of the modal belief operators. It is shown how their properties do indeed correspond with our intuitions about what should be an adequate formalization of the doxastic attitude of a non-ideal, non-logically omniscient agent. In section 5, a comparison of our proposal with two well-known approaches (Levesque's *logic of explicit and implicit beliefs* ([5]) and Thijsse's *hybrid sieve systems* ([6])) is performed. The paper finishes with a brief summary and the bibliographical references.

---

[3] This research has been supported by the CICYT project *SMASH: Multi-agent systems and its application to hospital services (TIC96-1038-C04-04)*.

2 Considering Subjective Situations

One of the ways of solving the logical omniscience problem is to revise the concept of possible world[4]. In the classical view, a possible world is a logical model (*e.g.* in a propositional setting, a possible world is an interpretation of the basic propositions). Some authors have tried to alleviate logical omniscience by changing this notion; for instance, a possible world may be seen as a situation in which some basic propositions may be considered true and some basic propositions (not necessarily different from the previous ones) may be considered false ([5]), or it may be represented as a *partial* assignment of truth values to the basic propositions ([6]) or simply as the set of formulas that are assumed to be true in it ([8], [9]).

Regardless of the way the concept of possible world is modified, there is something that does not change: the formal representation of a possible world is not related in any way with the notion of *agent*. Thus, it may be said that all the approaches in the literature present an *objective* view of what a possible world is (*i.e.* a world is the same for all the agents). In a standard *Kripke structure*, the only item that depends on each agent is the *accessibility relation* between possible worlds. The traditional meaning attached to the accessibility relation R_i of an agent i is that it represents the uncertainty that agent i has about the situation in which it is located (*e.g.* ($w_0 R_5 w_1$) means that agent 5 cannot distinguish between worlds w_0 and w_1, see [1]). This situation is quite peculiar, because the formulas that are true in two worlds that are linked by an accessibility relation are, in principle, totally unrelated.

Our proposal may be motivated by the following scenario. Imagine two people (α and β) that are watching a football match together. In a certain play, the referee awards a penalty kick. α thinks that the referee is right, because a fault was made inside the penalty area (let's represent this fact with proposition P); at the same time, β is thinking that the referee was wrong, because, in its perception of the situation, the fault was made just an inch outside the penalty area. How can this situation (and the beliefs of the two agents) be formally represented? This state of affairs may not be described with an assignment of truth values to the basic propositions. The situation (s) is obviously the same for the two agents α and β (they are watching the same match together). From α's point of view, the description of s should make true proposition P; however, from β's perspective, in the present situation P should be considered false. Obviously, there would be many aspects of s in which α and β would agree; *e.g.* both of them would consider that the proposition representing the fact *"We are watching a football match on TV"* is true in s.

As far as beliefs are concerned, we argue that, in this situation, α should be capable of stating that $B_\alpha P$ (α has seen the fault and has noticed that it was made inside the penalty area). It would not seem very acceptable a situation in which α perceived the fault to have been made inside the penalty area and defended that it didn't believe that a penalty kick should have been awarded. It also seems reasonable to say that α cannot

---

[4] Other alternatives, such as getting rid of the Kripke semantics or changing the underlying consequence relation, have also been considered in the literature. A detailed review of the most interesting proposals that have been made to solve the logical omniscience problem may be found in [7].

fail to notice that it believes that the fault was made inside the penalty area; thus, α may also assert in s that $B_\alpha B_\alpha P$. In a similar way, in this situation β cannot state that $B_\beta P$ (β cannot defend that it believes that the referee is right, in a situation in which it perceived the fault to have been made outside the penalty area).

In our framework we want to include the intuition that agents are smart enough to know that other agents may not perceive reality in the same way as they do. In the previous example, without further information (e.g. β shouting *Penalty!*), α should not be capable of supporting (or rejecting) that $B_\beta P$; analogously, β could not affirm (or deny) that $B_\alpha P$.

A final reflection on the meaning of the accessibility relation between situations for agent i (R_i) is necessary. It will be assumed that an agent cannot have any doubts about its own perceptions and beliefs in a given state. E.g. if, in situation s, α looks at the match and thinks P, then it surely must realise this fact and believe P in s (and even believe that it believes P, were it to think about that). Thus, if R_α links s with all those situations that α cannot tell apart from s, it must be the case that α also perceives P as true in all those states as well (otherwise, those states would be clearly distinguishable by α, because in some of them it would support P whereas in some of them P would be rejected). The only uncertainty that α may have is *about the perception of s by the other agents*. In the example, α does not know whether it is in a situation in which β supports P or in a situation in which β rejects P. Therefore, α's accessibility relation must reflect this uncertainty.

Summarising, the main points that have been illustrated with the previous discussion are the following:

- A situation may be considered not as an entity that may be objectively described, but as a piece of reality that may be perceived in different ways by different agents. Thus, it is necessary to think of a *subjective* way of representing each situation, in which each agent's point of view is taken into account. In the previous example, the description of s should include the fact that α is willing to support P, whereas β isn't.
- The beliefs of an agent in each situation also depend on each agent's point of view. In the situation of the example, $B_\alpha P$ would hold from α's perspective, whereas it would not be either supported or rejected by β. Thus, we argue that it does not make sense to ask whether $B_\alpha P$ holds in s or not; that question must be referred to a particular agent's point of view.
- The interpretation of the meaning of each agent's accessibility relation is slightly different from the usual one.
  Each accessibility relation R_i will keep its traditional meaning, *i.e.* it will represent the uncertainty of agent i with respect to the situation in which it is located. However, our intuition is that an agent may only be uncertain about the other agents' perception of the present state, not about its own perception.

3 Formalizing Subjective Situations

These intuitive ideas are formalized in the *structures of subjective situations*:

Definition 1 (Structure of Subjective Situations)

An structure of subjective situations E is a tuple

$$< S, R_1, ..., R_n, T_1, ...T_n, \mathcal{F}_1, ..., \mathcal{F}_n >, where$$

- *S is the set of possible situations.*
- *R_i is the accessibility relation between situations for agent i.*
- *T_i is a function that returns, for each situation s, the set of propositional formulas that are perceived as true by agent i in s.*
- *$\mathcal{F}_i$ is a function that returns, for each situation s, the set of propositional formulas that are perceived as false by agent i in s.*

$\mathcal{E}$ is the set of all structures of subjective situations.

The presence of T_i and $\mathcal{F}_i$ allows agent i to consider *partial* situations (those in which i does not have any reason to support or to reject a given formula) as well as *inconsistent* situations (those in which i may have reasons to support and to reject a given formula).

The accessibility relation between situations for agent i has to reflect its uncertainty about the way that the actual situation is perceived by the other agents. Thus, R_i has to link all those states that i perceives in the same way but that may perceived in different ways by other agents. This intuition is formalized in the following condition:

Definition 2 (Accessibility Relations)

$$\forall s, t \epsilon S, (sR_i t) \text{ if and only if } (T_i(s) = T_i(t)) \text{ and } (\mathcal{F}_i(s) = \mathcal{F}_i(t))$$

This condition forces each R_i to be an equivalence relation, thereby linking this approach with the classical $S5$ modal system, in which this condition also holds. In $S5$ the presence of this condition makes true axiom 4 (positive introspection), axiom 5 (negative introspection) and axiom T (the axiom of knowledge); the modal operators of the system proposed in this article will have similar properties, as will be shown in section 4.

3.1 Satisfiability Relations

A simplified version of the doxastic propositional language for n agents is considered, as shown in the following definition:

Definition 3 (Doxastic Modal Language $\mathcal{L}$)

Consider a set of modal belief operators for n agents (B_1, ..., B_n). $\mathcal{L}$ is the language formed by all propositional formulas (built in the standard way from a set $\mathcal{P}$ of basic propositions and the logical operators $\neg, \vee, \wedge, \rightarrow$), preceded by a (possibly empty) sequence of (possibly negated) modal operators. $\mathcal{L}_{PC}$ is the subset of $\mathcal{L}$ that contains those formulas that do not have any modal operator. The modal formulas of $\mathcal{L}$ are called linearly nested.

Thus, $\mathcal{L}$ contains formulas such as $P, B_3Q, B_1B_5(R\lor T), B_3\neg B_2S$ and $\neg B_1B_1\neg T$, but it is not expressive enough to represent formulas such as $(B_2P \to B_3Q)$ or $(P \lor B_5Q)$. In most practical applications, an agent in a multi-agent system will only need to represent what it believes (or not) to be the case in the world and what it believes (or not) that the other agents believe (or not). This is just the level of complexity offered by linearly nested formulas.

Following the previously outlined intuitions, two relations (of satisfiability, $\models_i$, and unsatisfiability, $=|_i$) between situations and formulas will be defined for each agent i. Given an structure of subjective situations E and a situation s, $E, s \models_i \phi$ should hold whenever agent i has some reason to think that ϕ is true in situation s. Similarly, $E, s =|_i \phi$ should hold whenever agent i has some reason to reject ϕ in situation s.

Notice that $E, s \not\models_i \phi$ should not imply that $E, s =|_i \phi$ (i.e. i not having any reason to support ϕ does not mean that it must have reasons to reject it). In the same spirit, $E, s \models_i \phi$ should not imply $E, s \neq|_i \phi$ (agent i could have reasons both to support and to reject a certain formula in a given situation).

The clauses that define the behaviour of these relations are the following:

Definition 4 (Relations $\models_i$ and $=|_i$)

- $\forall E\epsilon\mathcal{E}, \forall s\epsilon S, \forall agent\, i, \forall\phi\epsilon\mathcal{L}_{PC}$

$$E, s \models_i \phi \Leftrightarrow \phi\epsilon\mathcal{T}_i(s)$$
$$E, s =|_i \phi \Leftrightarrow \phi\epsilon\mathcal{F}_i(s)$$

- $\forall E\epsilon\mathcal{E}, \forall s\epsilon S, \forall agents\, i, j, \forall\phi\epsilon\mathcal{L}$

$$E, s \models_i B_j\phi \Leftrightarrow \forall t\epsilon S\, ((sR_it)\; implies\; E, t \models_j \phi)$$
$$E, s =|_i B_j\phi \Leftrightarrow \exists t\epsilon S\, ((sR_it)\; and\; E, t =|_j \phi)$$

- $\forall E\epsilon\mathcal{E}, \forall s\epsilon S, \forall agents\, i, j, \forall\phi\epsilon\mathcal{L}$

$$E, s \models_i \neg B_j\phi \Leftrightarrow E, s =|_i B_j\phi$$
$$E, s =|_i \neg B_j\phi \Leftrightarrow E, s \models_i B_j\phi$$

Thus, in a given situation s, agent i supports that j believes ϕ just in case j supports ϕ in all the situations that are considered possible by i in s. Similarly, i may reject the fact that j believes ϕ if it may think of a possible situation in which j rejects ϕ.

4 Properties of the Belief Operators

The definition of a structure of subjective situations, the fact that the accessibility relations are equivalence relations and the clauses that describe the behaviour of the satisfiability (and unsatisfiability) relations imply that the modal belief operator of each agent i has several interesting logical properties (that, in our opinion, make it an appropriate operator to model the notion of belief for a non-ideal agent). Some of these properties are described in this section[5].

---

[5] The proofs of the following propositions are quite straightforward; they have not been included in the final version of the paper due to lack of space.

General Results

Proposition 1 (Lack of Logical Omniscience)

In the framework of subjective situations, none of the following forms of logical omniscience ([1], [7]) holds:

- *Full logical omniscience.*
- *Belief of valid formulas.*
- *Closure under logical implication.*
- *Closure under logical equivalence.*
- *Closure under material implication.*
- *Closure under conjunction.*
- *Weakening of beliefs.*
- *Triviality of inconsistent beliefs.*

These properties do not hold because T_i and $\mathcal{F}_i$ are defined on sets of (arbitrary) formulas (not on basic propositions). It is possible to impose any of the above properties on the belief operators by requiring these sets of formulas to satisfy some conditions (e.g. if $(\phi \wedge \psi)\epsilon T_i(s)$ implies that $\phi \epsilon T_i(s)$ and $\psi \epsilon T_i(s)$, then the set of beliefs of agent i would be closed under conjunction).

Proposition 2 (Relation between $\models_i$ and $=|_i$)

The following properties do not hold:

$$E, s \not\models_i \phi \text{ implies } E, s =|_i \phi$$
$$E, s \models_i \phi \text{ implies } E, s \neq|_i \phi$$

This result is due, as suggested above, to the fact that an agent may have reasons to support *and/or* deny a formula in a given situation.

Results on Positive Introspection

Proposition 3 (Single-agent Positive Introspection)

$$E, s \models_i B_i\phi \text{ implies } E, s \models_i B_iB_i\phi$$

This proposition states that axiom 4 (the classical axiom of positive introspection) holds for each belief operator B_i (*i.e.* every agent has introspective capabilities on its own positive beliefs).

Proposition 4 (Inter-agent Positive Introspection)

$$E, s \models_i B_j\phi \text{ implies } E, s \models_i B_jB_j\phi$$

This is a more general result (the previous proposition reflects the case $i = j$). It states that each agent is aware of the fact that the other agents also have introspective capabilities.

Proposition 5 (Multi-agent Positive Introspection)

It does not hold (for three different agents i, j, k) that

$$E, s \models_i B_j \phi \text{ implies } E, s \models_i B_k B_j \phi$$

This proposition states a negative result. It is telling that even if agent i has reasons to support that j believes something, that is not enough for i to think that any other agent will have that belief. This proposition is essentially expressing the uncertainty of agent i about the beliefs of a different agent k.

Proposition 6 (Generation of Positive Beliefs)

$$E, s \models_i B_j \phi \text{ implies } E, s \models_i B_i B_j \phi$$

If an agent has reasons to support a certain belief, then that belief will be included in its belief set. This proposition is similar to the following one, that characterizes an agent's set of propositional positive beliefs in a given state.

Proposition 7 (Characterization of Positive Beliefs)

For any propositional formula ϕ,

$$E, s \models_i \phi \text{ if and only if } E, s \models_i B_i \phi$$

This result states that agent i believes ϕ in state s if and only if ϕ is one of the facts that are perceived as true by that agent in that state (in fact, the "only if" side of the proposition is the classical axiom of knowledge, axiom T).

Results on Negative Introspection

Proposition 8 (Single-agent Negative Introspection)

$$E, s \models_i \neg B_i \phi \text{ implies } E, s \models_i B_i \neg B_i \phi$$

This proposition states that axiom 5 (the classical axiom of negative introspection) holds for each belief operator B_i (*i.e.* every agent has introspective capabilities on its own negative beliefs).

Proposition 9 (Inter-agent Negative Introspection)

For two different agents i, j, it does not hold that

$$E, s \models_i \neg B_j \phi \text{ implies } E, s \models_i B_j \neg B_j \phi$$

This result states that each agent i is aware of the fact that, even if it has reasons to think that j does not believe ϕ, it may just be the case that j believes ϕ indeed (and, therefore, j would believe that it believed ϕ). Thus, it is another expression of the uncertainty that an agent has about the beliefs of the other agents. However, the following fact does hold:

situations that could be the actual one and T and F are functions from the set of primitive propositions into subsets of S. Intuitively, $T(P)$ contains all the situations that support the truth of P, whereas $F(P)$ contains the ones that support the falsehood of P. A situation s can be *partial* (if there is a primitive proposition which is neither true nor false in s) and/or *incoherent* (if there is a proposition which is both true and false in s). A situation is *complete* if it is neither partial nor incoherent. A complete situation s is *compatible* with a situation t if s and t agree in all the points in which t is defined. B^* is the set of all complete situations of S that are compatible with some situation in B.

The relations $\models_T$ and $\models_F$ between situations and formulas are defined as follows:

- $M,s \models_T P$, where P is a primitive proposition, if and only if $s \in T(P)$
- $M,s \models_F P$, where P is a primitive proposition, if and only if $s \in F(P)$
- $M,s \models_T \neg\varphi$ if and only if $M,s \models_F \varphi$
- $M,s \models_F \neg\varphi$ if and only if $M,s \models_T \varphi$
- $M,s \models_T (\varphi \wedge \psi)$ if and only if $M,s \models_T \varphi$ and $M,s \models_T \psi$
- $M,s \models_F (\varphi \wedge \psi)$ if and only if $M,s \models_F \varphi$ or $M,s \models_F \psi$
- $M,s \models_T B\varphi$ if and only if $M,t \models_T \varphi \ \forall t \in B$
- $M,s \models_F B\varphi$ if and only if $M,s \not\models_T B\varphi$
- $M,s \models_T L\varphi$ if and only if $M,t \models_T \varphi \ \forall t \in B^*$
- $M,s \models_F L\varphi$ if and only if $M,s \not\models_T L\varphi$

There are some similarities between our approach and Levesque's logic of implicit and explicit beliefs. However, they are more apparent than real, as shown in this listing:

- Levesque also considers a satisfiability and an unsatisfiability relation between situations and doxastic formulas.
  However, these relations are not considered *for each agent.*
- Levesque also describes each situation with two functions $\mathcal{T}$ and $\mathcal{F}$.
  Again, these functions are not indexed by each agent, as our functions are (Levesque considers an objective description of what is true and what is false in each situation). Another important difference is that Levesque's functions deal with basic propositions, and not with formulas as our functions do.
- Both approaches allow the presence of *partial* or *inconsistent* situations.
  However note that, in our case, it is not the (objective) description of the situation that is partial or inconsistent, but the *subjective* perception that an agent may have of it. Thus, the notions of partiality and inconsistency have a much more natural interpretation in our framework.
- Both approaches avoid all the forms of logical omniscience.
  The reason is different in each case, though. In Levesque's logic of explicit and implicit beliefs, it is the presence of incoherent situations that prevents logical omniscience. In our proposal, there is no need to have inconsistent situations to avoid logical omniscience. In fact, we solve that problem by defining $\mathcal{T}_i$ and $\mathcal{F}_i$ over arbitrary sets of formulas, and not over basic propositions.
- There are accessibility relations between situations for each agent in both systems.
  Levesque's accessibility relation between situations is left implicit; our accessibility relations are explicit. Furthermore, the intuition underlying these relations is somewhat different, as explained in section 2.

Many differences with Levesque's approach have just been outlined. Other differences that may be mentioned are the following:

- Levesque only considers one agent, and does not allow nested beliefs[6]. Thus, his agents do not have any introspective capabilities.
- Levesque defines *explicit* and *implicit* beliefs, whereas we do not make this distinction.
- Even though Levesque avoids logical omniscience, his agents must necessarily believe all those tautologies that are formed by *known* basic propositions (those propositions P for which the agent believes $(P \lor \neg P)$), regardless of their complexity. This is not the case in our approach, because we deal directly with formulas.
- There is a different treatment of the unsatisfiability relation when applied to beliefs, because he transforms $\dashv$ into $\not\models$, whereas we don't.

5.2 Thijsse's Hybrid Sieve Systems

Thijsse ([6]) proposes a way of using *partial logics* to deal with various forms of logical omniscience. He defines a *partial model* as a tuple $(W, \mathcal{B}_1, \ldots, \mathcal{B}_n, V)$, where W is a set of worlds, $\mathcal{B}_i$ is the accessibility relation between worlds for agent i and V is a *partial* truth assignment to the basic propositions in each world. $\top$ is a primitive proposition that is always interpreted as *true*. Truth ($\models$) and falsity ($\dashv$) relations are defined in the following way:

- $M, w \models \top$
- $M, w \not\dashv \top$
- $M, w \models P$, where P is a primitive proposition, iff $V(P, w) = 1$
- $M, w \dashv P$, where P is a primitive proposition, iff $V(P, w) = 0$
- $M, w \models \neg \varphi$ iff $M, w \dashv \varphi$
- $M, w \dashv \neg \varphi$ iff $M, w \models \varphi$
- $M, w \models (\varphi \land \psi)$ iff $M, w \models \varphi$ and $M, w \models \psi$
- $M, w \dashv (\varphi \land \psi)$ iff $M, w \dashv \varphi$ or $M, w \dashv \psi$
- $M, w \models B_i \varphi$ iff $M, v \models \varphi$ $\forall v$ such that $(w, v) \in \mathcal{B}_i$
- $M, w \dashv B_i \varphi$ iff $\exists v$ s.t. $(w, v) \in \mathcal{B}_i$ and $M, v \dashv \varphi$

The most important similarities between our approach and Thijsse's are:

- n agents and n explicit accessibility relations are considered.
  However, as in Levesque's case, there are no restrictions on these relations, and the intuitive meaning of our accessibility relations is slightly different.
- Two relations (of satisfiability and unsatisfiability) are defined. Moreover, a similar clause is used to provide a meaning to the unsatisfiability relation with respect to the belief operator.
  As before, the main difference is that we provide two relations *for each agent*.

---

[6] However, similar logics that deal with many agents have been considered by Halpern and Lakemeyer, see *e.g.* [10].

- There are no tautologies in Thijsse's system; therefore, he does not have to care about some forms of logical omniscience (closure under valid implication and belief of valid formulas).
- Closure under material implication and closure under conjunction do not hold in Thijsse's approach either.

The main difference with Thijsse's proposal is that he uses *partial* assignments of truth values *over basic propositions* for each state; thus, a proposition may be true, false or undefined in each state. We deal with formulas, not with basic propositions, and each formula may be supported *and/or* rejected by *each agent* in each state. Therefore, Thijsse's approach is three-valued, whereas ours is more of a four-valued kind, such as Levesque's.

6 Summary

It has been argued that each agent perceives its actual situation in a particular way, which may be different from that of other agents located in the same situation. This intuitive idea has been formalized with the notion of *subjective situations*. These entities are the base of a doxastic logic, in which the meaning of the belief operators seems to fit with the general intuitions about how the doxastic attitude of a non-ideal agent should behave. In particular, logical omniscience is avoided while some interesting introspective properties are maintained.

References

1. R. Fagin, J. Halpern, Y. Moses, M. Vardi, *Reasoning about knowledge*, MIT Press, 1995.
2. J. Hintikka, *Knowledge and belief*, Cornell University Press, Ithaca, N.Y., 1962.
3. S. Kripke, A semantical analysis of modal logic I: normal modal propositional calculi, *Zeitschrift für Mathematische Logik und Grundlagen Mathematik* 9 (1963), 67-96.
4. J. Hintikka, Impossible possible worlds vindicated, *J. of Phil. Logic* 4 (1975), 475-484.
5. H.J. Levesque, A logic of implicit and explicit belief, *Proceedings of the Conference of the American Association for Artificial Intelligence, AAAI-84* (1984), 198-202.
6. E. Thijsse, Combining partial and classical semantics. A hybrid approach to belief and awareness, in P. Doherty (Ed.), *Partiality, modality, and nonmonotonicity*, Studies in Logic, Language and Information, Center for the Study of Language and Information Publications (1996), 223-249.
7. A. Moreno, Avoiding logical omniscience and perfect reasoning: a survey, *AI Communications* 2 (1998), 101-122.
8. A. Moreno, T. Sales, Dynamic belief analysis, in J. Müller, M. Wooldridge, N. Jennings (Eds.), *Intelligent Agents III: Agent theories, architectures and languages*, Lecture Notes in Artificial Intelligence 1193, Springer Verlag (1997), 87-102.
9. A. Moreno, T. Sales, Limited logical belief analysis, in L. Cavedon, A. Rao, W. Wobcke (Eds.), *Intelligent Agent Systems: Theoretical and Practical Issues*, Lecture Notes in Artificial Intelligence 1209, Springer Verlag (1997), 104-118.
10. J. Halpern, G. Lakemeyer, Multi-agent only knowing, in *Proceedings of the Sixth Conference on Theoretical Aspects of Rationality and Knowledge, TARK-96* (1996), 251-265.

Formal Analysis of Models for the Dynamics of Trust Based on Experiences

Catholijn M. Jonker and Jan Treur

Vrije Universiteit Amsterdam, Department of Artificial Intelligence
De Boelelaan 1081, 1081 HV Amsterdam, The Netherlands
Email: {jonker, treur}@cs.vu.nl   URL: http://www.cs.vu.nl/{~jonker,~treur}

Abstract. The aim of this paper is to analyse and formalise the dynamics of trust in the light of experiences. A formal framework is introduced for the analysis and specification of models for trust evolution and trust update. Different properties of these models are formally defined.

1   Introduction

Trust is the attitude an agent has with respect to the dependability/capabilities of some other agent (maybe itself) or with respect to the turn of events. The agent might for example trust that the statements made by another agent are true. The agent might trust the commitment of another agent with respect to a certain (joint) goal. The agent might trust that another agent is capable of performing certain tasks. The agent might trust itself to be able to perform some tasks. The agent might trust that the current state of affairs will lead to a state of affairs that is agreeable to its own intentions, goals, commitments, or desires.

In [1], [2] the importance of the notion trust is shown for agents, multi-agent systems, and their foundations. From the viewpoint of the users of agent systems Ousterhout [10] makes clear that work can only be delegated to such systems if they can be trusted without there being a constant need for inspection of their work. Elofson [4] states that the reach and effect of trust in the affairs of individuals and organizations is largely pervasive. Elofson continues with the problem that trust is somewhat illusive, difficult to define, difficult to create, and difficult to measure. Before focusing on the difficulties regarding the creation and measurement of trust, a brief survey is made of definitions of trust, for more information see [4], [5].

Trust of an agent in another agent (social trust) is sometimes defined as a kind of binary property, for example, an agent A trusting another agent B means that A believes that B will act in a way that is favorable to A, even though that act might not be most convenient to B at that moment [5]. A shorter variant is that of Demolombe [3]: "We can understand trust as an attitude of an agent who believes that another agent has a given property." Another definition of trust, describes the notion as a subjective probability [5]. Common in these definitions is that the trusting agent A has a specific interest in the actions of the agent B that is trusted by A, and that B will act with respect to this interest even though it might seem that doing so is not favorable with respect to B's own interests. In [1], [2] this paradox is solved by the following definition of trust: "Trust is a theory and an expectation about the kind of motivations the agent is endowed with, and about which will be the prevailing motivations in case of conflict." This implies that an agent can have interests on several levels like economic interests, emotional and social interests (love, friendship, norms). They state that the mental ingredients of social trust are relative to the competence of the other agent, to the predictability of the behaviour of the other agent, and on the agents own faithfulness.

In the above definitions trust finally depends upon some sort of beliefs, predictions, or expectations. However, it is not clear (not meant as a criticism) where these beliefs and expectations come from. The definition of Lewis and Weigert [6] does not refer to beliefs or expectations, but to observations which in turn lead to expectations: "observations that indicate that members of a system act according to and are secure in the expected futures constituted by the presence of each other for their symbolic representations." Elofson [4] agrees that observations are important for trust, and he defines trust as: "trust is the outcome of observations leading to the belief that the actions of another may be relied upon, without explicit guarantee, to achieve a goal in a risky situation." Elofson notes that trust can be developed over time as the outcome of a series of confirming observations. From his experimental work, Elofson concludes that information regarding the reasoning process of an agent, more than the actual conclusions of that agent affect the trust in the conclusions of that agent.

The evolution of trust over time, also called the dynamics of trust, as mentioned by Elofson, is also addressed in [2]: "there is a circular relation, and more precisely a positive feedback, between trust in reciprocal delegation-adoption relations (from commerce to friendship)." An implication of this is that if an agent A trusts an agent B, then communicating his trust in B to B, can lead to an increase of B's trust in A. Of course, a similar feedback relation exists for distrust.

In this paper we consider trust from the perspective of the software agent, that is, trust within software agents regarding the reliability of objects and tools, their own work, the behaviour of others, and in the evolution of their environment (events and effects of actions performed by the agent).

Trust is based on a number of factors, an important one being the agent's own experiences with the subject of trust; e.g., another agent. Each event that can influence the degree of trust is interpreted by the agent to be either a *trust-negative experience* or a *trust-positive experience*. If the event is interpreted to be a trust-negative experience the agent will loose his trust to some degree, if it is interpreted to be trust-positive, the agent will gain trust to some degree. The degree to which the trust is changed depends on the trust model used by the agent. This implies that the trusting agent performs a form of continual verification and validation of the subject of trust over time. For example, you can trust a car, based on a multitude of experiences with that specific car, and with other cars in general. For this paper a formal analysis of the dependency of trust on experiences will be the central focus.

One of the key issues for the design of intelligent software agents is how trust is represented within the agent, and how the effect of experiences is specified. Representations can be *qualitative*, using specific qualitative labels (or term structures), or *quantitative*, using numbers as a representation. For example, trust could be measured by a real number between -1 and 1.

For a first analysis, a simple qualitative model is discussed in Section 2. In Section 3 the formal notion of trust evolution function is introduced, and properties of trust evolution functions are defined. In Section 4 trust update functions are introduced, and some properties are defined. Section 5 introduces a quantitative example model which takes into account an inflation rate on experiences.

2   A Simple Qualitative Model for Trust Update

In this section a simple qualitative trust model is discussed. The main purpose of this example is to identify a number of issues for further analysis.

2.1   The Representation of Trust

In the model considered in this section four trust values are distinguished and ordered in the following way:

unconditional distrust < conditional distrust < conditional trust < unconditional trust

The minimal trust value is unconditional distrust , the maximal value is unconditional trust. So, a first assumption on trust models is that there exists a set of trust values and they are partially ordered and maximal and minimal trust values exist.

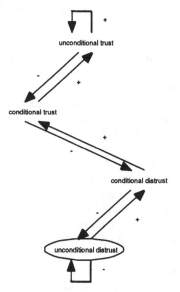

Fig. 1. A simple qualitative model for trust dynamics

2.2   Trust Characteristics

As discussed above, agents can have their own characteristics with respect to trust dynamics. There are many possible trust types of agents. To define these types two aspects can be taken into consideration:
(1) initial trust
(2) trust dynamics

Initial trust. With respect to initial trust the following possibilities can be distinguished:
1.   *initially trusting*
       a)   without previous trust influencing experiences the agent has unconditional trust: maximal trust value
       b)   without previous trust influencing experiences the agent has conditional trust: a positive trust value, below the maximal trust value
2.   *initially distrusting*
       a)   without previous trust influencing experiences the agent has unconditional distrust: maximal distrust value
       b)   without previous trust influencing experiences the agent has conditional distrust: a negative trust value, above the minimal trust value

Note that the actual trust values used by the agent can differ from the ones mentioned above. However, the trust values used will be partially ordered, and have maximal and minimal values.

Types of trust dynamics. The following trust dynamics types can be distinguished:
1.   *blindly positive*:
a)   always unconditional trust
b)   definitive having trust: after a certain number, or sequence of positive trust experiences, the agent reaches the state of unconditional trust and will remain in this state indefinitely.
2.   *blindly negative*:
a)   always unconditional distrust
b)   definitive losing trust: after a certain number, or sequence of negative trust experiences, the agent reaches the state of unconditional distrust and will remain in this state indefinitely.
3.   *slow positive, fast negative* dynamics: it takes a lot of trust-positive experiences to gain trust, it takes only a few trust-negative experiences to lose trust.
4.   *balanced slow*: slow dynamics both in positive and in negative sense
5.   *balanced fast*: fast dynamics in positive and in negative sense. The *tit-for-tat* strategy is an example of a strategy that can be used for a balanced fast trust-type
6.   *slow negative, fast positive* dynamics: it takes a lot of trust-negative experiences to lose trust, it takes only a few trust-positive experiences to gain trust.

Within the example used as an illustration in this section, the trust representation is just sufficiently rich to specify a difference in characteristics between slow and fast dynamics, but it is not rich enough to specify more subtle differences in characteristics. For example, it is not possible to specify that in an unconditional positive trust state, after three positive experiences trust will be blindly positive.

3   Trust Evolution Functions

In this paper trust is considered a mental agent concept that depends on experiences (evaluated events). One way to formally model the dynamics of trust is to formalise the dependency of trust on past experiences by a mathematical function that relates sequences of experiences to trust representations: a *trust evolution function*. Another way to formally model the dynamics of trust is in an inductive manner by a mathematical function relating a current trust representation and a current experience to the next trust representation: a *trust update function*. A natural question is whether these formalisations can be represented in terms of each other. In principle, any trust update function generates for any initial trust value a trust evolution function, but not every trust evolution function can be represented as a trust update function. Both ways of formalisation and their relations will be analysed in more depth in this (trust evolution functions) and the next sections (trust update functions and relations).

To obtain a formal framework, the following sets are introduced:

E   A partially ordered set of experience classes
      Examples are:
         - $E = \{-, +\}$ with $- < +$, as in Section 2, or
         - an interval in the real numbers (e.g., [-1, 1]), or
         - more dimensional variants.
      Actually these representations denote evaluated events; for shortness
      the word experiences will be used.
      In addition, E may have one or both of the following structures:
         - two sets E_{pos} and E_{neg} indicating positive and negative elements of E,
            with ev1 negative and ev2 positive implies ev1 < ev2.
         - a neutral element 0_E of E, such that
                $E_{neg} = \{ev \in E \mid ev < 0_E\}$ and $E_{pos} = \{ev \in E \mid ev > 0_E\}$

N   The set of natural numbers.

ES   The set E^N of experience sequences $e = (e_i)_{i \in N}$ with $e_i \in E$; this set ES is
      partially ordered by:
                $\forall e, f \in ES:$ $e \bullet f \Leftrightarrow \forall i\ e_i \bullet f_i$
      For $e \in ES$ and $k \in N$ by e↾k the finite sequence $(e_i)_{i \in k}$ is denoted

T   A partially ordered set of trust qualifications
      Examples are
         - the set of trust qualifications in the example in Section 2, or
         - an interval in the real numbers (e.g., [-1, 1]), or
         - more dimensional variants.
      In addition, T may have one or both of the following structures:
         - two sets T_{pos} and T_{neg} indicating positive and negative elements of T ,
            with tv1 negative and tv2 positive implies tv1 < tv2.

- a neutral element 0_T of T, such that

$$T_{neg} = \{tv \in T \mid tv < 0_T\} \text{ and } T_{pos} = \{tv \in T \mid tv > 0_T\}$$

Using these sets, the notion of trust evolution function can be formally defined; see Definition 3.1.

Definition 3.1 (Trust Evolution Function)

(a) A *trust trace* is a sequence

$$tt : N \rightarrow T$$

(b) A *trust evolution function* is a function

$$te : ES \times N \rightarrow T$$

Let $e \in ES$ and $i \in N$, then $te(e,i)$ denotes the trust after experiences $e_0,...,e_{i-1}$. Associated with every trust evolution function te, there is a function

$$te' : ES \rightarrow (N \rightarrow T)$$

defined by:

$$te'(e) = (te(e,i))_{i \in N} \text{ and } te'(e)(i) = te(e,i)$$

I.e., $te'(e)$ is a trust trace for every experience sequence e. Sometimes te is used to refer to te' as well.

(c) Trust traces and trust evolution functions are *ordered* by:

$tt1 \bullet tt2$	iff	$tt1(i) \bullet tt2(i)$ for all i
$te1 \bullet te2$	iff	$te1(e) \bullet te2(e)$ for all e

In Definition 3.2 a number of possible properties of trust evolution functions are formally defined. In this definition, *future independence* (see 1.), expresses that trust only depends on past experiences, not on future experiences. This is a quite natural assumption that is assumed to hold for all trust evolution functions; in particular, it holds for the example in Section 2. Also *monotonicity* (see 2.) is a quite natural assumption. It expresses that if the experiences are at least as positive (compared to a given sequence of experiences), also trust will be at least as positive (compared to the trust related to the given sequence of experiences). The example model discussed in Section 2 satisfies monotonicity.

The property *indistinguishable past* expresses that only the experiences themselves count and not the point in time at which they were experienced; in fact this property abstracts from the temporal aspect. We consider this not a natural property. Only in very simple cases it might be relevant, for example a trust evolution function in which just the number of all positive and negative experiences are counted and compared has this property; for example:

$$te(e, i) = [\#\{i \mid e_i \bullet 0\} - \#\{i \mid e_i \bullet 0\}] / i$$

Since this property expresses that experiences far back in time count just as strong as very recent experiences, all trust evolution functions that take into account some notion of inflation or forgetting of experiences will not satisfy this property (see, for example, Section 5). Also the simple example in Section 2 does not satisfy indistinguishable past. For example, a sequence of experiences

$$+ \; + \; + \; - \; + \; - \; + \; - \; +$$

leads to the value unconditional trust, whereas the sequence

$$+ \; + \; + \; + \; + \; + \; - \; - \; -$$

leads to unconditional distrust.

The properties *maximal* or *minimal initial trust* (see 4. and 5. in Definition 3.2) express the starting point of the trust evolution process. The properties of *positive* (or *negative) trust extension* (see 6. and 7.) express that after a positive (or negative) experience, trust will become at least as much (or as less) as it was. The example in Section 2 satisfies these properties.

The property *degree of memory based on window n back* expresses that only the last n experiences are relevant. All earlier experiences are forgotten. The example of Section 2 does not satisfy this property, not for any n. For example, the two experience sequences of arbitrary length

$$+ \ + \ + \ - \ + \ - \ + \ - \ + \ \ldots\ldots\ldots\ldots\ - \ +$$

and

$$- \ - \ - \ - \ + \ - \ + \ - \ + \ \ldots\ldots\ldots\ldots\ - \ +$$

will always lead to different trust values, even while the last part is equal. However, for not too sophisticated models for trust dynamics, this property might be relevant. It provides an easy way to specify the evolution, just by looking at the most recent experiences; e.g., the tit-for-tat strategy.

The property *degree of trust dropping* (or gaining) (see 9. and 10.) expresses after how many positive (or negative) experiences trust will be positive (or negative). The example of Section 2 satisfies degree of trust gaining and dropping 2: always after two positive experiences, trust will be positive, and always after two negative experiences, trust will be negative.

Four properties (see 11. to 14.) concern *limit behaviour*. They express, for different cases, conditions under which trust will become maximal (respectively, minimal). Essentially they express that it is always possible to reach maximal trust, if a sufficiently long period with only positive experiences is encountered, and the same for the negative case. The example in Section 2 satisfies the properties 12. and 14.; just take $N = M + 3$. Models for trust dynamics in which it is possible that a form of *fixation* occurs, i.e., so much of distrust is acquired that trust will not be possible anymore, independent of further experiences, do not satisfy these properties (see also the blindly positive or negative characteristics in Section 2.3.2). Properties 15. and 16. express this phenomenon of trust fixation.

Definition 3.2 (Properties of Trust Evolution Functions)

The following properties (in which $e, f \in ES$, $i, j, k, n \in N$) are defined

1. *future independence*

    a trust evolution function te is *future independent* if its values only depend on the experiences in the past:

    if $e|k = f|k$ then $te(e, k) = te(f, k)$

2. *monotonicity*

    $e \bullet f \Rightarrow te(e) \bullet te(f)$

3. *indistinguishable past*

    if $e|k$ is a (temporal) permutation of $f|k$ then $te(e, k) = te(f, k)$

4. *maximal initial trust*

    $te(e, 0)$ is maximal in T

5. *minimal initial trust*

    $te(e, 0)$ is minimal in T

6. *positive trust extension*

    $\forall i, j \ [\forall k \in N : i \bullet k < j : e_k \text{ positive}] \Rightarrow te(e, i) \bullet te(e, j).$

7. *negative trust extension*

    $\forall i, j \ [\forall k \in N : i \bullet k < j : e_k \text{ negative}] \Rightarrow te(e, i) \bullet te(e, j).$

8. *degree of memory based on window n back* (forgetting about the past)
   $\forall i \; [\forall k \in N : i\text{-}n < k \bullet i : e_k = f_k \;] \Rightarrow te(e,i) = te(f,i)$
   extreme cases:
   a) $n = 1$: only last experience counts
   b) $n = 0$: no experience counts

9. *degree of trust dropping* n
   $\forall i \; [\forall k \in N : i\text{-}n < k \bullet i : e_k \text{ negative }] \Rightarrow te(e,i) \text{ negative}$
   extreme cases:
   a) $n = 1$: trust drops after 1 bad experience
   b) $n = 0$: trust is never given

10. *degree of trust gaining* n
    $\forall i \; [\forall k \in N : i\text{-}n < k \bullet i : e_k \text{ positive}] \Rightarrow te(e,i) \text{ positive}$
    extreme cases:
    a) $n = 1$: trust is given after 1 good experience
    b) $n = 0$: trust is always given

11. *positive limit approximation (continuous metric case)*
    if there exists an M such that for all $m > M$ it holds e_m is maximal, then for all $\varepsilon > 0$ there exists an N such that $te(e, n)$ is within at most ε from maximal for all $n > N$.

12. *positive limit approximation (discrete case)*
    if there exists an M such that for all $m > M$ it holds e_m is maximal, then an N exists such that $te(e, n)$ is maximal for all $n > N$.

13. *negative limit approximation (continuous metric case)*
    if there exists an M such that for all $m > M$ it holds e_m is minimal, then for all $\varepsilon > 0$ there exists an N such that $te(e, n)$ is within at most ε from minimal for all $n > N$.

14. *negative limit approximation (discrete case)*
    if there exists an M such that for all $m > M$ it holds e_m is minimal, then an N exists such that $te(e, n)$ is minimal for all $n > N$.

15. *negative trust fixation of degree* n
    if for some i the trust value $te(e, k)$ is minimal for all k with $i \bullet k < i + n$, then $te(e, k)$ is minimal for all $k \bullet i$.

16. *positive trust fixation of degree* n
    if for some i the trust value $te(e, k)$ is maximal for all k with $i \bullet k < i + n$, then $te(e, k)$ is maximal for all $k \bullet i$.

4   Trust Update Functions

From a mentalistic perspective, the notion of trust evolution function suggests that an agent builds a representation for sequences of past experiences, and at each moment in time uses these representations of experiences to determine its trust. Another, from a computational perspective maybe more desirable model is that an agent does not build a representation of the (past) experiences, but only of trust itself, and that a new experience instantaneously leads to an update of the trust representation, without maintaining the experience itself. This perspective was also the perspective used in

Section 2, and is addressed in more depth below. First the definition of a trust update function:

Definition 4.1 (Trust Update Function)

A *trust update function* is a function $tu : E \times T \to T$.

Note that Fig. 1 depicts an example specification of a trust update function. For a given trust update function, any initial trust value it generates by induction a unique trust evolution function te with $te(e,0) = it$. This relation between trust update functions and trust evolution functions will be addressed in more depth in Section 6.

Definition 4.2 (Properties of trust update functions)

The following properties are defined:

1. *monotonicity*
   $$ev1 \bullet ev2 \ \& \ tv1 \bullet tv2 \qquad \Rightarrow \qquad tu(ev1, tv1) \bullet tu(ev2, tv2)$$
2. *positive trust extension*
   $$ev \ positive \Rightarrow tu(ev, tv) \bullet tv$$
3. *negative trust extension*
   $$ev \ negative \Rightarrow tu(ev, tv) \bullet tv$$
4. *strict positive monotonic progression*
   $$ev \ positive \ and \ tv \ not \ maximal \Rightarrow tu(ev, tv) > tv$$
5. *strict negative monotonic progression*
   $$ev \ negative \ and \ tv \ not \ minimal \Rightarrow tu(ev, tv) < tv$$

Note that all properties defined in Definition 4.2 hold for the example in Section 2. From a trust update function, by iteration for each initial trust value a trust evolution function can be generated. The following definition shows how.

Definition 4.3 (Trust evolution generated by a trust update function)

Let tu be a trust update function and it any (initial) trust value. The trust evolution function te *generated by* tu for initial value it is the trust evolution function te inductively defined by:

$$te(e,0) = it \qquad \text{for all } e \in ES$$
$$te(e, i+1) = tu(e_i, te(e, i)) \qquad \text{for all } e \in ES, i \in N$$

This generated trust evolution function is denoted by $te_{tu,it}$.

Properties of $te_{tu,it}$ relate to properties of tu, for example, in the following sense:

Proposition 4.4

Let tu be a trust update function. Then the following hold:

1. $te_{tu,it}$ is future independent

2. If tu is monotonic, then $te_{tu,it}$ is monotonic

3. If tu satisfies positive trust extension, then $te_{tu,it}$ satisfies positive trust extension

4. If tu satisfies negative trust extension, then $te_{tu,it}$ satisfies negative trust extension

5. If tu has strict positive monotonic progression and T is finite, then $te_{tu,it}$ has positive limit approximation

6. If tu has strict negative monotonic progression and T is finite, then $te_{tu,it}$ has negative limit approximation

Note the condition on finiteness of the set of trust values in 5. and 6. in Proposition 4.4. If T is infinite, then the condition of strict monotonic progression is not strong enough. For example, it might well be the case that the progression decreases to such an extent that it stays under a bound tv less than the maximal value. However, for the continuous case stronger notions of progression can be defined that guarantee that the maximal value is reached, for example: there exists a $\partial > o$ such that $tu(ev, tv) - tv > \partial$ (maxtv - tv).

5   A Quantitative Example

The model for trust dynamics introduced in this section has as a basic assumption that there is some rate of inflation of experiences. Experiences further back in the past count only for a fraction of the recent experiences. For both E and T the closed interval [-1, 1] is taken. We assume there is an inflation rate of d (between 0 and 1; for example 0.5) per experience step. The following trust update function is defined:

$$g_d(ev, tv) = d\ tv + (1 - d)\ ev$$

In this trust function, after each new experience the existing trust value is multiplied by d (this expresses the inflation), and the impact of the new experience is added, normalised in such a manner that a 2-ary function from the interval [-1, 1] to [-1, 1] results.

(a) For a fully positive experience with value 1, the comparison with maximal trust value 1 is:

$$
\begin{aligned}
1 - g_d(1, tv) \quad &= \quad 1 - [\,d\ tv + (1 - d)\,] \\
&= \quad d\,(1 - tv)
\end{aligned}
$$

This means that the distance of the trust value to the maximal trust value 1 is decreased to a fraction d of the old distance.

(b) For a fully negative experience with value -1, the comparison with maximal distrust value -1 is:

$$
\begin{aligned}
1 + g_d(-1, tv) \quad &= \quad 1 + [\,d\ tv + (1 - d)\,(-1)\,] \\
&= \quad d\,(1 + tv)
\end{aligned}
$$

This means that the distance of the trust value to minimal trust -1 is decreased to a fraction d of the old distance.

(c) For a zero-experience, the following can be found:

$$g_d(0, tv) \quad = \quad d\ tv$$

This means that for a zero-experience the distance of the trust value to 0 is decreased to a fraction d of the old trust value.

The example trust update function defined in this section has the following properties: monotonicity, positive and negative trust extension, strict positive and negative progression. The trust evolution function generated by the example trust update function can be determined in an explicit formula as a sum of powers of d as follows:

$$f_d(e, k) \quad = \quad it\ d^k + (1-d)\ \Sigma_{i=0}^{k-1}\ e_{k-1-i}\ d^i$$

7 Discussion

In this paper a framework is presented that supports formal analysis of the dynamics of trust based on experiences. The formal models made within this framework can also be used for the specification of trust evolution and trust update for software agents as part of their design. The requirements imposed on models for trust dynamics can highly depend on the individual characteristics of agents, therefore, a variety of models that capture these characteristics is needed. The formal framework enables the explication of these characteristics. Both qualitative and quantitative example models are given that are based on explicit trust evolution functions and trust update functions with which these characteristics can be formally specified.

Trust may be influenced by experiences of different types. This paper models differences between experiences by mapping them into one overall set of distinct experience 'values'. In addition, more explicit distinctions between different dimensions of experience could be made. Also other cognitive or emotional factors could be integrated. The work presented in [7], [8], [9] addresses some of these other aspects of trust, which could be integrated. This is left for future work.

References

1. Castelfranchi, C., and Falcone, R., Principles of Trust for MAS: Cognitive Anatomy, Social Importance, and Quantification. In: Demazeau, Y. (ed.), Proceedings of the Third International Conference on Multi-Agent Systems, IEEE Computer Society, Los Alamitos, 1998, pp. 72-79.
2. Castelfranchi, C., and Falcone, R., Social Trust: Cognitive Anatomy, Social Importance, Quantification, and Dynamics. In: Proceedings of the First International Workshop on Trust, 1998, pp. 35-49.
3. Demolombe, R., To trust information sources: a proposal for a modal logical framework, In: Proceedings of the First International Workshop on Trust, 1998, pp. 9-19.
4. Elofson, G., Developing Trust with Intelligent Agents: An Exploratory Study, In: Proceedings of the First International Workshop on Trust, 1998, pp. 125-139.
5. Gambetta, D., Trust. Basil Blackwell, Oxford, 1990.
6. Lewis, D., and Weigert, A., Social Atomism, Holism, and Trust. In: Sociological Quarterly, 1985, pp. 455-471.
7. Marsh, S., Trust and Reliance in Multi-Agent Systems: a Preliminary Report. In: Proc. of the Fourth European Workshop on Modelling Autonomous Agents in a Multi-Agent World, MAAMAW'92, Rome, 1992.
8. Marsh, S., Formalising Trust as a Computational Concept. Ph.D. Thesis. Department of Mathematics and Computer Science, University of Stirling, 1994
9. Marsh, S., Trust in Distributed Artificial Intelligence. In: C. Castelfranchi, E. Werner (eds.), Artificial Social Systems. Lecture Notes in AI, vol. 830, Springer Verlag, 1994, pp. 94-112
10. Ousterhout, J., Virtual Roundtable. In: Internet Computing on-line Journal, July-August issue, 1997.

Author Index

Springer
and the
environment

At Springer we firmly believe that an
international science publisher has a
special obligation to the environment,
and our corporate policies consistently
reflect this conviction.
We also expect our business partners –
paper mills, printers, packaging
manufacturers, etc. – to commit
themselves to using materials and
production processes that do not harm
the environment. The paper in this
book is made from low- or no-chlorine
pulp and is acid free, in conformance
with international standards for paper
permanency.

Springer

Lecture Notes in Artificial Intelligence (LNAI)

Lecture Notes in Computer Science